SIATISTA MACEDONIA

THE SPIRIT OF HELLENISM

To my devoted sister Katherine

July 29, 2001

James C. Siotas

SIATISTA MACEDONIA

James C. Siotas

THE
SPIRIT
OF
HELLENISM

www.pentlandpressusa.com

PUBLISHED BY PENTLAND PRESS, INC.
5122 Bur Oak Circle, Raleigh, North Carolina 27612
United States of America
919-782-0281

ISBN 1-57197-221-8
Library of Congress Control Number: 00-130908

Copyright © 2000 James C. Siotas
All rights reserved, which includes the right to reproduce this book or portions thereof in any form whatsoever except as provided by the U.S. Copyright Law.

Printed in the United States of America

Dedicated to Siatista's Macedonian Hellenism

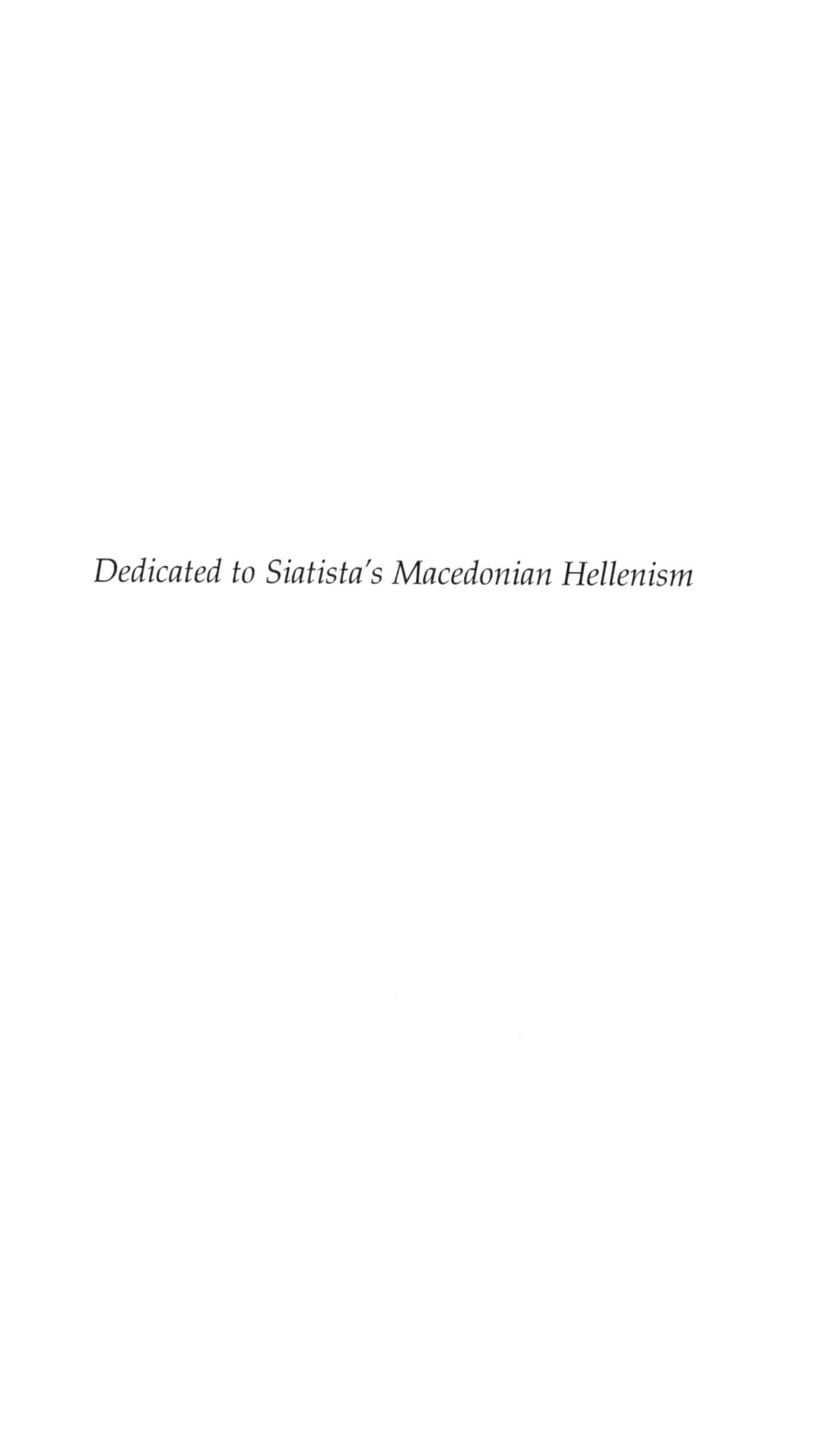

TABLE OF CONTENTS

Introduction 1

PART A
Chapter 1 – Region in Antiquity 7
Chapter 2 – Development of Hellenism 11
Chapter 3 – Macedonian Rule 15
Chapter 4 – Rome and Byzantium 21
Chapter 5 – Byzantium and Slavs 27
Chapter 6 – Ottomans and Balkans 33

PART B
Chapter 7 – Upper Macedonia 39
Chapter 8 – Eastern Orthodoxy 45
Chapter 9 – Survival Adjustment 53
Chapter 10 – The Golden Years 61
Chapter 11 – Ambitious Efforts 67
Chapter 12 – The Explosion 73

PART C
Chapter 13 – Local Autonomy 81
Chapter 14 – Homes and Mansions 87
Chapter 15 – The Enlightenment 97
Chapter 16 – Social Development 113
Chapter 17 – Model Community 121
Chapter 18 – Liberalism and Revolutions 131

PART D
Chapter 19 – Greek Revolution 143
Chapter 20 – Barons, Bankers, Benefactors 159
Chapter 21 – Achievements and Mayors 173
Chapter 22 – Education – An Objective 179
Chapter 23 – Cultural Behavior 187
Chapter 24 – Annual Festivals 195

Bibliography 205

Introduction

A person's character is formed by childhood experiences among other factors. Parental love and affection provide psychic comfort and security. Environmental behavior broadens understanding and acceptability. Exposures to noticeable but not easily understood events stipulate curiosity.

My early years in Siatista certainly provided all of the above. Fatherly guidance was only an abstract symbol. My father left Paris for New York when I was forty days old in February 1928. It was nothing unusual. For centuries Siatistians worked as expatriates in foreign lands, leaving their families behind. Wives and relatives, mainly grandparents, reared their children. Fathers provided necessary income and guidelines through correspondence and proxy. It was the beginning of the second quarter of the twentieth century. The area won its freedom from centuries-long foreign occupation only fifteen short years earlier. Foreign lands were ever present in Siatistian society. Children repeatedly questioned: Where is Bucharest? Why does the next-door neighbor live in Belgrade? Am I going to school in Italy or Germany when I grow up? Why is almost everybody talking against the Turks? All of these questions demanded answers. It was difficult to understand. I made it my objective to learn the answers through study. During preschool years, my training consisted of exposures to the above experiences. Relatives of expatriates provided answers to the questions above during my mother's visits to exchange news with them. Mother often brought my sister and me to expatriates returning home for a short visit and rest. She hoped through this action to deliver, upon the visitors' return to their foreign base, a favorable comment to our father struggling in a foreign land. The postman was a constant source of courage and hope. At the time we moved to Salonica I was ten years old.

When I registered for elementary school I realized the significance of being born in Paris, France. Was I Greek or French? It did not really matter. The school recorded both and emphasized "son of an immigrant" in America. Neighborhood playmates and classmates did not care. Playing had top priority after school and homework. In summer evenings, being tired after hours of rough running all over dirt and rocky roads, we would settle under star-shiny skies. We often discussed the solar system. The subject, never mentioned in school but overheard in adult discussions, fascinated us. Repeated previous gatherings covered history, especially geography. Everyone was an expert on that one. Generations upon generations of Siatistians accumulated it through necessity and passed it down. It was a matter of survival.

Our family's relocation to Salonica in 1938 was a necessity. It permitted mother to be with her brother and sisters' families already there. Pressures for learning increased further. Our destination was America. The Second World War turmoil shattered our dreams for early family unification. Untold suffering endangered our health and strengthened our willpower. In 1946, we arrived in America. The family reunited after eighteen years of protracted separation. New York City housed a strong and thriving Hellenic community. Siatistians, Kastorians, and Kozanetes were part of it. They had their own societies. Siatistians formed the Siatistian Brotherhood of New York City. Its members were mostly fur craftsmen, but they engaged in other commercial activities as well. In Bradford, Pennsylvania, Siatistians formed the Siatistian Businessmen Association. Similar clubs and societies of Siatistians existed in Lowell, Massachusetts, Washington D.C., and other cities. In Jamestown, New York, the Hellenic community, whose origin was Korytsa (Korce) of Northern Epirus — part of Southern Albania — prospered. Syracuse, New York, had a considerable number of Greeks hailing from Asia Minor, part of Turkey. Ithaca, New York, was home of many immigrants hailing from Tsintzina of Peloponnese, a small village near Sparta. Two groups of Greek settlers, one from Chios Island and another from Tsakonia, an isolated area in eastern Peloponnese, chose Elmira, New York. All groups had their own characteristics and customs. They all, however, belonged to the Greek Church and spoke Greek. Tsakonians spoke their own dialect as well, an ancient version preserved through centuries in villages located in the eastern shores of central Peloponnese, south of Epidaurus.

Twenty years of continuous living in Elmira, New York, strengthened my ties in the community. High school and college education, military service with the U.S. Army, and participation in the Korean War between 1950 and 1952 accentuated my world understanding. Commercial activity along with Chamber of Commerce involvement enhanced my perspective. Daily contact with Elmira's professional and business families, maintained through my fur retail business, supplied comfort and vision. Immeasurable satisfaction derived from active membership in the Greek community provided plenty of contentment. I had no regret, and I sacrificed plenty of time, effort, and money to support its social activities.

My marriage and subsequent family circumstances necessitated my expatriation to Greece in 1966. My son and family continue to live in the United States. I feel an obligation, however, to add my contribution to understanding—by my grandchildren and by all readers worldwide—the efforts made by our ancestors, Siatistians and Upper Macedonians, to the well-being of their next-door neighbors and the world. Once I settled back into Greece, I began to think over my life and how much the town of Siatista is responsible for the way things worked out the way they did. My efforts and research to write my first book, Siatista, Macedonia, and Our Ancestors, exposed me to impressive findings. Very little of it is known to the world. I felt I had an obligation to look into it further. This book is an attempt to understand my parents' hometown and to put it into perspective.

Greek escapees, following invasion and capture of the region by Ottoman Turks, established the town of Siatista. Hard-pressed, independence-minded individuals, greatly influenced by the spirit of Hellenism, settled this hidden mountainous location seeking safety. Its strategic intersection of mountain trails, fairly close to the ancient Roman road Egnatia leading from the Adriatic seaport Durres (presently of Albania) to Constantinople, led to all geographical directions. Absence of water was not a deterrent. Caravan mule and horses led to the close-by, lower-altitude Aliakmon River and nearby springs alleviated the situation. Political conditions favored development of similar communities in the area. Siatista's leading growth in size matched its leading role in trading activities. Accumulation of wealth accompanied its educational advances. Heretofore existing communities accepted Siatistians' impressive spiritual, economic, and political leadership.

Siatistians maneuvered successfully through occupational objectives and appetites of local Ottoman governors. Events are discussed in several books published in Salonica by the Macedonian Studies Society, by the Institution for Balkan Studies, and by independent authors. I attempted to use all items I read about Siatista during my research and tried to mention every source of my information. I emphasized and perhaps repeated items most appropriately fitting the book and my comprehension and presentation of my thoughts.

In order to understand events discussed in the book the following clarifications are necessary:
1. The area's political entity at the time Romans captured it was Macedonia.
2. Hellenic scientific achievements continued to thrive throughout Alexander's and his successors' rule, as well as in Roman and Byzantine empires.
3. Residents of the area as well as all Hellenic people were called Romans during Roman, Byzantine, and Ottoman Empire administrations.
4. Ottoman subjects were all nationalities under Ottoman rule, including Hellenes.
5. Turk(s) and Turkish refer to originators and founders of the Ottoman Empire and their actions.
6. The international powers used the name Greek to identify Hellenes, including Macedonians, living in Ottoman Empire.
7. Greeks, or Hellenes, used ancient Hellenic spirit and achievements to secure a revival of their national entity.
8. Modern-day Greece is called Hellas both at home and the European Union.
9. The words Buda and Pest are mentioned representing events in them at the time they were separate cities prior to uniting and forming Budapest in 1873[1].
10. Hellenic achievements and glory remained as reference to classical advancements. Ancient Isocrates best described Hellenism at his Panegyricus as follows: "The name Hellene no longer connotes the race but the mental attitude, and men are called Hellenes when they share our education rather than merely our common blood[2]."

[1] *The Golden Home Encyclopedia*, p. 447
[2] Methodius G. Fugias, *Hellenism, The Pedestal of Christianity*, p.12

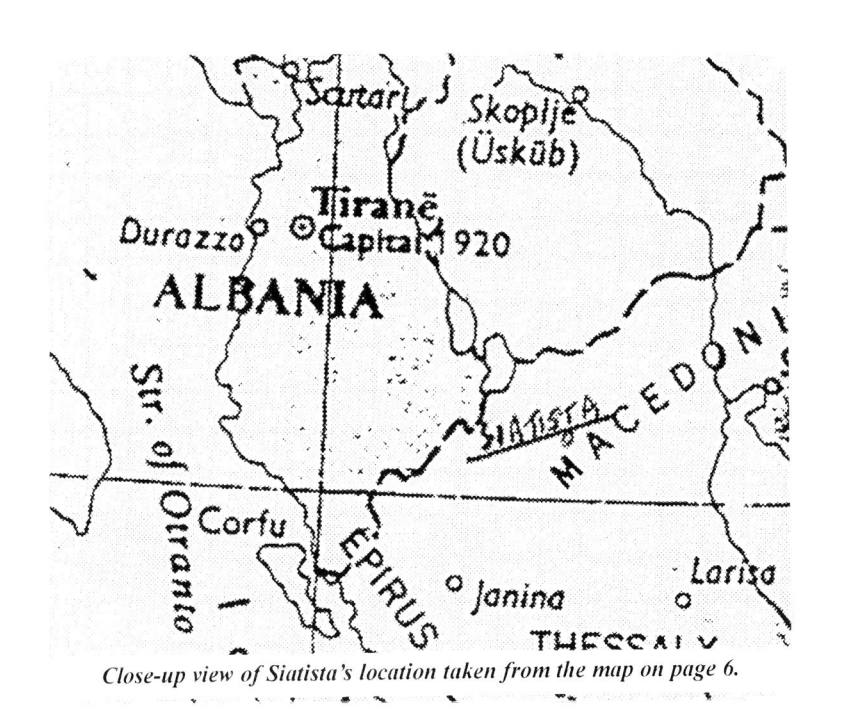

Close-up view of Siatista's location taken from the map on page 6.

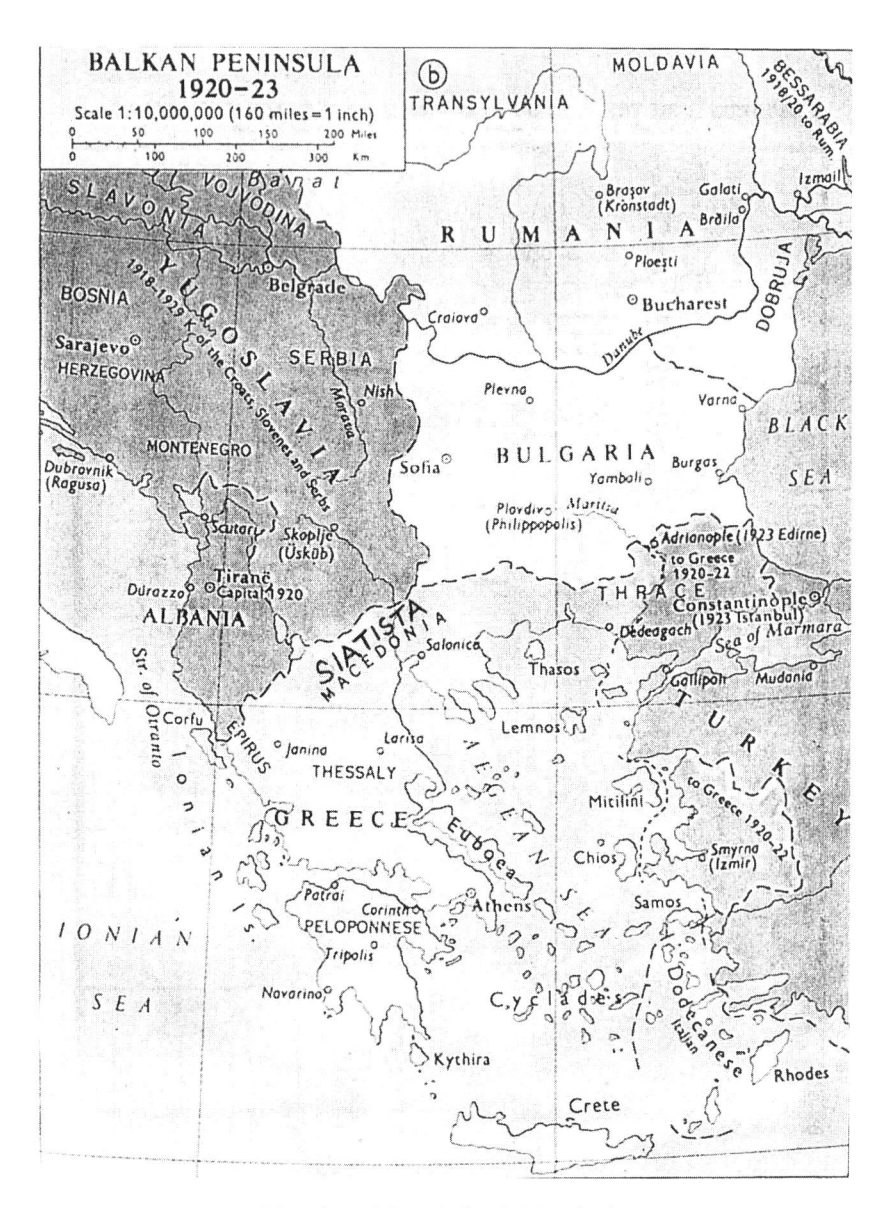

Map from Martis's book *Macedonia*

PART A
Chapter 1
Region in Antiquity

The area between parallels forty and forty-one and meridians twenty-one and twenty-two of the Northern Hemisphere of our planet is part of Northwestern Greece. This area was home base to Alexander the Great's Macedonian Empire during the fourth century B.C. The original Macedonian region first formed around the Aliakmon River extended to Mount Olympus[1]. The terrain is mostly mountainous with beautiful peaks and valleys traversed by the river and its tributaries. The river begins south of Prespa Lakes, flows from northwest to southeast for about one hundred miles, turns eastward, follows a northeastern direction and after about seventy miles, passing west of the town of Vergina, continues its course to empty its waters in the North Aegean Sea. To the east of the river are the mountain crests of Mouriki and Siniatsiko. To the south, Vellia and Bourinos Mountains dominate the area. At Bourinos's southern tip the river turns eastward.

Mountain Bourinos offers lovely scenery with marvelous biotopes. Its flora and fauna preserved even today prompted in 1996 publication in English of Bourinos, a very informative 128-page book, by George Sfekas of the Mountaineering Club of Siatista. The book contains listings of 555 species or subspecies of plants, Spermatophytes, Pteridophytes, and Gymnosperms. Eight of these species don't exist anywhere in the world[2]. Approximately half of all types of butterflies living in Greece are found in the area. Eighty-six of them are presented by name. Amphibians and reptiles are represented by several colorful photos[3]. The prevailing belief that mammals are rare in Greece is challenged by the presence in Bourinos of wolf, brown bear, roe deer and wild boar[4]. One hundred thirty-two bird species are

---

[1] George N. Hammond, *Problems and Achievements of the Great Macedonian Kings Philip and Alexander*, p. 17
[2] George Sfekas, *Bourinos*, p. 21
[3] George Sfekas, *Bourinos*, p. 87
[4] George Sfekas, *Bourinos*, p. 97

listed as residents or passers-by stopping over on their migration from and to Africa. Many of these birds are rare in Greece, even in Europe[5]. The ecological importance of the area can not be overemphasized.

The first Hellenic tribes lived in this region in antiquity. Historians in antiquity claimed the tribes that inhabited Epirus, the area west of Prespa Lakes, included a group called Makednoi, named so from the word makos, meaning long, tall people. During the migration periods the tribes moved to more fertile grounds. Around fourteenth century B.C. they moved north and east, settling on the eastern slopes of the mountainous range of Pindus. These tribes retained the name Macedonians[6]. The expansionist movement south during the thirteenth and twelfth centuries B.C. brought others to the southernmost areas of the Balkan Peninsula, all the way to the Peloponnese. Ancients named these settlers Dorians. The ancient city-state Sparta hailed from this Hellenic tribe. The ancient historian Plutarch wrote that Rome was a colony of Arcadians who, in turn, hailed from the Hellenic tribe Dorians[7]. The Macedonians remained in areas on the eastern side of the Pindus mountains. The abundant supply of water and densely wooded areas found in the region provided plenty of lumber for the settlers' needs and livelihood. They lived by raising sheep and goats. All tribes originating from this area spoke Greek. The Macedonians retained their own dialect, in contrast to the evolution that occurred to dialects of other tribes that moved south. They lived in small, independent groups and opposed slavery as it developed in cities formed in southern Greece[8]. Hard living conditions existing in these isolated areas prevented early development of Macedonians settled around the Aliakmon River. The level of civilization attained by other Hellenic tribes of southern lowlands and coastal strips reached Macedonians much later. Settlers to the south developed their communities and civilizations much

[5]George Sfekas, *Bourinos*, p. 106
[6]Nikolaos K. Koutras, *The Truth About the Central Region in the Balkans* , p. 10
[7]Methodius G. Fugias, *Hellenism, The Pedestal of Christianity*, p. 266
[8]George N. Hammond, *Problems and Achievements of the Great Macedonian Kings Philip and Alexander*, p. 7

earlier than the ones who stayed north. This attracted the interest of the Persians, who repeatedly attempted to conquer them. Macedonian chieftains and lords, leading the groups that stayed behind, united around the fifth century B.C. to protect their own interests. This development came about through their contact with their neighboring communities and states.

The expansionist movements of Asian powers, Persia in particular, presented a threat to all Hellenes, including the Macedonians. The Persians exerted pressure on the flourishing, newly established North Aegean Sea colonies of the Hellenic city-states. Macedonians' realistic determination to defend their safety, their advancement, and well-being was profound. Able Macedonian leaders quickly identified the problems facing them. They realized the need for their participation in the affairs of their neighboring communities. Their involvement in the Peloponnesian War against the Athenian alliance intended to protect their interest in the neighboring city of Potidea, a colony of Athens. Macedonians exported their lumber through Potidea[9]. Their initial interest resulted in continuous involvement in conflicts taking place among various Hellenic city-states. Prolonged fighting lasted for decades and weakened all Greek city-states. When the Persian troops came, the Hellenic cities were unable to effectively defend themselves. Macedonians, because of their ability to recruit hardened warriors unbeatable in horse riding even at the age of sixty, strengthened their power. Strongmen and their elite, controlling until then all Macedonian groups, formed an alliance. Four small independent states—Elimeia, Orestis, Lyggistis, and Pelagonia—formed Upper Macedonia[10]. Their leader, Philip II, father of Alexander the Great, emerged as a very powerful man. Philip spent several of his youth years at Thebes, a southern Hellenic city-state, prior to his elevation to power. He received his education from a student of philosopher Plato[11]. His military tactics followed the strategy of Epameinondas, a Theban general. He was continually

---

[9]B. Grafurof, D. Tsiboukides *Alexander the Macedon and the Orient*, translation G. Stergiou, p. 41

[10]Papathemelis, Stelios, "Macedonia, The Historical View," *Elimeiaka* magazine 16-19, p. 5

[11]B. Gafurof, D. Tsiboukides, *Alexander the Macedon and the Orient*, translation G. Stergiou, p. 43

victorious over neighboring kings. Additionally, he used his diplomatic approaches and moves, such as recognizing all Macedonian chieftains as his equals, to strengthen his powers at home. He succeeded in converting all area strongmen and elite into a governing council with himself as first among equals. Eventual weakening and/or elimination of privileges of dissenting forces elevated him to a powerful position. He hired Aristotle to educate his son Alexander and all the elite's sons, and enhanced the operation of his government. Philip introduced unprecedented changes in his kingdom's organizational structure. The improvements he imposed on his Armed Forces (he was the first to introduce a military uniform for his troops) enabled him to create an unbeatable army. He expanded his control over all neighboring lands. Within years, he annexed his eastern neighbors. His kingdom tripled from fourteen thousand to forty thousand square kilometers. The lands he captured included mountain Paggeon, location of rich gold- and silver-producing mines. Athenians exploited the mines up to that time. Philip's newly formed kingdom included the original four mountainous counties called Upper Macedonia and its annexed areas of Lower Macedonia. Annexation of the Thessaly region in the south added another fifteen thousand square kilometers to Philip's control. The kingdom's original area quadrupled. Its population grew from approximately three hundred thousand to eight hundred thousand people[12]. It was only natural his progress continued to grow.

---

[12]B. Gafurof, D. Tsiboukides, *Alexander the Macedon and the Orient*, translation G. Stergiou, p. 54

Chapter 2

Development of Hellenism

The inhabitants of Upper Macedonia lived in their ancestors' lands isolated for centuries. Their harsh mountains and valleys, rich in lumber and water, were ideal for cattle raising. The groups that migrated south dispersed at all directions, settling in lower altitude and more fertile lands. Through navigation, they came in contact with other, more advanced peoples living in the Eastern Mediterranean, the Middle East, and on African shores. They developed their own communities and ideas about life and the world.

The civilizations created by them through study and research benefited all mankind. Their knowledge reached the highest level known. Working on whatever they could hear, understand, observe, or study, they developed their own sound theories. Step by step they elevated the level of their society by employing logical approaches to problems facing them. They researched all possible avenues with fantastic results. Philosophers Plato and Aristotle, among others, studied life and death questions. Their objective was complete elimination of human dependence on ignorance and superstition. Scientists researched and improved medicine to appreciable levels. Hippocrates became famous for his oath and commitment to medicine. There was immense advancement with Democritus' accomplishments on the atom theory in the area of physics. Multitudes of scientists, including Euclides and Pythagoras, perfected mathematics through their theorems. Appreciable advances occurred in agriculture, botany, and astronomy as well. The arts reached magnificent levels, remaining unequaled even to this date. Political science and government, however, made a significant impact on the Greek masses. The people were free to express themselves and elect their own government. Laws were passed, imposed, altered, or abolished as per voters' wishes. Commerce flourished and society's living standards improved. Humans engaged in all sorts of activities to their heart's content. Historians Herodotus, Thoucydides, Xenofon, and others wrote about activities they experienced, heard about, or conceived. Homer's centuries-old works of *The Iliad* and *The Odyssey* are immortalized. Playwrights Sophocles, Eschylos, Euripides, and Aristofanes among many, created all sorts of human agonies, anxieties, pleasures, bitterness, sufferings, and tragedies. Society established guidelines and directions leading to human fulfillment and satisfaction in all phases of life. They questioned and researched everything, even theology. Nothing was absolute, not even luck. Scientists conducted their research employing reason and proof. The accumulation of knowledge was immense. The accumulation of art pieces was even greater. Artists worked on statues of gods, public figures, mythical scenes, and animals. They produced anything worth immortalizing through their work. More than five hundred pieces of art decorated the rock of Acropolis in Athens. Displayed inside the Parthenon, the Erechtheum, in other temples, or in the open, they made Athens world famous. Hellenes' observation, thinking, and efforts to study and research, to understand and express, to promote and enhance, to develop and introduce products and ideas, and to differ and coexist transformed humanity. Hellenism was on the go.

Hellenes' advances continued to grow for centuries, promoting dignity and respect. They occurred in many city-states and in their colonies. Wherever Hellenes settled, they brought with them their own way of life. Their improved shipbuilding industry enabled them to travel to the North Aegean, Black Sea, and to all Mediterranean points. They established innumerable colonies on their shores. They lived there and prospered for centuries. Athenians and Corinthians colonized the North Aegean coastline in the middle of seventh century B.C.[1] These colonies traded with their northern neighbors and with Upper Macedonia's merchants. King Philip II of Macedonia conquered the area in the middle of fourth century B.C. Recent archaeological excavations by Professor Andronikos of Salonica University unearthed golden wreaths, bracelets, swords, necklaces, and precious personal objects of King Philip II. These items confirm early commercial transactions between southern Hellenes and the Macedonians. This activity provided

[1] Nikolaos K. Koutras, *The Truth About the Central Region in the Balkans*, p. 23

an opportunity for more advanced Hellenes of the colonies to make inroads into Upper Macedonia. The traders brought with them their ambitions and enthusiasm, and stimulated the heretofore easygoing thoughts and ideas of hard-working Macedonians.

Medical doctors provided their services to Macedonian government officials and elite groups. Aristotle's father, Nicomachos, served as a doctor in the royal court of Philip II's father, King Amyntas. Peoples everywhere in the known world religiously followed Hellenism as a way of life. Macedonian kings were no exception. Aristotle's theory was simple. He considered the political organization of civilized Hellenism superior to whatever had come before. Freedom of thought and speech were basic requirements. Thirteen-year-old Alexander and his classmates, all sons of the Macedonian elite (local chieftains, generals, and other government officials), received Aristotle's tutoring for four years. They absorbed whatever there was to know from philosophy to medicine, to government, to war. Alexander respected Aristotle. Father Philip, along with Aristotle, continued to guide him. At the age of eighteen, Alexander won his first battle. In a brilliant performance he defeated Hellenic cities' allied forces at Chaeronia in 338 B.C. The Macedonians, themselves of Hellenic decent, did not destroy their opponents. Instead, they proposed to them establishment of a Hellenic Community to include all Hellenic cities, similar to today's European Union[2]. All city-states were to retain their own independence and self-governments, but had to jointly fight non-Hellene aggression. They promoted the concept they experienced themselves of getting together, of maintaining peace, and attacking the Persians, the Hellenes' enemies in Asia.

Philip's assassination in 336 B.C.[3] and Alexander's rise to power advanced that intent. Hellenic city-states' representatives in a conference held in Corinth voted for an all-Hellenic campaign against the Persians. They elected Philip's son Alexander as their leader. Sparta, although it participated in the

---

[2]George N. Hammond, *Problems and Achievements of the Great Macedonian Kings Philip and Alexander*, p.10
[3]Arrian, translation of A. De Selincourt, *The Campaigns of Alexander*, p. 41

conference, could not accept Alexander's leadership on grounds of principles. Spartans could not compromise their leadership.

Alexander's campaigns began by solidifying Macedonian conquests in the Balkan Peninsula. He advanced conquering all lands all the way to Danube River[4]. Alexander crossed into Asia chasing the enemy and triumphantly fought, defeated, captured, resettled, rehabilitated, and attempted to Hellenize the multitude of peoples he conquered. A plethora of scientists, philosophers, administrators, and historians supplemented his soldiers. He utilized their presence and instituted changes that vastly improved the lives of the population. His troops and technicians cleared virgin lands, constructed roads, opened canals, built cities, and restored temples. He performed sacrifices to Gods, held symposiums, and arranged marriages of his soldiers with Asian women, intermingling populations and societies. He advanced Hellenic values of acceptance, understanding, and respect. Nothing escaped Alexander's advisers' attention. Their efforts concentrated in passing their own knowledge to locals. Simultaneously, they absorbed everything they considered useful and beneficial. Asian civilizations offered new opportunities for study. The enormous wealth of the rich royal courts' treasuries financed all the above projects. Their money paid all of his multinational troops' salaries and wages[5]. The aged Macedonian troops returned to their homes endowed with whatever types of items they could carry. Additionally, they enjoyed all privileges given to them by their state. Their fellow men extended to them recognition and honors. A large number of veterans, including the sick and wounded, however, settled in the newly established communities in conquered lands. They married Asian women and made new families. They manned the guards on these far-from-Macedonia posts. Alexander married an Asian princess. He adopted Asian customs and attire but remained a Hellene. His spirit of Hellenism was ever present. By the time he died, he was well on his way to being the top citizen of a new, unified, and integrated world with Babylon as his capital. His dream of Hellenizing the whole known world was at the point of attainment.

[4]J. G. Droysen, translation of R. H. S. Apostolides, *History of the Heirs of Alexander the Great*, p. 670
[5]Arrian, translation of A. De Selincourt, *The Campaigns of Alexander*, p. 355

Chapter 3
Macedonian Rule

Alexander's death in 323 B.C.[1] occurred eleven years after his invasion of Asia. All these years the king was leading his troops away from home to distant lands. Eleven years is an extremely short period for any person, leader, or system to affect profound changes in any society. The changes taking place during this period at Alexander's initiative in the entire known world, however, were immense. The newly instituted reforms resulted in uncontrollable repercussions. Individuals and merchants traveled extensively in all corners of the conquered land, bringing products and ideas from Europe all the way to India.

Alexander's death brought an end to the carefully cultivated divinity concept nourished by Olympias, Alexander's mother. God Ammon of Egypt no longer represented Alexander's biological father. Cavalrymen, infantry soldiers, and special unit troops making up Philip's original army obeyed only their immediate officers. Ancestry formed the basis of their allegiance. Alexander's Advisory Council, at a meeting called after his death to determine the empire's future, failed to agree as to who would replace the king. Alexander, lying in his bed, handed his authority ring to Perdikkas, his eldest general[2]. However, the shattered divine force unifying all Macedonians was no longer among them. Human ambitions surfaced. The king's lieutenants and partners in battle divided the huge empire among themselves. Most conquered peoples already enjoyed semi-independent status with very little or no central governmental authority. A triumvirate composed of a governor—sometimes the same Asian king who elected to surrender rather than fight Alexander's forces—a finance administrator, and a post guard commander formed the governing body. Non-Macedonians, members of the huge supply of talented individuals who followed Alexander's armies, often received appointments to

[1] Arrian, translation A. De Selincourt, *The Campaigns of Alexander*, p. 405
[2] J. G. Droysen, translation R. H. S. Apostolides, *History of the Heirs of Alexander the Great*, p. 4

top positions. Disobedience or questioning Alexander's absolute authority brought severe punishment, sometimes by beheading the guilty.

Alexander's Advisory Council divided this vast territory for administrative purposes. It established twenty-six departments with corresponding governors and armies. Perdikkas, with an honor guard of one thousand men, became the titular head of the central government in Babylon[3]. The new organization resulted in a similar or parallel arrangement to the Persian royal court administration or a combination of the two. It reflected the one-world-order concept pursued by Alexander. His home base, Macedonia, was one of the twenty-six departments, however, that retained all its characteristics and idiosyncrasies of the centuries-old kingdom.

Alexander's lieutenants and generals challenged each other's entitlement of governmental authority. Conflicts broke out not only in Macedonia proper, but also in all departments of the empire. Local commercial interests of Hellenic cities, interwoven with personal political ambitions cultivated in all walks of life, surfaced. Surplus military manpower, ready to join the ranks of any leader offering more money, moved the wheels for the upcoming battles. Alliances formed from the Mediterranean shores to the Indu River, and from the shores of the Danube River to Cyprus attempted to maintain the balance of power. Competition for projection and success remained the driving force. Horse-riding messengers and runners with almost primitive means performed all communications.

The power struggle continued among Alexander's lieutenants and generals for years. Each one of them gave his own interpretation to Alexander's dreams and objectives. Hellenism, however, prevailed throughout these years. Its spirit, with all it represented, commanded everyone's objectives and actions. The Asians' captured wealth financed the generals' campaigns and built ships, war machines, and installations. Utilization of the huge wealth the Asian public treasuries possessed stimulated the economy. Commerce among East and West improved through usage of new inland and navigational

---

[3] J. G. Droysen, translation R. H. S. Apostolides, *History of the Heirs of Alexander the Great*, p. 14

routes.

Everyone spoke the Hellenic language to do business. Alexander had previously given instructions to his troops: Children of intermarried couples, settlers of newly established cities and army posts were to be taught the Hellenic language. Their proper training was mandatory in anticipation of their contribution to the new nation's administrative nucleus and its army. Hellenic education, ideas, and philosophy joined the Asiatic mind and filled vacuums wherever such existed. Coined moneys depicted Hellenic Gods, Alexander, his general Antigonos, and Hellenic objects. These coins circulated along with previously issued Doric and Phoenician coins. Alexander's heirs to the throne, Macedonians, Hellenes, and Asians, absorbed and thoroughly practiced Hellenism during their power struggle and for centuries thereafter. Governmental officials, local and regional authorities, merchants, doctors, scholars, and philosophers employed the Hellenic language. Historians, true to Alexander's intentions to have everything recorded, followed the newly reorganized Macedonian armies. A considerable portion of these troops consisted of Asiatics or Helleno-Asians. Historians observed and recorded in detail all events.

In 322 B.C. Perdikkas advanced his control in Kappadokia, central Asia Minor region, and appointed Eumenes governor. Antigonos and Antipatros resisted Perdikkas's plans favored also by Alexander's mother Olympias. Olympias, to strengthen Perdikkas's position to the throne, proposed to him to marry her daughter Cleopatra, widowed queen of Epirus. Ptolemeos, governor of Egypt, broke ties with Babylon's authority of Perdikkas and expanded his control over North Africa. In 321 B.C. general Krateros moved from Macedonia against Eumenes. In the battle that followed the governor of Armenia, Neoptolemos came to the assistance of Eumenes. Neoptolemos defeated Krateros's Macedonian troops and strengthened Eumenes's and Perdikkas's position.

These conflicts and battles lasted for almost half a century. Back in the area where it all originated, Hellenic cities continued their debate to determine what was best for their own interests. Regional alliances formed in Thebes, Attica, and Peloponnese.

Macedonians reconstructed the city of Thebes that they destroyed when they first drove south twenty years earlier, selling its inhabitants as slaves to raise funds. Macedonia proper, after years of civil disorder, witnessed the death by stoning of Alexander's mother in 316 B.C. It happened in the city of Pydna where she maintained her palace[4]. Political instability followed, having a succession of ten kings within thirty years from 306 to 277. Then, Antigonos Gonatas took over and governed for thirty-eight years. Gonatas was the grandson of the one-eyed general who played an important role in all of Philip II army's drives to Alexander's campaigns. In the post-Alexander era, grandfather Antigonos became a governor-then-king and, at eighty-four, led his troops in battle, getting killed by opposing Macedonian soldiers[5].

The death of old-guard officers who somehow cherished Alexander's dream of unifying and solidifying Hellenism in the entire known world brought an end to the civil strife. Their sons carried their dreams only to some extent. Their grandsons finally faced reality. Hellenism thrived even though the one-world idea failed. Merchants continued to trade their goods, traveling to all known regions. Caravans followed newly developed routes in bringing goods back and forth. Merchants and educators universally utilized the Hellenic language. Integration occurred even in religious beliefs. Many people living in remote Asiatic regions cultivated vineyards and honored Dionysus, the Greek god of wine and fun.

Another century passed with Macedonia and other regions, including the Hellenic cities, trying to find their destiny. The governors of the twenty-six administrative units were busy with their own departments. The Macedonian kings felt the growing power and pressure of Rome west of their border. It was only a matter of time for new powers to emerge back home. The areas of Sicily and Italy in the Adriatic Sea, themselves part of the ancient Hellenic world, grew stronger and stronger. Their close ties to developments in the entire Macedonian Empire,

---

[4] J. G. Droysen, translation R. H. S. Apostolides, *History of The Heirs of Alexander the Great*, p. 242

[5] J. G. Droysen, translation R. H. S. Apostolides, *History of the Heirs of Alexander the Great*, p. XII

especially in its regions in the Mediterranean Sea, prompted them to act. They moved and defeated in the battle of Pydna in the year 168 B.C.[6] whatever remained of the Macedonian forces. The Macedonian symbol, Philip's bright sun, stopped shining. It lay buried with Macedonia for twenty-three centuries at the modern town of Vergina. Excavations under archeologist Andronikos unearthed it from its grave along with a reborn hope for a lasting peace.

---

[6]Konstantinos E. Siabanopoulos, *The Museum of Kozane*, p. 4

Photo of the golden larnax where Philip's bones were stored in his grave, unearthed in the town of Vergina.

Chapter 4
Rome and Byzantium

Defeat of Macedonian armies in the battle of Pydna signaled capitulation of its military forces to Rome but did not affect the growth of the Hellenic spirit. The Roman armies utilized the Macedonian-established roads to rapidly expand their conquests. To control their new subjects the Romans relied on existing educators, scholars, and merchants, and on their Hellenic language and culture. The Romans continued for centuries to build on the knowledge accumulated in Hellenic cities of the Macedonian Empire. They concentrated on improving their own organization and approach. Hellenic thought and culture in the meantime experienced further growth. Termination of Rome's civil strife during the first half of the first century resulted in the long period of peace, the Pax Romana as it is known, which enhanced development of remarkable political, social, and intellectual standards[1]. Kamara Galery, built in 297 to commemorate Galerius Maximilian's victory against the Persians even today reminds Salonica's visitors of the Hellenistic and Roman cooperation.

Hellenes continued to produce and to export statues and other art pieces to Asiatic regions. Sculpturing grew to such proportions that Rome, the new center of world power, was full of marble exhibitions. They depicted all types of scenes from Hellenic mythology. Scholars, intellectuals, and artists continued to study the Hellenic language. It was profoundly essential for businessmen for promotion and expansion of their trade. Plato's Academy in Athens established in 387 B.C. was still in operation. The school, highly respected throughout the known world first of Alexander's empire and the Roman conquerors later, attracted and accepted students from all races. It dealt with all areas of knowledge. It cultivated all sciences, art, political institutions and ethics, strategy, diplomacy, navigational and international laws. Philosophy and religion dominated its deliberations.

[1]Apostolos E. Vacalopoulos, *The History of Thessalonike*, p. 13

Explosion of accumulated knowledge resulted in many philosophical interpretations and approaches to religion. Alexandria, the city Alexander built in Egypt, developed into the most advanced educational center. It paralleled, even excelled, Plato's Academy in Athens. It fused together civilizations from Asiatic lands, Egypt, and the Hellenes. Hellenism provided the fuel for such intellectual intercourse. Crucial interpretations and philosophical trends of perennial values shaped contemporary society and culture.

Hellenism's twelve gods allowed space for the Unknown God whom Apostle Paul lost no time to promote in his visits to Athens and other Macedonian cities. His appearance and lectures delivered to congregations of Salonica's Jewish synagogue in A.D. 50 for three Sabbaths in succession, had a positive response. Many converted into Christianity[2]. Jewish intellectuals dispersed throughout the Mediterranean seaports already practiced monotheism. Their holy Old Testament translated into Hellenic language from Hebrew contributed to greater understanding and assimilation of Christianity. Jewish intellectuals perfected the new religion whose destination was transformation of humanity. Philosopher Philon, Hellenized Jew and contemporary of Jesus, supporting his thesis claimed, directly or indirectly, one god alone was the source for both Moses's Laws and Hellenic philosophy[3]. Innumerable common characteristics developed between the two peoples, Jews and Hellenes. They both benefited from each other's philosophies yet they retained their identities. Winston Churchill's words, "Athens' and Jerusalem's messages on religion, philosophy, and art have been the main guiding lights of modern faith and culture" (The Second World War, vol. , pages 470, 471) are worth repeating[4]. J. G. Droysen, a nineteenth-century historian wrote regarding Hellenism and Christianity: "Development of a Christian World Church would have been extremely difficult, if not impossible, without the achievements made by the Hellenes[5]."

[2]Apostolos E. Vacalopoulos, *The History of Thessalonike* , p. 17
[3]Methodius G. Fugias, *Hellenism, The Pedestal of Christianity*, p. 103
[4]Winston S. Churchill, *The Second World War, Vol. V*, p. 470-71
[5]Methodius G. Fugias, *Hellenism, The Pedestal of Christianity*, p. 124

The city of Tarsus, Apostle Paul's birthplace and residence, included among its Jewish population a good number of settlers hailing from the Hellenic city of Argos. Alexander's general Antiochos brought them over during the post-Alexander era. They operated their own schools, offering a first-class Hellenic education. Paul, a son of Jewish parents, most likely studied Hellenism along with his Jewish education. Many of Apostle Paul's writings paralleled the thoughts and expressions of Xenophon, Euripides, and Plato[6]. Origenes, the greatest exponent of Hellenic knowledge, after a bright teaching career at the school of Alexandria went to teach at Kesareia schools in the third century. His teachings and influence expanded to Asia Minor, Syria, and Palestine. The Antiochian school in Syria, established in the fourth century, developed a different interpretation on Hellenic works and philosophy. John Chrysostom, a Syrian Christian "who merits a higher rating than (ancient) Aristides and can be compared with Demosthenes," of Athens, as per U. von Wilanovitz-Mollendorf, attended the Antiochian school. The school of Gaza, established towards the end of the fifth century, was a brainchild of the Alexandrian school, which itself was a brainchild of Athens school. Both Plato's and Aristotle's theories were dominant in all of these schools. The professors taught and debated through a Christian interpretation[7]. Fundamental achievements and trends developed through debate and elaboration throughout the Hellenistic period continued. Mohammedanism, which appeared in the Arab world in the seventh century, utilized existing Hellenic and Roman intermingled thought communications to expand. By the eleventh century Mohammedanism translated most Hellenic works, including Plato and Aristotle, into Arabic. Mohammedamism's sacred book, the Koran, accepted and respected Jews and Hellenes. It even acknowledged, in the Chapter of the Cave, Alexander the Great (or the Dul-el-Karnein meaning two-horned one) as one of the good men sent to earth to instruct the people[8]. Its followers

[6]Methodius G. Fugias, *Hellenism, The Pedestal of Christianity*, p. 78-81
[7]Methodius G. Fugias, *Hellenism, The Pedestal of Christianity*, p. 118
[8] Konstantinos Metsakis, *Macedonia Throughout the Centuries*, p. 13

were to protect Jewish and Hellenic places of worship and their estates[9].

While intellectual activity of scholars, historians, and theologians regarding Hellenic, Jewish, Christian, and Islamic virtues continued, the Latin language began to make inroads into the Roman church. The exclusive use of the Hellenic language prevailed in the church throughout both the East and West Roman Empire, until A.D. 180[10]. Slowly over the centuries, Latin replaced the Hellenic language in the Roman church. Hellenic, however, remained the operational tongue until the fourth century for philosophers, educators, and merchants as well as for slaves originating in the eastern regions of the Roman Empire. Emperor Constantine between 324 and 330 built Constantinople at the crossroads of Asia and Europe. The intent was to improve administration by overcoming the huge distances. Contrary to his wishes it resulted in splitting the empire in two, the Western and Eastern parts.

The elimination of the Hellenic language by the Roman church resulted in poor spiritual communications between East and West. Complete lack of understanding occurred in the fifth century and thereafter. The eastern part, with Constantinople as its capital, continued to use the Hellenic language. Eventually the two, eastern and western parts, drifted further apart. Even the Roman Imperial Court at Constantinople converted to Hellenization as per A. Hamman[11]. Lack of spiritual exchanges between eastern and western independent forces and administrative division caused by emperor Theodosius' death in A.D. 395[12] resulted in a complete partition in the two Roman Empires. The eastern Roman Empire eventually became Byzantine, named after the Greek colony Byzantium, a small community preceding Constantinople's construction on the site. The ancient Hellenic civilization that carried forward first by Alexander, and then continued its expansion by Romans, prevailed even though emperor Justinian closed Plato's Academy in A.D. 529 after being in operation for nine hundred years. The residents of the Byzantine Empire were Roman citizens. People residing in the outer eastern lands referred to them as Unanis, a modified word from the original

[9]Methodius G. Fugias, *Hellenism, The Pedestal of Christianity*, p. 277
[10]Methodius G. Fugias, *Hellenism, The Pedestal of Christianity*, p. 132
[11]Methodius G. Fugias, *Hellenism, The Pedestal of Christianity*, p. 155
[12]Apostolos E. Vacalopoulos, *The History of Thessalonike*, p. 26

Iones, the name of the ancient Hellenic groups that traveled and settled their lands, bringing to them the spirit of Hellenism.

Chapter 5
Byzantium and Slavs

The transformation of Eastern Roman into the Byzantine Empire occurred because of severe social, economic, and political pressures experienced by governments and populations residing within its borders. All ethnic groups, civic leaders, and vested interests tried to improve their position in the new world order. Macedonian Hellenism and subsequently Rome no longer used the word "barbarian," common in Hellenic cities one thousand years ago. Alexander's internationalization of trade resulted in the authorities' acceptance, even encouragement, of freedom of movement of laborers to satisfy demands in agriculture and related areas.

The Slavic people, a branch of the Indo-European group, lived in areas north of the Black Sea east of the Dneiper River. They moved west and south early in the sixth century A.D. They first settled in northeast Germany and north Austria[1]. Slavs inhabited Bohemia, Saxony, and Poland[2]. The groups engaged mostly in agriculture eventually moved south. They lived peacefully with the local populations. Byzantine authorities did not object to these settlers. In 535 Emperor Justinian, in an effort to promote Christianity and assist them, established the First Justinian Autocefalus Eastern Orthodox Archepiscopate of Achris. The city of Achris lies on the east shore of Lake Achris in the area of ancient Upper Macedonia[3]. Slav immigrants kept on moving south in substantial numbers. Their strength reached considerable proportions in areas around Salonica[4]. The greatest number of immigrants settled in areas adjacent to the northern borders of the Byzantine Empire. The state of Bulgaria was established in the southern lands of the River Danube in the second half of the seventh century[5]. Repeated military excursions

---
[1]Fedon Maligoudes, *Thessalonike and The World of Slavs*, p. 36,37
[2]*Encyclopedia Avlos*, p. 2124
[3]Donald M. Nichol, translation by Perikles Lefkas, *The Despotate of Epirus*, p. 73
[4]Fedon Maligoudes, *Thessalonike and The World of Slavs*, p. 56
[5]Apostolos E. Vacalopoulos, *The History of Thessalonike*, p. 38

of Slav leaders followed, occupying Byzantine lands. They did not, however, perpetuate their rule and their stay on the lands they captured. They nevertheless left many settlers as far south as the Peloponnese. All of them eventually became Hellenes. Byzantine authorities, in an effort to control them—parallel to military measures—proceeded to educate these people. After the Russians' attack on Constantinople in 860 with twelve hundred men and two hundred vessels[6], Byzantine emperor Michael, at the request of Moravia's ruler Radislav, commissioned in 862 Cyril and Methodius from Salonica to upgrade the Slavs' standards[7]. The two brothers, sons of a Byzantine army officer, were graduates of the Imperial School of Constantinople. They were well versed in the Slavic tongue. Cyril composed an alphabet for them where none existed before. The new alphabet included Greek, Jewish, and Armenian elements. The two brothers then translated into Slavic the Bible and other liturgical books. Upon Cyril's death, Methodius, who at a time had served as governor and had administrative experience, continued Cyril's work. The actions of these two brothers from Salonica laid the foundations for the remarkable achievements that the Slavic nations show today. "Cyril and Methodius introduced the Hellenic and Byzantine cultures in Europe and made the Slavs Christians," stated Pope John-Paul in his speech in Moravia on April 22, 1990[8]. The central church authority at Byzantium guided and assisted the Slav Hellenization and Christianization process.

Byzantium's political turmoil, however, continued. The self-confidence of the Bulgarian leaders led them to repeated attacks to the south against Byzantine areas. Salonica and surrounding areas finally fell in their hands in 900. Their power, however, quickly disintegrated upon their leaders' death[9]. Hellenism prevailed over their numbers remaining behind by assimilation. Hellenic values of social acceptance and enhancement of individual excellence prevented racial prejudice. Available records confirm Slav families settled in Chalcidike in the tenth

[6]Elias Laskaris, *Byzantine Emperors*, Vol. I, p. 157
[7]Konstantinos Metsakis, *Macedonia Throughout the Centuries*, p. 24
[8]Nikolaos Martes, *Macedonia, Hellenism's Advanced Shield, Macedonia Themata*, issue 3-4/1995
[9]Apostolos E. Vacalopoulos, *The History of Thessalonike*, p. 38

century. They lived harmoniously with their neighbors. They worked on land belonging to the Holy Monastic community of Mt. Athos. Their only obligation was payment of their tax[10]. Byzantium, towards the end of the tenth century, in an effort to strengthen its defenses, requested assistance from its northern neighbors. The ruler of Kiev, Vladimer—who controlled vast regions each with its own pagan religion—readily responded. An arrangement, worked out between the two powers, introduced Christianity to these northern people. The Eastern Orthodox Church extended its influence to all former eastern Roman Empire regions plus all land masses to the north. The Slavia Orthodoxa became a reality[11].

Byzantium's concentration on church matters at the expense of civil administration caused repeated setbacks and defeats of the Byzantines[12]. Their eastern neighbors, the Persians, during the first half of the seventh century fought a ten-year war against the Byzantines. The Persians weakened the Byzantines, who constantly repelled them. The Byzantines paid no attention to the rise of Mohammedanism originating in Arabia. They underestimated its importance and potential. Byzantine authorities had abandoned Hellenic values in many areas of the empire. Pressure on residents of Syria and Palestine to become Christians substituted the Hellenic principles of respect to individuals and human rights[13]. This brought resentment to inhabitants of these lands. They sided with the Arabs upon their appearance. The new conquerors honored their Jewish religion. In 636, the Byzantines experienced defeat in the battle near Yarmuk. Damascus already fell a year earlier. By the middle of the eighth century, the Arab world stabilized itself and Baghdad became the center of the Islamic Empire[14]. Their driving force was theocratic Islam. All political entities maintained their existence in contrast to Byzantium's policy, which incorporated them all into the empire.

Saracen pirates repeatedly stormed the Mediterranean and Aegean shores in the early part of the tenth century. Destruction,

---

[10] Fedon Maligoudes, *Thessalonike and The World of Slavs*, p. 116
[11] Fedon Maligoudes, *Thessalonike and The World of Slavs*, p. 134
[12] Methodius G. Fugias, *Hellenism, the Pedestal of Christianity*, p. 31
[13] Methodius G. Fugias, *Hellenism, the Pedestal of Christianity*, p. 95
[14] Methodius G. Fugias, *Hellenism, the Pedestal of Christianity*, p. 32

suffering, and slavery of the population were everyday phenomena[15]. While these were going on towards the end of the tenth century, the Bulgarians under King Samuel moved. They renewed their attempt to stabilize their authority in areas all the way south including Macedonia[16]. The Serbs won their autonomy in 1190[17]. The European crusaders arriving later with the stated purpose of liberating the holy lands from the Mohammedans dealt a catastrophe to Byzantium. The first invasion by Normans took place at Durres, the western shore port in the Balkans. The ancient Roman road east, Egnatia, began from Durres. In 1204, they advanced through Macedonia, captured Constantinople[18], and demolished the Byzantine Empire. Destruction and loss of wealth were immense. Loss of dignity, however, became irreparable. The empire broke into several kingdoms and principalities[19]. Among them were two distinct Greek states, the Kingdom of Nicea in the East and the Despotate of Epirus in the West. The Franks' Kingdom of Macedonia, with Salonica as its capital, found itself in the center. Its life lasted only twenty years. In 1224 it succumbed to the Despotate of Epirus. Much later, in 1261, the emperor of the kingdom of Nicea liberated Constantinople, fifty-seven years from its capture from the crusaders. The empire technically reunited[20]. The new situation allowed continuation and improvement of trade between the Venetians and the empire. In 1277, Venetians won commercial rights, including quarters facilities, through a treaty signed with the emperor's officials. The treaty included rights to maintain a church in Constantinople and Salonica[21]. In a balancing move for trade competition and political purposes, Byzantine authorities extended trading privileges to the cities of Genoa and Pizza[22].

The threat to the empire continued to be serious. Franks, Bulgarians, and later the Serbs became important military and political powers[23]. In 1283, Serbian forces conquered Upper

---

[15]Apostolos E. Vacalopoulos, *The History of Thessalonike*, p. 37
[16]Apostolos E. Vacalopoulos, *The History of Thessalonike*, p. 39
[17]Elias Laskaris, *Byzantine Emperors*, Vol. II, p. 206
[18]Apostolos E. Vacalopoulos, *The History of Thessalonike*, p. 47
[19]Konstantinos Metsakis, *Macedonia Throughout the Centuries*, p. 27
[20]Konstantinos Metsakis, *Macedonia Throughout the Centuries*, p. 28
[21]Apostolos E. Vacalopoulos, *The History of Thessalonike*, p. 49
[22]Donald M. Nicol, translation by Perikles Lefkas, *The Despotate of Epirus*, p. 8
[23]Konstantinos Metsakis, *Macedonia Throughout the Centuries*, p. 29

Macedonia areas[24]. Thirteen years later, in 1296, their occupation extended to Durres at the Adriatic Sea. The Serbs forced Andronicos, the Byzantine emperor, to offer his six-year-old daughter in marriage with middle-aged King Milotin of Serbia. A dowry of lands north of Achris and Perlepe already in the hands of the Serbs accompanied the deal[25]. In 1331 Stephen Dousan, emperor of Serbia and Romania, invaded considerable parcels of Byzantine land in the lower Balkans. His intention was to be crowned emperor in Constantinople. His Hellenized Serbian state, writes modern Greek historian Professor A. Vacalopoulos in *History of Macedonia* (1354–1833), was Greek in its structure and character. It was inevitable for it to later submit completely to the Greek cultural influence[26]. Hellenic language was necessary in administering all captured lands.

Serb expansionism ended as the Ottomans invaded the continent of Europe in 1354. The Serbs' defeat in 1371 and again in 1389 in the battle of Kosovo resulted in the taking over by the Ottomans of the whole region[27]. Serbs, Bulgarians and Byzantines capitulated. In addition to paying the Ottomans tribute, they all accepted an obligation to assist their rulers with their military campaigns[28]. Ottoman presence in the Balkans continues.

---

[24]Elias Laskares, *Byzantine Emperors*, Vol. II, p. 206
[25]Elias Laskares, *Byzantine Emperors*, Vol. II, p. 162
[26]Konstantinos Metsakis, *Macedonia Throughout the Centuries*, p. 33
[27]Konstantinos E. Siabanopoulos, *The Museum of Kozane*, p. 4
[28]Apostolos E. Vacalopoulos, *The History of Thessalonike*, p. 60

Chapter 6
Ottomans and Balkans

The invasion of European lands by Ottoman forces was gradual and methodical. The city of Salonica, Macedonia's capital, first came under their rule in 1387. After sixteen years, in 1403, Salonica reverted to previous status when the Ottomans, preoccupied with internal power struggles, had to withdraw. Ottomans and Byzantines faced internal instability within their ranks. Venetians became rulers of Salonica in 1423 at the invitation of the local Byzantine governor. He made the arrangement in an effort to stabilize the situation and discourage the Ottomans[1]. Repeated efforts by Byzantine emperors to negotiate differences with European leaders ended up in failure. Inefficient administration of Salonica by the Venetians and reorganization of the Ottomans enabled them to recapture the city in 1430[2]. It remained under their rule for 482 years. All European crusades organized to repel the Ottoman advances proved fruitless. The Ottomans defeated Hungarian King Ladislas in Varna in 1444. They also managed a devastating blow to John Hunyard in Kosovo in 1448[3]. Constantinople, the empire's capital, resisted the pressure until 1453, the year it fell to the Ottomans. Its capture blocked all commercial overland routes from Europe to Asia and vice versa. This development led to the landing on America in 1492.

Upon conquering Constantinople the Ottoman troops, contrary to their religion, slaughtered, looted, destroyed, and burned whatever was on their way. They based their administration on humiliation, abuse of power, forced labor, prison sentences, execution, and high taxation[4]. Large segments of populations living in the lands they captured left their homes. Their cities emptied and the villagers retreated to more mountainous and defensible locations where they could hope for

[1] Konstantinos Bakalopoulos, *Macedonia and Turkey*, 1830-1878, p. 29
[2] Konstantinos Metsakis, *Macedonia Throughout the Centuries*, p. 36
[3] Konstantinos Metsakis, *Macedonia Throughout the Centuries*, p. 37
[4] Konstantinos Metsakis, *Macedonia Throughout the Centuries*, p. 36

safety. Many relocated to areas occupied by the Franks. Intellectuals and scholars, unable to live and work under guidance and pressure, migrated to Western cities. Freedom of expression and favorable conditions encouraged their literary endeavors[5]. Many migrated to Serbia, Austria, Hungary, Wallachia, Moldavia, and other lands. Some individuals gave up Christianity and accepted Mohammedanism but retained their language and culture. Others converted to the new religion in order to save either their estates or their positions of power[6].

Massive waves of Asian settlers followed the forced or voluntary migration of original residents to outlying areas and hidden mountainsides. The conquerors brought these Asians in to inhabit vacated communities and to work the land[7]. The Ottomans distributed to them all abandoned fertile farmlands. Northern migrant workers provided the seasonal agricultural labor requirements. A significant group, however, the Jews, settled in Macedonia. They arrived from Germany and Hungary in 1470, from Spain in 1492, from Italy in 1493, and from Portugal in 1497 by the thousands[8]. They settled in Constantinople, Andrianople, Salonica, and other cities supplementing the Romanic Jews, i.e., the ones living there since antiquity. The revitalized Jewish community of Salonica strengthened its trade connections with Venice, Genoa, Amsterdam, and other commercial centers in Europe. Jewish efforts were instrumental in making the Macedonian capital the bustling city it was in ancient times of Rome and Byzantium[9]. European languages, mostly Spanish and French, dominated its market, but they spoke Greek, Turkish, Wallach, Albanian, and other languages as well[10]. Of the 5,605 families living in Salonica in 1519, a huge 56 percent was Jewish, 25 percent Turkish and 19 percent was Greek[11]. These population percentages continued through the seventeenth century[12]. Salonica welcomed all Diaspora Jews. The schools they operated provided instruction in various sciences,

[5] Apostolos E. Vacalopoulos, *The History of Thessalonike*, p. 79
[6] Konstantinos Bakalopoulos, *Macedonia and Turkey*, 1830-1878, p. 30
[7] Konstantinos E. Siabanopoulos, *The Museum of Kozane*, p. 4
[8] Apostolos E. Vacalopoulos, *The History of Thessalonike*, p. 76
[9] Apostolos E. Vacalopoulos, *The History of Thessalonike*, p. 77
[10] Apostolos E. Vacalopoulos, *The History of Thessalonike*, p. 93
[11] Konstantinos Bakalopoulos, *Macedonia and Turkey* 1830-1878, p. 35
[12] Apostolos E. Vacalopoulos, *The History of Thessalonike*, p. 81

especially in philosophy. Their student communities included non-Jews hailing from aristocratic families[13]. These schools contributed considerably to economic prosperity and the brilliant intellectual development of Salonica. The attendance by the children of the commerce-oriented Greeks resulted in the self-confidence, wealth, and social advancement necessary to later stimulate the Greek national aspirations.

The re-inhabitation of vacated lands and cities by Asiatics, Slavs, and Jews slowly diminished. The reorganization of society under the Ottoman administration eventually provided calmness and security. People engaged in business activity, which resulted in prosperity and tranquillity in most areas in the Balkans[14]. The Ottomans provided a greater marketing area by expanding their borders north when they began capturing Hungary in 1526[15]. They completed its conquest in 1687. The Ottomans threatened but failed to capture Vienna in 1529 as well as in 1683[16]. The Austrian capital was a thriving commercial center in Europe. It remained so throughout the entire, 160-year-long occupation of Hungary by the Ottomans. Poet Schmetzl in 1547 stated among the languages heard in Vienna were German, Hungarian, Dutch, French, Bohemian, Slovenian, Croatian, Serbian, Latin, Greek, Jewish, Spanish, Italian, Polish, Turkish, Syrian, even Ancient Chaldean[17]. Vienna merchants, from all trading points, traveled freely within the Ottoman Empire. Ottoman authorities, by promoting security in the countryside, encouraged freedom of movement of individual traders and laborers first introduced by ancient Hellenes and continued through Macedonian, Roman, and Byzantine administrations. It was an effective method of preventing resenting individuals from forming powerful opposition groups with possible threat to established rule.

A gradual alteration in the composition of populations occurred throughout all occupied lands[18]. The Balkan areas experienced the greatest population movements. Intermingling,

[13]Apostolos E. Vacalopoulos, *The History of Thessalonike*, p. 90
[14]Apostolos E. Vacalopoulos, *The History of Thessalonike*, p. 90
[15]George Laios, *Siatista and Its Commercial Houses Hadje-Michael and Manouses*, p. 42
[16]George Laios, *Siatista and Its Commercial Houses Hadje-Michael and Manouses*, p. 40
[17]George Laios, *Siatista and Its Commercial Houses Hadje-Michael and Manouses*, p. 40
[18]Konstantinos Metsakis, *Macedonia Throughout the Centuries*, p. 40

consequently, altered considerably its population composition[19]. Responsible for this were its geographical location and its relationship to the Western World's center of intellectual activity. All western civilizations—Mesopotamian, Phoenician, Egyptian, Hellenic, Roman, and Arabic—flourished in direct proximity to this area. All major religions originated in the area as well.

Venetian traders continued their activities in all sea routes. Their industrious character, devotion to sea trade, and efficiency greatly contributed to trade between the East and West. The Pope and the Spanish fleet assisted them in neutralizing the Ottoman's challenge to their sea sovereignty. They defeated the Ottoman fleet in 1571 in the battle of Naupactus[20]. Venetians remained the dominant power until the second half of the seventeenth century. In 1669 they lost the island of Crete in the eastern Mediterranean to the Ottomans. Loss of Crete and development of new routes directly to Asian ports by English and Dutch vessels eliminated utilization of middlemen traders located in eastern Mediterranean ports. This development impacted adversely on the commercial activities of Jewish businessmen in Salonica. Growth in competition by Greek merchants operating in many European cities such as Ancona, Dubrovnik, and Venice took a toll as well. Reduced activity in the area brought an economic upheaval even to Venetians, the commercial lords of the Mediterranean. In 1686 the French Consul Gleize advised "all trade in Salonica was done by Greeks and a few Jews" with representatives of Greeks living in cities of Europe[21].

The war between the Venetians and the Ottomans lasted for twenty-five years. It culminated in the fall of Crete to the Ottomans. It created, however, restlessness, opposition, and determination. The mobilization of residents of occupied regions against the Venetians imposed by the Ottomans involved active participation. The coastal cities carried an extra heavy burden. They had to organize their own defenses in order to repel Venetian attacks. Forced conscription strengthened the

---

[19]Stephan J. Papadopoulos, *Educational and Social Activities of Macedonian Hellenism During the Last Century of Ottoman Occupation*, p. 7
[20]Apostolos E. Vacalopoulos, *The History of Thessalonike*, p. 79
[21]Apostolos E. Vacalopoulos, *The History of Thessalonike*, p. 91

objections of many locals. The Greeks formed guerrilla bands and looked to Russia, their fellow Orthodox Christians, for assistance. Political instability precipitated the decline in economic activity in Balkan ports. Armand, French Consul in Salonica, wrote in 1699 "in the five years I have been staying here in Salonica I have never seen a foreign vessel[22]."

The Ottomans failed to capture Vienna in 1683. The Hungarians also defeated them, and in 1687 regained their freedom[23]. In a few years, however, the Ottomans defeated the Russians and in 1711 negotiated a settlement. Five years later, in 1716, the Ottomans faced the Venetians and the Austrians.

Confrontation of the opposing forces for two continuing years ended up in the Passarowitz pact of 1718 between Austro-Hungarian and Ottoman empires[24]. This agreement gave to Ottoman subjects operating in the Austro-Hungarian Empire various incentives. The Austrians lowered their import custom duties to only 3 percent of their value. Importers of these products were mostly Jewish, Greeks, Armenians, and a few Turks. This stimulus was beneficial to Greek, mostly Macedonian, merchants who further enhanced their already successful operations. The Greeks traded in all fifty-three districts of Hungary. During the Russo-Ottoman war of 1768–1774, Greek sailors and traders, protected by Russia, increased their activities. They achieved considerable economic prosperity[25].

Greeks of Diaspora adopted the lands they settled as their mother countries. They reinforced the previously existing Hellenism throughout the East and West in the Ottoman and the Austro-Hungarian empires. Their contribution to these lands was enormous. The contribution to the country of their ancestors, however, was even greater.

[22] Apostolos E. Vacalopoulos, *The History of Thessalonike*, p. 92
[23] George Laios, *Siatista and Its Commercial Houses Hadje-Michael and Manouses*, p. 42
[24] George Laios, *Siatista and Its Commercial Houses Hadje-Michael and Manouses*, p. 41
[25] Apostolos E. Vacalopoulos, *The History of Thessalonike*, p. 97

PART B
Chapter 7
Upper Macedonia

In 1390, Asians settled Upper Macedonia's lowlands around the Aliakmon River[1], where ancient prefectures of Elimeia and Eordea were, between the Siniatsiko and Bermio mountains. The plateaus found in this rugged region were heaven for many who abandoned their homes and fertile fields and ran for safety and freedom. Rugged individuals carried their tools and household items uphill. They established themselves in cave shelters and huts that they built as time went on. They preoccupied themselves with cattle raising. They later carved small plots of land on mountainsides, enabling them to plant wheat and corn. They also planted trees and vineyards adaptable to the local adverse climatic conditions.

The interdependence of these small groups quickly resulted in the development of small communities. Their family-operated shops fulfilled their technical tool requirements. Hard work and perseverance helped these groups survive and even prosper. New arrivals from other localities augmented their numbers. The relatively secure environment they created kept away punishment by the enemy. Persecution by the conquerors in other areas and subsequent uprisings in 1495 brought new refugees. Defeat of the Ottoman fleet in 1571 in Naupactus created additional turmoil and more relocations of Greeks[2]. The revolt in Epirus and Thessaly of 1612[3] sent additional waves of refugees, unable to return to their hometowns. They settled in the new communities. Together they formed the new towns of Siatista, Kozane, Vlaste, Bogatsiko, Galatine, and others. The failures of 1710 and 1748 uprisings sent fleeing Greeks from Parga, Souli, Ioannina, Fourka of Epirus, and even as far south as Peloponnese to these communities. Approximately thirty lowland villages, existing in the region as per available records

[1] Konstantinos E. Siabanopoulos, *The Museum of Kozane*, p. 4
[2] Parmenion N. Tzifras, *Brief History of Bogatsiko*, p. 12
[3] Panagiotes N. Lioufes, *History of Kozane*, p. 14

of the area monastery of Zaborda[4], disappeared because of relocation of their residents.

The influx of such big numbers in the area stimulated growth in economic activity. Among the indigenous population were villages whose residents considered themselves Greeks, attended Greek Orthodox church services, practiced Hellenism, and spoke a unique, unwritten dialect. They lived in isolated areas where Slavs settled when they moved south in Byzantine times. Their dialect, developed over centuries of intermingling with various groups, mainly combined ancient Homeric Greek and Slavic. It also contained Albanian and Latin words to a lesser degree[5]. Marshal Tito of Yugoslavia in 1945 used this dialect to establish a written language for his Yugoslav Republic of Macedonia. Presence of this group in the area proved an asset to newcomers. This group provided manpower familiar with the area's conditions and its possibilities. These Greeks, perhaps remnants of ancient Macedonia, served as the vehicle for expansion of the newcomers' commercial activities north.

Equally important was the existence of another group who lived in these mountains. The Wallachs, often called Koutsovlachs, raised sheep and goats in large numbers, moving about over long distances. To protect themselves from extreme cold, snow blizzards, and ice, they moved to lower altitudes in the winter. The Wallachs spoke a version of Latin related to the languages of Western Europe[6]. It is possible this language developed because of Roman settlers or through their dealings with them[7] at the time of constant Roman movements. It should be remembered that the ancient Roman road Egnatia passed through this area from west to east.

In the center of all these people was the ancient city of Keletron, renamed Kastoria by Roman emperor Justinian in the sixth century[8]. Kastoria's residents occupied themselves mainly

---

[4]Committee of N. Liamades, D. Makris, A. Bellos, L. Papaioannou, K. Siabanopoulos, *Acquaintance With Prefecture of Kozane*, p. 17
[5]Paraskevas J. Meliopoulos, "The Slavo-Macedonians of Skopja, Descendants of Homeric Greeks," *Dytike Macedonia*, 1992
[6]John A. Papadrianos, *The Greek Settlers of Semlin*, p. 242
[7]George N. Filios, "Naming of Siatista," *Efemeris* (newspaper of Siatista) #133, 11-12/1995
[8]Panos Gr. Tsolakes, *The Boats of Kastoria*, p. 34

with fishing in their own lake, adjacent to the city[9]. The local ruler had exclusive rights over the lake and collected from the fishermen one-third of their catch. The remaining two-thirds provided their livelihood and maintenance of their fishing fleet. Kastorians sold their catch to Siatista, Kozane, Servia, Monastere, et cetera. Of continued special interest is the boat construction used by local craftsmen in this lake. It did not resemble the boats used in other lakes of the same region[10]. Constructed from thick boards, the boats had no inner frame nor keel.

Nature provided another positive asset to local residents. Their densely wooded mountains, richly endowed with fur-bearing animals— especially foxes and stone martens— provided fur skins, a status symbol of all societies. Inhabitants of Kastoria and Achris developed the art of skin processing and fur garment construction since antiquity. Both men and women widely used fur coats in the area. Prevailing weather conditions made this a necessity. Fur craftsmen specializing on maintenance and service traveled extensively to big cities in the Balkans and Central Europe. They visited royal courts and wealthy families and serviced their fur garments. Natives of Kastoria and Siatista promoted this craft into a worldwide fur industry with immense wealth brought to their towns.

All of these isolated groups lived with the spirit of Hellenism. They were alert and industrious, willing to understand and coexist with others. They opened their hearts and souls to the new settlers who became their customers and employers. Shops established in all new communities served their interests well. Sales and consumption of cheese and other products increased. Traders carried these products to neighboring towns. Tool makers, locksmiths, gunsmiths, candle makers, wool weavers, skin and leather processors, shoe makers, cloth makers, rug producers, and others operated in these semi-industrialized towns. Horseshoe installing, travelers inns, taverns, coffee shops, barber shops, yard goods stores, seamstresses, tailors, wineries, bakeries, and groceries served every imaginable need and satisfied the population's requirements. Open-air markets operated weekly in all towns.

[9]Panos Gr. Tsolakes, *The Boats of Kastoria*, p. 21
[10]Panos Gr. Tsolakes, *The Boats of Kastoria*, p. 11

They earmarked a specific day for each town. Traders exhibited a variety of products for sale either in small or big quantities. Sales were final on a cash-and-carry basis. People visiting the neighboring towns walked over accessible mountain paths. Loaded horses, mules, or donkeys carrying their wares and goods led the way. A system of brotherhood and reciprocity ensured their safety. In days-long caravans destined for distant lands they employed hired guards, mostly trusted Albanians[11]. For short journeys, the trip was an excuse for gossip and singing.

A festive mood prevailed, especially on the way back, after the sale of their merchandise. Increased trading activity in all sectors of the economy followed. Mule caravans carried excessive quantities of wine, cheese, and other products on a regular basis. They traded with Thessalian cities of Ambelakia, Tsaritsane, Elassona, Larisa, Tyrnavos and Wallach communities of Samarina, Perivoli, Avdella, and Smixe, as well as Ioannina of Epirus and Korytsa, Moschopolis and Monastere, as far as Durres on the north.

Annual fairs held in the town of Servia early in September, Elassona on Good Friday, Grevena on May 17, Tsotyli on July 17, Mavrovo (near Kastoria) on September 25, and in other towns provided an important stimulus. Traders visited these fairs with greater interest because of huge participation and their magnitude. The one held in Perlepe became famous for its animal trading and availability of quality horses[12].

Avoidance of tax payment to Ottoman authorities preoccupied the traders' thinking. The newly formed communities had no Turkish residents. Ottoman authorities, however, devised their own system of tax collection. Area governors (pashas) assigned this burden to individuals who bought the right to collect taxes for a lump sum. Often the taxes imposed were excessive and unrealistic. In such cases overpressed groups rebelled. Many times protesting debtors moved to mountain hideouts to evade payment. They defied the tax collector and fought to force him to compromise their severity. In time of war, additional stiff assessments could not

---

[11]George Laios, *Siatista and Its Commercial Houses Hadje-Michael and Manouses*, p. 51
[12]Mich. Ath. Kalinderis, *Life in the Community of Vlaste During the Turkish Occupation*,p.29

possibly be met. Armed conflicts constantly developed between subjects and occupiers.

The Russia-Ottoman war of 1768 influenced the Greeks. Intellectuals hoped for an opportunity to develop so they could advance their national goals. Pressed hard for greater tax payments and incited by Russian promises for help, they revolted against the Ottomans[13]. Their retreat resulted in quick and harsh punishment. Turkish-Albanian forces in 1769 destroyed Moschopolis, a populous and prosperous Greek city (near today's Albanian city of Korce) in Epirus, full of keen-judgment merchants and traders throughout the Balkans. The population vacated the city within three days[14]. Its inhabitants moved in all directions. A good number of them relocated to Siatista, Vlaste, Kozane, Bogatsiko, and other area towns. Moschopolitans took with them whatever they could carry or smuggle out by bribing local authorities at the time of their escape. Most importantly, they brought to their new towns their rich trading experiences and contacts, their knowledge of other lands, their education and ingenuity.

---

[13]Konstantinos Metsakis, *Macedonia Throughout the Centuries*, p. 43
[14]John A. Papadrianos, *The Greek Settlers of Semlin*, p. 52

View of Chora, Upper Siatista, with St. Demetrios chuch in the center.
Big building on the left is the elementary school.
Photo by G. Logdanides

Chapter 8
Eastern Orthodoxy

Byzantine emperor Constantine the Great, the builder of New Rome (or Constantinople), first accepted Christianity as the legal religion of the empire in the year 330. Constantine the Great was born in Nis, Serbia. His father was a Roman ruler of Britain and Spain, and his mother was Helen, a Greek from Vithynia, a region in north Asia Minor[1]. Constantine summoned the First Ecumenical Synod of Christianity held in Nicea in 325. This Synod composed the Symbol of Faith first written in Hellenic language[2]. Emperor Theodosius I, after fifty-seven years, called the second Ecumenical Synod held in Constantinople in 382[3]. This Synod finalized the Symbol of Faith and upheld Orthodox Christianity. Theodosius, in an effort to advance Christianity, implemented a strict policy of eliminating institutions operating contrary to or ignoring the new religion. He even abolished the Olympic Games held for over one thousand years at Olympia in Peloponnese. He specifically ordered the destruction of Olympia's renowned (and still-impressive remnants) temples of antiquity. The world-famous gold and ivory statue of God Zeus, or Dias suffered the same fate. Theodosius appointed only Christians to public positions.

Another Roman emperor followed the same policy one hundred years later. Emperor Zenon directed the burning of 120,000 volumes of books assembled in the Julian public library in Constantinople. He also attempted to unite the two warring factions of Orthodox and Monophysic Christians, whose dispute ended in the first Ecclesiastical Schism (484–519)[4]. The ups and downs of Eastern Orthodoxy continued. In 482, Justinian, another great Byzantine emperor in office between the years 527 and 565, was born in the Balkan village of Tavris, close to the birthplace of Constantine the Great[5]. This region of the southwest Balkan

[1] Elias Laskares, *Byzantine Emperors*, Vol. I, p. 10
[2] Elias Laskares, *Byzantine Emperors*, Vol. I, p. 18
[3] Elias Laskares, *Byzantine Emperors*, Vol. I, p. 38
[4] Elias Laskares, *Byzantine Emperors*, Vol. I, p. 58
[5] Elias Laskares, *Byzantine Emperors*, Vol. I, p. 64

Peninsula gave birth to Alexander the Great, Constantine the Great, and Justinian.

Hellenized Justinian promoted Christianity and Hellenism. His education in philosophy, theology, law, and architecture plus his marriage to Theodora, a Greek Cypriot woman, enabled him to develop his brilliant administration. His many accomplishments included doubling the size of the empire, establishment of the Roman Law[6], and expansion of industry and commerce. Justinian constructed, as did Alexander, many public buildings, roads, bridges, and water systems, and hundreds of defense forts. Over fifty of them went up in Macedonia alone. His target was to re-establish the original Roman Empire. His objective remained to promote Eastern Orthodoxy throughout its jurisdiction. He constructed churches in many cities of the empire, including the famous St. Sophia[7] in Constantinople. St. Sophia today is a museum. In 535, Justinian established the First Justinian Autocefalus Eastern Orthodox Archepiscopate in Achris, a town near the village where he was born. The Pope recognized the Achris Archepiscopate, thus becoming the third center of Christianity after Rome and Constantinople. The neighboring city of Kastoria's episcopate, existing since the fifth century, became part of Achris Archepiscopate[8]. Many of Kastoria's Byzantine churches are still in operation today[9].

Christianity, following the endorsement of Constantine the Great, flourished. Clergymen and individuals seeking devotion and solitude found serenity in Chalkidike's eastern peninsula of Mt. Athos. Monks established in Mt. Athos their first monastery in 337. Its monastic life attracted Christians from all parts of the empire. Theologists, laymen, and clergy—intellectuals or not — continued to settle there over the centuries. In 885, the Macedonian Byzantine emperor Vasilios I decreed the area "protected" and turned it over to the monks. The monks formed their first commune in 963[10]. Christians from all Balkan lands arrived in this multinational community.

[6]Elias Laskares, *Byzantine Emperors*, Vol. I, p. 72
[7]Elias Laskares, *Byzantine Emperors*, Vol. I, p. 74
[8]Anastasios N. Dardas, "Episcopate of Sisani (?-1686)," *Siatista* 1/1989, p. 40
[9]Panos Gr. Tsolakes, *The Boats of Kastoria*, p. 19
[10]John P. Panagiotou, *Mt. Athos, The Holy Mountain*, p. 4

The First Justinian Archepiscopate of Achris provided spiritual leadership when Bulgarian Slavs under Samuel's control expanded their political activity all the way up to Savo River, a tributary of the River Danube. The Archepiscopate of Achris expanded its jurisdiction to serve these lands. The Ecumenical Patriarchate of Constantinople issued new directives in 1019 to clarify the clergy's rights and obligations in these communities[11]. In an atmosphere of brotherly love and Hellenic values, Eastern Orthodoxy utilized the Holy Scripture translations into Slavic of Byzantine brothers Cyril and Methodius to cultivate intellect and promote human dignity. The Ecumenical Patriarchate of Constantinople oversaw, encouraged, and assisted all regional multidialect group and individual initiatives. Parishioners in all communities assisted their priests' efforts to build churches in which to practice their faith. Parishes and clergy often followed ambitious and decisive political and military leaders in their campaigns to pursue their objectives. Many leaders built churches in order to influence their constituents or followers. Christopher Protospatharius, the governor of Lombardy, built in Salonica in 1044 the famous well-preserved church of the Virgin of Coppersmiths[12]. The church is still adored today. In 1114 emperor Alexios, in conjunction with the Ecumenical Patriarch, decreed Mt. Athos a Holy Mountain. In 1195 the ruler of Serbia, Stephan Nemanya, declared Orthodoxy as the official church of his country,[13] and established the Holy Monastery of Chilandariou at Mt. Athos[14]. The Ecumenical Patriarchate recognized the Serbian Church in 1219 as the First Autocefalus Serbian church[15]. Stephan Nemanya's son Savas, head of the Monastery that his father established in Mt. Athos, became its first Archbishop.

The First Justinian Autocefalus Eastern Orthodox Archepiscopate of Achris, however, continued to provide spiritual leadership. Its clergy preached love, understanding,

---

[11]John A. Papadrianos, *The Greek Settlers of Semlin*, p. 25
[12]Apostolos E. Vacalopoulos, *The History of Thessalonike*, p. 41
[13]Konstantinos Babouskos, *Ecclesiastical Relationship of Serbs and the Ecumenical Patriarchate the Nineteenth Century, Helleno-Serbian Symposium*, p. 22
[14]John P. Panagiotou, *Mt. Athos, The Holy Mountain*, p. 4
[15]Konstantinos Babouskos, *Ecclesiastical Relationship of Serbs and the Ecumenical Patriarchate the Nineteenth Century, Helleno-Serbian Symposium*, p. 264

patience, and hope. Archbishop Demetrios of Achris crowned Theodore, the Despotate of Epirus ruler, as Emperor of the Byzantine Empire when in 1224 he defeated the Franks and terminated their twenty-year rule in Salonica[16]. Political leaders often influenced religious developments and vice versa. Bulgarians defeated Emperor Theodore in 1230 when he campaigned against them. Bulgarian king John Assan conquered among other lands, the entire peninsula of Mt. Athos[17]. The Holy Community gained independence five years later, in 1235, when the princess Helen, daughter of John Assan, married Theodore Laskaris, son of the emperor of Nicea, the eastern state of the Byzantine Empire[18]. Mt. Athos's Holy Community eventually enhanced its status. Monastic life sought wide learning and stimulated refined intellect whose impact reached other centers of Christianity. Reunification of the Byzantine Empire in 1261 rekindled the spiritual leadership of the Ecumenical Patriarchate. The Patriarchate again sanctioned Mt. Athos in 1313. The Holy community's primate exercised his full authority to appoint/elect its clergy and spiritual leaders[19].

A new challenge to Mt. Athos's independence, however, reappeared in 1340. Serbian forces under Stephan Dousan took advantage of the empire's political instability and internal strife, and invaded it[20]. The local Synod of Skopje elevated the Serbian church to Patriarchate status six years later in 1346[21]. The Serbs since then derived spiritual strength and guidance from their Patriarchate. Mt. Athos Holy Community later returned to the jurisdiction of the Ecumenical Patriarchate of Constantinople. The emperor John Kantakouzenos in 1355 resigned his throne to become a monk at the monastery of Vatopediou[22].

The number of Mt. Athos's monasteries increased in 1363 with Serbian King John Ugles's financial assistance. He built the

[16] Apostolos E. Vacalopoulos, *The History of Thessalonike*, p. 48
[17] John P. Panagiotou, *Mt. Athos, The Holy Community*, p. 4
[18] Donald M. Nicol, translation of Perikles Lefkas, *The Despotate of Epirus*, p. 107
[19] John P. Panagiotou, *Mt. Athos, The Holy Community*, p. 4
[20] Konstantinos Metsakis, *Macedonia Throughout the Centuries*, p. 30
[21] Konstantinos Babouskos, *Ecclesiastical Relationship of Serbs and the Ecumenical Patriarchate the Nineteenth Century, Helleno-Serbian Symposium*, p. 264
[22] John P. Panagiotou, *Mt. Athos, The Holy Community*, p. 4. Elias Laskares states in his Vol. II of *Byzantine Emperors*, John Kantakouzenos changed his name to Ioasaf and lived in Mystra monastery in Peloponnese until 1383.

great monastery of Simon Petra. The Holy Community at Mt. Athos consisted of twenty-five monasteries by the end of the fourteenth century[23]. The Ecumenical Patriarchate and the Balkan peoples placed tremendous prestige on the Holy Community. Nearby Salonica experienced impressive growth in religious activity that paralleled its commercial and social advancement. Its location in close proximity with Mt. Athos's peninsula benefited both centers through their spiritual and economic intercourse. Among the earliest churches established in Salonica, the most notable one is the Rotunda, a round building called church of Asomate (translated: "without body") later dedicated to Holy Angels and finally to St. George. Rotunda's construction took place around 300[24]. Construction of St. Demetrios' Church in the fifth century followed Demetrios's martyrdom in the same city. Believers built the church on the site of his grave. Construction of Acheiropoietos Church (translated: "constructed by no hands") took place in the fifth century[25]. St. Sophia Church followed in the eighth century[26]. By the end of the fourteenth century the additional churches of St. Taxiarchs, St. Nickolas, Holy Savior, Holy Apostles, and the monastery of Vlatades served the people in Salonica[27]. Eastern Orthodoxy's ecclesiastical performance was part of Salonica's religious cultivation and development.

The Ecumenical Patriarchate in Constantinople continued to oversee, guide, and appoint all Metropolitans including those of the Russian Orthodox Church. In 1439, an all-Christianity Synod held in Florence stipulated/approved reunification of the church worldwide under the spiritual leadership of the Pope[28]. Most of the Eastern Metropolitans who attended it were signatories to this resolution. In 1448, the Orthodox Synod of the Russian Bishops elected their own head, Metropolitan Ionas. Four years later, in 1452, the Ecumenical Patriarchate declared Autocefalus the Russian Church at the request of Russian ruler Vassily Vasiliewitz[29]. This formalized a policy of respect and recognition.

[23]John P. Panagiotou, *Mt. Athos, The Holy Community*, p. 4
[24]Apostolos E. Vacalopoulos, *Macedonia Throughout the Centuries*, p. 19
[25]Apostolos E. Vacalopoulos, *Macedonia Throughout the Centuries*, p. 21
[26]Apostolos E. Vacalopoulos, *Macedonia Throughout the Centuries*, p. 29
[27]Apostolos E. Vacalopoulos, *Macedonia Throughout the Centuries*, p. 51
[28]Elias Laskares, *Byzantine Emperors*, Vol. II, p. 176
[29]Konstantinos Babouskos, *Ecclesiastical Relationship of Serbs and the Ecumenical Patriarchate the Nineteenth Century, Helleno-Serbian Symposium*, p. 264

The Byzantines endorsed it in hope of receiving assistance to repel the threat displayed by Mohammedanism through its political leader. In the same year the Eastern Orthodox Mt. Athos Holy Community denounced the Synod of Florence decision for worldwide Christian unification. Its attitude appeased the threatening Ottoman Turks, who prayed for the continuation of Christians' division. A year later, in 1453, Constantinople fell and still is in the Ottomans' hands. The Holy Community's attitude ensured its recognition and independent status. Upon Constantinople's fall and capture of the Ecumenical Patriarchate, Mt. Athos's maintained all its previous privileges.

The Holy Community's efforts were at the service of Eastern Orthodoxy. Mt. Athos communal system of work, study, and intellectual activism minimally satisfied the individuals' material needs. It perpetuated a positive contribution to Christianity and to humanity. Its existence continues to implement and project Hellenism.

The Mt. Athos monastery of Dionysios pictured from southwest.
It was found around 1370-1374 by holyman Dionysios who hailed from the town of Korysos, near Kastoria of Macedonia.
(from the book of Soteris Kadas, published by Ekdotike of Athens.)

Chapter 9

Survival Adjustment

Civil disorders and dislocations caused throughout the years of Mohammedan expansion brought stress to Christianity. Eastern Orthodox faith and its Ecumenical Patriarchate in Constantinople felt its consequences. The Ottomans, following the Koran, encouraged continuation of the Patriarchate's existence and operation. This policy considerably advanced their objectives. Perpetuation of divided Christianity between Eastern Orthodoxy and Roman Catholicism was their first objective. Their second one was to control manipulation of church affairs and their parishes. A third and equally important reason, if not the original objective, was utilization of its existing mechanism for collection of money for the Ottoman treasury.

The First Ecumenical Patriarch elected/confirmed by the Ottomans was George Scholarios. He was a signatory to the church reunification agreement of the 1439 Holy Synod, yet he denounced it upon becoming a Patriarch. He led the fight against reunification instead[1]. Many subordinates supported his views, seeking promotion within the hierarchy. Other clergymen, however, along with scholars, educators, and intellectuals fled to western cities. Their first concern, wherever they moved, was performance of their religious duties. The Holy Community of Mt. Athos managed to maintain its privileges. Ottoman chief-of-state Salem I restated its status during his visit to Mt. Athos in 1513[2].

Bishop Pavlos of Voivodina in 1530 challenged the expanded jurisdiction the First Justinian Archepiscopate of Achris had as far north as the Savo and Danube rivers. He quickly succeeded in taking this area to the Serbian Church's authority[3]. It was a stimulus to its setback due to Mohammedan expansion. Greeks and Serbs practiced their religion jointly in communities with mixed population. The Protestant clergyman Stephan Gerlach

---
[1] Elias Laskares, *Byzantine Emperors*, Vol. II, p. 176
[2] John P. Panagiotou, *Mt. Athos, The Holy Mountain*, p. 4
[3] John A. Papadrianos, *The Greek Settlers of Semlin*, p. 27

visited their poor, small church in Semlin near Belgrade in 1578[4]. Many Serbs moved to Mt. Athos' monasteries. Serb monks served even in top hierarchy positions, always utilizing the Hellenic language. Wallachia and Moldavia rulers, enjoying semi-autonomous status within the Ottoman Empire, replaced the financial assistance to Holy Community previously given by Byzantine Emperors. The Wallachia ruler's grant in 1535 covered Karakalos monastery's restoration[5]. Russian clergy, with their rulers' consent, collected huge sums and assisted the monasteries, and through them, Eastern Orthodoxy.

Religious authorities, bishops, and priests, with Ottoman supervision at highest levels, organized the communities' education and civil administration. Very little, scattered information survived the clergy's reaction during the first years of the protracted, four-hundred-year long occupation. It is widely accepted in Greece that priests stayed in their jobs. After all, it was a matter of survival. They comforted the old and sick, encouraged the healthy ones, and taught the young ones to read and write. The church mechanism had to be maintained at all costs. The Greek language, therefore, was essential. Candidates and persons selected for higher church positions were careful not to offend Ottoman authorities. Regional metropolitans and bishops singled out promising students for promotion and appointment to lower-level positions. The phenomenon of bribing officials existed[6]. Questionable quality cadre satisfied, however, the minimal needs of the population. Priests taught students the language and religion in low-profile schools. Children of relatives, or families that could afford it, pursued education on a private basis. In nonoccupied lands, individuals and societies established schools for Greek children.

Spiritual stagnation in Eastern Orthodoxy resulted in an agonizing re-evaluation of Christianity by western Theologians. Martin Luther (1483–1546) issued his ninety-five-point position in 1517[7] and John Calvin (1509–1564)[8] questioned existing

[4]John A. Papadrianos, *The Greek Settlers of Semlin*, p. 28
[5]John P. Panagiotou, *Mt. Athos, The Holy Mountain*, p. 4
[6]Anastasios N. Dardas, "Zosimas' Episcopal Service in Siatista," *Siatistina* 2/1989, p. 50
[7]Demetres Fotiades, *The Revolution of 1821*, Vol. IV, p. 282
[8]Zacharias N. Tsirpanlis, *Macedonian Students of the Greek College in Rome and Their Activities in Greece and in Italy*, p. 7

Catholicism. Pope Gregorius XIII, in an effort to promote obedience through understanding, established several colleges in Rome[9]. The German College came first in 1573, followed by the Greek College St. Athanasius in 1576[10]. The establishment of Hungarian and English colleges by the same pope followed in 1578 and 1579, respectively. Saint Athanasius Greek College was the pope's positive step to Hellenism. His intent was to find ways and means to pursue reunification decided by the 1439 Synod. Saint Athanasius's instructors taught Greek children in their language, the ancient Hellenic classics of Isocrates, Demosthenes, Sofocles, Thoucydides, Xenophon, and others[11]. The original student body[12] of six grew in numbers. Many graduates held outstanding positions in the educational circles of Italy and Greece[13]. By the turn of the century, 125 students, mostly from the Greek islands and Peloponnese, registered. Constantinople's elite sent seven students. Alexander and Constantine Laskaris, nephews of the Ecumenical Patriarch Jeremiah II[14], attended it in 1581. Patriarch Jeremiah II evaluated favorably Saint Athanasius College. He estimated it would strengthen the spirit of Hellenism and have a positive effect to Hellenism in general[15]. In 1593, Patriarch Jeremiah II and his Constantinople Holy Synod decided on establishment of Greek schools in all parts of Greece[16]. They requested all local bishops' assistance[17]. The Greek community of Venice responded the same year. Iasi and Bucharest of Wallachia established Greek-speaking Academies in 1629. Top educators and scientists devoutly taught

[9]Zacharias N. Tsirpanlis, *Macedonian Students of the Greek College in Rome and Their Activities in Greece and in Italy*, p. 37
[10]Zacharias N. Tsirpanlis, *Macedonian Students of the Greek College in Rome and Their Activities in Greece and in Italy*, p. 8
[11]Zacharias N. Tsirpanlis, *Macedonian Students of the Greek College in Rome and Their Activities in Greece and in Italy*, p. 59
[12]Zacharias N. Tsirpanlis, *Macedonian Students of the Greek College in Rome and Their Activities in Greece and Italy* p. 40
[13]Zacharias N. Tsirpanlis, *Macedonian Students of the Greek College in Rome and Their Activities in Greece and Italy*, p. 77
[14]Zacharias N. Tsirpanlis, *Macedonian Students of the Greek College in Rome and Their Activities in Greece and Italy*, p. 46
[15]Zacharias N. Tsirpanlis, *Macedonian Students of the Greek College in Rome and Their Activities in Greece and Italy*, p. 56
[16]Zacharias N. Tsirpanlis, *Macedonian Students of the Greek College in Rome and Their Activities in Greece and Italy*, p. 34
[17]Demetres Fotiades, *The Revolution of 1821*, Vol. IV, p. 286

Greek and non-Greek children. Graduates of these schools formed the necessary cadre for education of Greeks in enslaved areas, more so in Epirus and Macedonia[18].

The Greek College in Rome continued to attract Greek students. Rome sent its graduates to various posts in Europe and in occupied Greece. Their mission was to proselytize Christians and to recruit candidates for Saint Athanasius College. Among ten Macedonian students who attended the college the first quarter of the seventeenth century were Nickolas and Constantine Logothetes, nephews of Eastern Orthodox Metropolitan of Nikopolis and Nevrokopi Daniel[19]. John Cottunios from the city of Veroia, recommended by the Ecumenical Patriarchate and certain German scholars and politicians[20], registered at the age of thirty-three, contrary to the institution's age requirements. Its directors utilized Cottunios's broad knowledge in philosophy and theology. Along with being a student he taught Greek grammar and Hellenic classics for four years[21].

John Cottunios developed into a brilliant scientist and a philosopher. With the assistance of Venetians in 1613 he attended the University of Padova to study medicine. In 1637 he became a professor of philosophy at the same university[22]. In 1653 he published his two volumes of Hellenic classics in both Greek and Latin. The same year Arsenios Souchanof, librarian of Russia's Holy Trinity monastery, visited Mt. Athos and carried back with him 519 handwritten Hellenic classics of Homer, Hesiodus, Aristotle, Aristophanes, Aischylus, Sofocles, Euripides and several Byzantine works[23]. All these enriched the Russian Patriarchal library. Today they are found at Moscow's National Historical Museum. Cottunios, four years prior to his death in 1657, established the Cottunian

---

[18]Fotes Vittes, *Stachyologemata* short story collection, p. 86
[19]Zacharias N. Tsirpanlis, *Macedonian Students of the Greek College in Rome and Their Activities in Greece and Italy*, p. 94
[20]Zacharias N. Tsirpanlis, *Macedonian Students of the Greek College in Rome and Their Activities in Greece and Italy*, p. 75
[21]Zacharias N. Tsirpanlis, *Macedonian Students of the Greek College in Rome and Their Activities in Greece and Italy*, p. 77
[22]Zacharias N. Tsirpanlis, *Macedonian Students of the Greek College in Rome and Their Activities in Greece and Italy*, p. 135
[23]A. Rogof, "Russian-Hellenic Political Relationship from the Second Half of 15th to 17th Century," International Chamber of Commerce *Symposium, Hellas-Russia,* p. 128

College in Padova[24]. Greek children could from now on study without any religious influence. Greek brothers Sofronios and Ioannikios Leihoudis, founders of the first Russian higher institution of learning, the Slavo-Helleno-Latin Academy, established in Moscow in 1687[25], were Padova school graduates. The school in Padova educated children from all parts of Greece for more than two and a half centuries[26].

Relations between Greeks of occupied territories and those from western lands improved in the second half of the sixteenth century. Businessmen and representatives of the Ecumenical Patriarchate[27] visited non–Ottoman-held areas. The First Justinian Archepiscopate of Achris had contacts with western countries since 1548[28] in an effort to explore the new theological tendencies of Martin Luther and John Calvin forming in Europe. Clergyman Demetrios, a Greek from Salonica, visited Wittenberg, Germany, in 1559. His contemporary, famous Dane professor Niels Hemmingsen (1513–1600), who studied in Wittenberg, stated Demetrios received his Hellenic education in Constantinople, prior to his ten-year service in Cairo. Demetrios was familiar with the organizations of Egyptian, Asian, and European churches. Demetrios was Ecumenical Patriarch Ioasaf II's convoy to Wittenberg. Demetrios's six-month association with Protestant theologians helped him understand and evaluate trends and developments. He forwarded to Constantinople his precious findings, messages, and letters from renowned personalities and philosophers, to help Patriarch Ioasaf understand what was going on. Ernst Benz in his *Wittenberg and Byzanz*, Marburg, 1949 book, pages 76–77, claimed Demetrios was a Serb rather than Greek. Demetrios

---

[24]Zacharias N. Tsirpanlis, *Macedonian Students of the Greek College in Rome and Their Activities in Greece and Itlay*, p. 145
[25]A. Rogof, "Russian-Hellenic Political Relationship from the Second Half of 15th to 17th Century," International Chamber of Commerce *Symposium, Hellas-Russia*, p.135
[26]Zacharias N. Tsirpanlis, *Macedonian Students of the Greek College in Rome and Their Activities in Greece and Italy*, p. 146
[27]Zacharias N. Tsirpanlis, *Macedonian Students of the Greek College in Rome and Their Activities in Greece and Italy*, p. 28
[28]Anastasios N. Dardas, "Zosimas' Episcopal Service in Siatista," *Siatistina*, 2/1989, p. 71

spoke Slav, Wallach, Turkish, and Greek[29]. His possible Serbian background did not prevent his Hellenization. Demetrios promoted communication and understanding between Eastern Orthodox and western theologians.

Clergyman Gabriel Kalonas from Corinth visited Martin Crusius (1526–1607), professor of Latin and Ancient and Modern Greek[30] at Tubingen University in Germany. Prior to his visit he served his fourteen-town ecclesiastical district at Orfani, near the city of Kavala. He practiced his teachings, but mainly obeyed his Hellenic feelings for brotherly love and assisted Italian prisoners of war to escape the Ottoman prison. His apprehension would equal death. In 1578, equipped with a letter of recommendation from Ecumenical Patriarch Jeremiah II, he visited Crusius. Gabriel Kalonas's long stay with Crusius benefited both. Kalonas taught Crusius his spoken Greek. Subsequent to Kalonas, priest John Tholoites from Salonica visited Crusius in 1585. A year later Daniel Paleologos, a monk from Mt. Athos Holy Community, followed. The above visits to Crusius preceded Archbishop of Achris Gabriel's visit in 1587. Gabriel's party included his assistants Jeremiah, Metropolitan of Pelagonia and Perlepe, Archimandrite of Achris Anthimos, and Ioasaf from Veroia. Ioasaf later became bishop of Aetos and Angelocastro[31].

The First Justinian Archepiscopate then consisted of thirty-two episcopates. Twelve of them, including Siatista's episcopate of Sisani, were in Macedonia[32]. Siatista, built at an altitude of three thousand feet, experienced a rapid growth from the very start. Its settlers, versatile in all trades, traded with Trieste, Venice, and other Italian cities. Siatistians accumulated wealth and developed their self-confidence. Their children attended Padova schools. Upon their graduation and return home they proved well equipped to carry on their parents' trade. Their objective was to improve their self-respect and society's as well. They applied their scientific knowledge for the betterment of humanity. George

---

[29]Zacharias N. Tsirpanlis, *Macedonian Students of the Greek College in Rome and Their Activities in Greece and Italy,* pp. 29-30

[30]Demetres Fotiades, *The Revolution of 1821,* Vol. IV, p. 282. Crusius printed his Turcograecia in 1584.

[31]Zacharias N. Tsirpanlis, *Macedonian Students of the Greek College in Rome and Their Activities in Greece and Italy,* p. 32

[32]Anastasios N. Dardas, "The Episcopate of Sisani (?-1686)," *Siatistina,* 1/1989, p. 42

Parakeimenos from Kozane, Sevastos Leondiades from Kastoria, and the pillar of the Greek enlightenment in the eighteenth century[33] Eugene Voulgaris from the island of Corfu—all Padova graduates— offered important services to their people. Ottoman authorities concerned themselves mainly with prevention and avoidance of civil upheavals, insurrections, and certainly with collection of taxes.

In Upper Macedonia, establishment of new churches was in order. Ottoman authorities required their construction on the outskirts of the towns[34]. Mikrocastro's Virgin Mary's monastery, built in 1603 on the distant bank of the Aliakmon River, originally served as Mikrocastro's parish. Siatista's Holy Trinity Church, built in 1610[35], was also a fifteen-minute walking distance from the town. Saint Demetrios and St. Paraskevi, built in 1647[36] and in 1677[37], respectively, apparently ignored this rule. New churches built within fifteen miles were in Kozane, St. Anargyroi in 1612[38], St. Nickolas in 1664[39], and St. Athanasios in 1678[40]. In Vlaste they built St. Mark in 1643 and St. Nickolas in 1661[41]. In Eptahorio St. Nickolas was built in 1639 and in Sisani, Holy Virgin was built in 1662[42]. All these churches, except Kozane's, sought guidance from the First Justinian Archepiscopate of Achris. Kozane's churches belonged to Metropolis of Servia[43]. Their responsibility for resettling, civil administration, education, and spiritual enhancement was tremendous.

Absence of Turkish residents in these towns presented a definite advantage. Cooperation of the population and their respect for their archons ensured successful community operation.

[33]P. M. Kitromelides, "The Political Meaning of Helleno-Russian Spiritual Relationship During the Turkish Occupation," International Chamber of Commerce, *Symposium, Hellas-Russia*, p. 144
[34]Anastasios N. Dardas, "The Monastery of Virgin Mary of Mikrocastro," *Siatistina*, 5-6/1991 p. 37
[35]Anastasios N. Dardas, "Zosimas' Episcopal Service," *Siatistina*, 2/1989, p. 54
[36]Anastasios N. Dardas, *The Metropolitan Church of Saint Demetrios of Siatista*, p. 13
[37]Committee of M. Dainavas, A. Dardas, D. Batzios, G. Bodas, D. Siasios, *Siatista,* Acquaintance Invitation, p. 15
[38]Panagiotes N. Lioufes, *History of Kozane*, p. 42
[39]Panagiotes N. Lioufes, *History of Kozane*, p. 47
[40]Panagiotes N. Lioufes, *History of Kozane*, p. 34
[41]Michael Ath. Kalinderis, *Life in the Community of Vlaste During the Turkish Occupation*, p. 86-87
[42]Polykarpos Lioses, "The Metropolis of Siatista," *Siatista Memoirs*, p. A-45
[43]Panagiotes N. Lioufes, *History of Kozane*, p. 53

Siatista's religious and social development paralleled all close-by communities. Eratyra, a small village in 1481, belonged to the episcopate of Kastoria[44]. Its sufficient growth permitted the accommodation, jointly with Sisani, of the Archimandrite's seat. The existing—since the early fourteenth century—villages of Sopoton, Three Trees, and St. Athanasios formed the nucleus of Kozane[45]. The revolts in Thessaly and Epirus of 1612 forced several families to settle in the area. In 1646, Christian residents of Epirus's village of Charmovo experienced forced Islamization. Its two priests, father Papagikas and his son George, led its fifty armed families to Kozane. They all sought refuge in homes of earlier refugees from their village[46]. In 1649 similar circumstances forced another eighty-eight families from village Ktenion, destroyed by Moslem Albanians, to settle in Kozane. Their leader, wealthy shepherd John Trantas, carried with him twelve thousand sheep and goats. In 1664, Trantas's son Charises used his uncle's Russian estate (where he was an army officer)[47] for construction of Kozane's St. Nickolas church. Charises Trantas negotiated important privileges for Kozane residents, granted by Sultan's mother and Ottoman First-Lady[48]. The privileges specified: 1) No Moslem city residents allowed, 2) Kozane was exempt from payment of certain taxes, and 3) extension of freedom in performing religious duties as well as social and commercial fairs. In return the city agreed to 1) pay lump-sum zone rights, 2) refrain from all musical performances during transit of Ottoman troops through the city, and 3) install horseshoes to cavalry's horses upon their passing. The towns of Vlaste and Naousa enjoyed similar provisions under separate agreements whose documents did not survive[49].

To this date we don't know if Siatista claimed similar privileges under written or oral agreement. Its successes, however, following the 1686 election of Siatistian Archimandrite Zosimas as Bishop of Sisani's episcopate, are indeed impressive.

[44]Anastasios N. Dardas, "The Episcopate of Sisani (?-1686)," *Siatistina*, 1/1989, p. 40
[45]Panagiotes N. Lioufes, *History of Kozane*, p. 15
[46]Panagiotes N. Lioufes, *History of Kozane*, p. 44
[47]Panagiotes N. Lioufes, *History of Kozane*, p. 47
[48]Panagiotes N. Lioufes, *History of Kozane*, p. 45
[49]Michael Ath. Kalinderis, *Life in the Community of Vlaste During the Turkish Occupation*, p. 75

Chapter 10
The Golden Years

Population growth in the area and increased pressure to earn a living created an explosion in trading activities. At least fifty merchants[1] headquartered in Siatista traded with Venice[2]. The sizable Greek community in Venice included numerous settlers from Kastoria, Kozane, and Siatista. Marriage records of Eastern Orthodox Saint Georgios church of the Hellenic Brotherhood indicate parishioners hailed from these towns. Durres served as the shipping point of goods sold under transactions with Venice.

Area cities of Achris, Moschopolis, Monastere (Bitola), Kastoria, and Siatista utilized this port. Siatistians exported mainly wool, skins, furs, raw cotton, and crocus. They imported woolen and silk yard goods, crystal and porcelainware, jewelry, diamonds, gold-covered framed mirrors, and other industrial goods[3]. They sold imports locally and to further-away inland markets. Well-organized caravans operated overland from Upper Macedonia all the way to Vienna, Germany, and the Netherlands[4] carrying Macedonian goods east and to central Europe. In 1656, a Greek community consisting mostly of Upper Macedonian businessmen existed in Libin, Bohemia[5]. Archbishop Zosimas's diary of 1686 to 1746 recorded transactions with Istip, Serbia, in 1690, Dubrovnik in the Adriatic Sea in 1692, Adrianoupolis and Salonica in 1697, Durres, Veroia, Serres, Larisa, Kavala, Eleftheroupolis, and Thasos in 1700, Tsaritsane in 1714, and Tyrnavo[6]. His records include Sofia and Phillipoupolis of Bulgaria, and the regions Kraina, Kalocsa, and Tokaja of Hungary. The trading centers of Constantinople in 1719[7], Nis of Serbia, and Vienna in 1744[8] predominate. Siatistians

---
[1]George Laios, *Siatista and Its Commercial Houses Hadje-Michael and Manouses*, p. 14
[2]George Laios, *Siatista and Its Commercial Houses Hadje-Michael and Manouses*, p. 17
[3]John Apostolou, *The History of Siatista*, p. 14
[4]George Laios, *Siatista and Its Commercial Houses Hadje-Michael and Manouses*, p. 84
[5]Panagiotes N. Lioufes, *History of Kozane*, p. 338
[6]Michael Ath. Kalinderis, *Metropolis of Sisani and Siatista Register (1686-1746)*, pp. 29-82
[7]Michael Ath. Kalinderis, *Metropolis of Sisani and Siatista Register (1686-1746)*, pp. 88, 98
[8]Michael Ath. Kalinderis, *Metropolis of Sisani and Siatista Register (1686-1746)*, pp. 112

and Moschopolitans often formed partnerships between them[9]. A letter sent from Salonica to Venice in 1697 clearly stated: "Last year Siatistians and Moschopolitans came and got all the wax from our hands by offering more." The church offered not only spiritual guidance, but also cultivated humanism and Hellenism. Its target remained cooperation of all peoples through trade. The Ecumenical Patriarchate in Constantinople gained control over the First Justinian Autocephalus Archepiscopate of Achris in 1676[10]. It simultaneously reaffirmed its right to appoint or confirm its Archbishop. Siatistian Zosimas became an Archmandrite of the episcopate in Sisani, a small town near Siatista, in 1686. Son of a Siatistian priest named Nickolaos Rouses, Zosimas had one brother and two sisters[11]. Records of his formal education do not exist. It is possible he, too, studied in Padova. His family had both the education and the means to send him there. Available contacts in Venice turn this possibility into probability. The next nine years Siatistians, being part of Sisani's episcopate, experienced the leadership of a multitalented and broadly educated personality. His actions cemented the foundation of their progress and advancement. His guidance in all areas—religious, educational, civil, and judicial—reflected a person with sound judgment, understanding, and fairness as indicated by his diary's entries. Among the first thirty-three decisions recorded in his diary register during his first ten years in office, thirteen dealt with Last Will executions, nine dealt with settlements among individuals or partners, and four recorded filing legal complaints for debts. The following categories had one case each: recording an investment, repayment of loan, donation to Jesus's grave in Jerusalem, minutes of church committee, return of dowry to a bride's family, child adoption, and believe it or not, marriage annulment. Both spouses accepted the committee's counsel to end their twenty-year married life because they were blood relatives[12].

[9]George Laios, *Siatista and Its Commercial Houses Hadje-Michael and Manouses*, p. 14
[10]Konstantinos Metsakis, *Macedonia Throughout the Centuries*, p. 47
[11]Anastasios N. Dardas, "Zosimas' Episcopal Service in Siatista," *Siatistina*, 2/1989, p. 47
[12]Michael Ath. Kalinderis, *Metropolis of Sisani and Siatista Register (1686-1746)*, p. 33

When the local synod convened to choose and recommend to the Ecumenical Patriarchate three candidates, one of which was to head the First Justinian Archepiscopate of Achris, Zosimas's name led the list[13]. His confirmation followed their choice in 1695. Zosimas performed his duties very satisfactorily if we can judge by the fact that they elected him again in 1707 to serve another four-year term. Archbishop Zosimas served both offices, Bishop of the episcopate of Sisani and Siatista and Archbishop of First Justinian of Achris, simultaneously. He kept on visiting his episcopate in Siatista regularly. He held board sessions in Siatista as it appears from the decisions recorded subsequent to his election in his register. His influence among merchants, educators, and appointees to various community positions grew. Upon ending his first term as head of the Archepiscopate of Achris, Zosimas embarked in building the following churches in Siatista: St. John's in 1700, Prophet Elias in 1701, St. Menas in 1702, and St. Nicanor in 1709. He lived and held office long enough to build the St. Nickolas Church in 1743 and the Church of the Twelve Apostles in 1744[14]. The Saint Nicanor and Twelve Apostles churches serve as cemeteries even today.

Siatistians, residents and expatriates, living in nonoccupied and Ottoman-occupied lands felt Zosimas's impact. In 1702 Siatistian merchants, most likely with his suggestion or encouragement, wrote to Venice's consul in Durres. They briefed him on their preference and decision to have fellow Siatistians represent them in their dealings with the authorities, such as supervising, loading, and shipping their goods. In 1705 Siatistian Demetrios Hadje-Triantafyllou received an appointment of Port Secretary at Durres, a key position in export shipments control. This probably happened with the assistance of Siatistian George Peyos who in 1704–1705 served as president of the Greek community in Venice[15].

Zosimas's second term in the office of Archbishop started in 1707. In 1709, his predecessor, Archbishop Dionysios from the island of Chios, bribed Ottoman officials and won back the throne[16].

---

[13]Anastasios N. Dardas, "Zosimas's Episcopal Service in Siatista," *Siatistina,* 2/1989, p. 49
[14]Anastasios N. Dardas, "Zosimas's Episcopal Service in Siatista," *Siatistina,* 2/1989, p. 53
[15]Michael Ath. Kalinderis, *Metropolis of Sisani and Siatista Register (1686--1746),* p. 19
[16]George Laios, *Siatista and Its Commercial Houses Hadje-Michael and Manouses,* p. 19.
(Dionysios bribed Sultan's advisers and increased the "fee" by 300 grosia)

Ottoman authorities accepted the increased fee payment offered by Zosimas's opponent for the position. Zosimas's support from his followers and associates, however, remained solid. In 1710 Siatistian John Nerantzes, resident and representative in Durres of France's commercial interests, formed a partnership with Nick Poulemenos. The two contracted the collection of tobacco custom duties. In the war between Venetians and Ottomans of 1714 to 1718, Nerantzes served as British Consul in Durres. He looked after the Venetians' commercial interests from this position. In this capacity he joined the consuls of France, Denmark, and Venice who, in 1720, wrote to Ottoman officials at Durres regarding the Greek merchants' interests[17]. A year earlier, Zosimas helped elevate his friend Bishop Ioasaf of Korytsa to the throne of First Justinian Archepiscopate of Achris[18]. Ioasaf replaced Archbishop Philotheos who displayed a pro-Ottoman policy, thirst for money, and inadequacy in administration during his term in office from 1714 to 1718[19].

Zosimas demonstrated appreciation towards the proteges of Slav educators and Christianizers. He introduced and used extensively in Siatista, the names Naoum for men and Naouma for women, honoring Cyril and Methodius's assistant Naoum. A monastery of Saint Naoum located in the south shore of Lake Achris also honors the name. Area residents honored Zosimas's own name widely. These names even today are used by Siatistians, something that does not happen in other parts of Greece. Siatistians honored Zosimas's wife's name Triada (Trinity) by dedicating a church to Holy Trinity. Zosimas added "and Naoum[20]" to the name of the same church.

Trade with Venice presented a challenge to Zosimas. He decided to improve parish and private education by all means. No documents survived that prove operation of public schools in Siatista prior to Zosimas's time. In nearby Vlaste[21] and

---

[17]George Laios, *Siatista and Its Commercial Houses Hadje-Michael and Manouses*, p. 16
[18]Anastasios N. Dardas, "Zosimas's Episcopal Service in Siatista," *Siatistina.*, 2/1989, p. 51
[19]Anastasios N. Dardas, "Zosimas's Episcopal Service in Siatista," *Siatistina*, 2/1989, p. 74
[20]Anastasios N. Dardas, "Zosimas's Episcopal Service in Siatista," *Siatistina*, 2/1989, pp. 54-55
[21]Fortes Vittes, *Stachyologemata (Short Stories Collection)* p. 43

Kozane[22], public schools operated since 1668. Financial assistance from expatriate businessmen made this possible. Siatista operated similar schools under Zosimas between 1695 and 1699. Siatistians acquired advanced education and foreign languages in Balkan and European cities and in Constantinople. In 1698, Siatistian Kyprianos, member of Mt. Athos Holy Community then numbering six thousand monks[23], copied Holy Scriptures and documents. George Rouses, Zosimas's only son from his wife Triada, who died prior to Zosimas's becoming bishop in 1686, registered in Padova University in 1699. He received his degree in philosophy and theology in 1705[24]. He assisted Siatista's school to the point where the Ecumenical Patriarchate in 1718 recognized it compatible with the schools of Athens, Trikala, and the islands of Skopelos and Patmos[25].

Zosimas's efforts on education covered nearby communities of Vlaste, Tsotyli, and Pentalofos. In the town of Eratyra, much closer to Siatista, the "Museum of Knowledge and Virtues" school improved area education[26]. Kastoria's bishop supervised his episcopate's schools. A brilliant educator, Methodius Anthrakites, taught in Kastoria's George-Kyritzes school. Zosimas correctly assessed the advantages in hiring him for Siatista's school. Anthrakites's all-important eleven-year experience in the key position of priest in Venice's Greek Church weighted heavily. Anthrakites's contacts in Venice were precious. Zosimas ignored Anthrakites's liberal views. Anthrakites taught Siatistian youth the ancient Hellenic thought and Macedonian pride. Siatistians became self-confident, self-reliant, ambitious, energetic, and resourceful. Their humbleness, unselfishness, and understanding provided their contentment. They often displayed solidarity through personal sacrifices. Their disciplined austerity and hard work led them to proper disposition. Their tolerance and courage gave them an advantage. Their education enabled them to make prudent judgments. Free from prejudices and fears they developed their

[22]Panagiotes, N. Lioufes, *History of Kozane*, p. 49
[23]John P. Panagiotou, *Mt. Athos, The Holy Community*, p. 4
[24]George Laios, *Siatista and Its Commercial Houses Hadje-Michael and Manouses*, p. 23
[25]Anastasios N. Dardas, "Zosimas' Episcopal Service in Siatista," *Siatistina*, 2/1989, p. 61. (Theologian John wrote *Apocalypse*, in Patmos Island)
[26]Anastasios N. Dardas, "Zosimas' Episcopal Service in Siatista," *Siatistina* 2/1989, p. 69

inner satisfaction and strength. Men full of positive qualities went on with their business. Women stayed behind cultivating the same values. Their embroidered mottoes "Good-morning," "Keep Hoping," "Be Patient," and "Happiness Comes from Within," in gold-covered sculptured wooden frames hung on living-room walls. The motto "Know Thyself," which appeared on the ancient Temple of Apollo[27] at Delphi Sanctuary, was their favorite. Siatistian women supplemented their husbands' self-reliance and strength. The girls patiently waited for their man, who was carefully selected for them by their family. No records of crime whatsoever existed in this vibrant mountainous community of five thousand inhabitants.

---

[27]Konstantinos A. Plevris, *Socrates Facing His Death*, p. 46

Chapter 11
Ambitious Efforts

Siatista's location, bravery of its citizenry, education, liberal views, and power of money produced able local leaders who managed to maintain a rather secure semi-autonomous community. In the surrounding vicinity, illegal armed bands roamed the countryside. In 1682 an Ottoman directive declared: "For about fifteen years now, Greeks of Achris, Monastere, Skopje, Trikala, and Salonica areas, following their secret deliberations, formed armed bands of fifteen, twenty, or thirty men each. They roam around on foot or on horses attacking many Turks and Greeks of towns and villages. They grab money from caravan individuals and public funds and kill people[1]."

Considerable unrest existed throughout the Balkans when in 1683 Austria declared war against the Ottoman Empire. Oppressed individuals welcomed with patience and hope every foreign attack on the Ottomans. Austria recruited over fifty thousand volunteers—Orthodox residents of Nis, Pec, Pristeni, and Skopje—to fight the war. Many among them were Greeks. When the Ottoman troops defeated the Austrians in 1690 all these people, led by Archbishop Arsenije III, retreated to Belgrade[2]. Most of them finally settled in the Austrian Empire. Among the Greeks from Macedonia were Mark Krantas from Kozane and Demetrios Popovic from Salonica. They submitted a request to Leopold I of Austria for assistance. Austrian authorities recognized these peoples' service. They guaranteed their safety and granted them preference in employment along with other benefits. John Monasterlis, son of a Macedonian immigrant from Monastere, born in Komarom, Hungary, received an appointment as their officer. In 1691, he commanded ten thousand soldiers. Monasterlis's and Archbishop Arsenije III's constant requests for assistance alienated the King. Leopold

---
[1] Demetrios G. Siasios, "Siatistian Traders, Their Trips, Their Songs," *Siatistina* 13/1995, p. 38
[2] John A. Papadrianos, *The Greek Settlers of Semlin*, p. 34

I removed Monasterlis from office, compensating him with a title of Baron and sufficient land[3].

The Austrian-Ottoman war ended in January 1699. Archbishop Zosimas was still head of the First Justinian Archepiscopate of Achris (he served until June 1699)[4]. Zosimas's ambition and his power to implement church directives impacted variously within the Ottoman Empire as well as to outside powers. Zosimas conceived a plan to form an independent state comprised of Upper Macedonia, Albania, and Southwest Serbia with Achris as capital under the protection of Austria. The Montenegrins' objective coincided with Zosimas's idea. Russia's defeat and subsequent treaty of 1711 disappointed many Greeks and Montenegrins. They renewed their hopes in 1716 when Austria, allied with Venice, declared war against the Ottomans[5].

A Siatistian merchant named Cyrus John Tsiporopoulos approached governor Baron von Cosa, general of the Austrian army, at the city of Arad (presently it belongs to Rumania). Tsiporopoulos presented his credentials signed by Patriarch Archbishop of First Justinian of Achris, three bishops, archons of the area, and soldiers[6]. His petition requested from the Austrians three written guarantees for protection and three Austrian flags, one each for the three counties of Macedonia. General von Cosa sent the Siatistian merchant, accompanied by a noncommissioned officer carrying his favorable comments on the case[7], to Futak, in Hungary, to meet with general-in-command Eugenius. Tsiporopoulos requested the commander to place the new state-to-be-formed under Austrian protection and guarantees, in the event the plan succeeded, with continuation of all privileges enjoyed by Greek Orthodox Christians. He stated Siatista was two days west of Salonica on foot. Siatista had the capability of organizing twelve thousand men, with their weapons, providing the Austrian army kept advancing. He emphasized that he represented Siatista, Kozane, Naousa,

[3]John A. Papadrianos, *The Greek Settlers of Semlin*, p. 37
[4]Anastasios N. Dardas, "Zosimas's Episcopal Service in Siatista,"*Siatistina*, 2/1989, p. 50
[5]John A. Papadrianos, *The Greek Settlers of Semlin*, p. 39
[6]Anastasios N. Dardas, "Zosimas's Episcopal Service in Siatista,"*Siatistina*, 2/1989, p.72
[7]George Laios, *Siatista and Its Commercial Houses Hadje-Michael and Manouses*, p. 31

Moschopolis[8] (which had seven thousand homes) and other cities.

On the same day, July 22, 1716, a Montenegrin named Nickolaos presented himself to commander Eugenius as ex-officer of the Russian army. Nickolaos stated he left the Russians upon their defeat and since resided in Fume, Italy. He claimed the Montenegrins authorized him to seek Austrian protection and stood ready to revolt. He promised he could deliver forty thousand troops with rifles but would need food and supplies. He specifically asked for: 1) continuation of religious privileges enjoyed up to now by Montenegrins, 2) dispatch of an Austrian army towards Serajevo from which his country is only six days distant by foot, and 3) assignment to Montenegrins of four experienced officers in order to take command of the revolutionaries. Furthermore, he requested provisions of food and supplies to be sent by sea to Ragousa (presently Dubrovnic). Nickolaos stated Montenegrin troops would wait for Austrian advance units before they took action.

Prince Eugenius approved the plan and prepared the relative proclamations in July 1716. He forwarded them to Vienna's Imperial War Council for confirmation. His troops defeated the Ottomans at Peterwardein in August. Austrian troops captured Temesvar (Timisoara) in October. In the eastern front, a cavalry regiment surprised Bucharest with an attack. It captured Wallachia's Greek governor Nickolaos Mavrokordatos. The Ottomans replaced him in a few months with his brother John. The Austrians advanced towards Belgrade and almost captured it in 1717. Diplomatic maneuvering by western European powers, however, forced the prince to discontinue his advance south[9]. All hostilities stopped in the summer of 1718. The Passarowitz pact recognized Austria's gains of lands north of Serbia and Bosnia. Cessation of hostilities brought an end to efforts on the part of the Greek team from Siatista and the one from Montenegro. Luckily the Ottoman officials were unaware of the secret negotiations taking place. There were no attempts to punish Siatistians for their moves.

[8]George Laios, *Siatista and Its Commercial Houses Hadje-Michael and Manouses*, p. 33
[9]George Laios, *Siatista and Its Commercial Houses Hadje-Michael and Manouses*, p. 35

Macedonian merchants and Zosimas made another attempt for freedom twenty years later. Russia's declaration of war against the Ottomans in 1735 provided a second opportunity. Political conditions in the area deteriorated. Ottoman authorities attempted to put on war footing all conquered peoples to help their effort. In 1736, local governors dispatched armed details supplied with Ottoman flags to towns where well-off Greeks lived. These details posted a flag in front of influential homes with a specific requirement: to organize and arm at their expense a band of twenty, thirty, or even fifty men and bring them to their regular units for induction. They applied pressures to residents of Achris, Elbasan, Tirana, Berate, Moschopolis, Siatista, Ioannina[10], and other towns.

Zosimas knew or correctly estimated the Russo-Austrian treaty of 1725 provisions. He expected Austria to get into the act on Russia's side. Correctly appraising Austria's Balkan policy for expansion to the Aegean Sea[11], Zosimas proceeded to negotiate with the Austrians. He prepared in Latin, and addressed to Emperor Karl VI of Austria, a letter on behalf of the First Justinian Archepiscopate of Achris. It contained the signatures of two Archepiscopate officers. Metropolitan and Archimandrite of Patras, Peloponnese, delivered the letter. Written very, very eloquently it utilized many exceedingly impressive titles. Most likely, consultations with the emperor's counselors for acceptance preceded its preparation. The letter was only an accreditation document for the clergymen visiting the Austrians. It mentioned no details of purpose regarding the visit. Perhaps another document outlined all details. George Kantakouzenos, a Greek and a general in the Russian army, facilitated the representatives in their meetings. Kantakouzenos hailed from an old imperial family of Byzantium (see earlier chapter on Eastern Orthodoxy)[12]. The extremely secret negotiations held in Vienna in 1737 between the Austrians and the Patriarch of Pec, Serbia, and Archbishop of First Justinian of Achris are mentioned in Austrian Friedrich Heinrich Seckendorff's biography. Both

---

[10]George Laios, *Siatista and Its Commercial Houses Hadje-Michael and Manouses*, p. 16
[11]Apostolos E. Vacalopoulos, *The History of Thessalonike*, p. 12. Vacalopoulos discusses a natural channel that leads from river Danube to Aegean Sea.
[12]Elias Laskaris, *Byzantine Emperors*, Vol. II, p. 172

clergymen assured the Austrians their nation would revolt as soon as Austrian troops advanced in areas near Nis of Serbia. Food supplies and armed assistance were available to Austrian troops to carry on the war. In return the petitioners requested Austrian protection and guarantees for their religious freedom. Zosimas claimed he hailed from the Kantakouzenos family of Byzantium. He insisted he had every right and an obligation for spiritual and civil authority over Bosnia, Serbia, Albania, and Macedonia as heir to Byzantine throne. He was interested in revitalizing the First Justinian Archepiscopate of Achris. Zosimas asked for his right to be represented in the German parliament. He also requested voting rights and favorable taxation terms[13] for the proposed state.

Unfortunately for Zosimas, the Ottomans won. Victorious General Eugenius of Austria died in 1736. Seckendorff and his staff proved unable to advance further south or even hold on to captured areas. The Ottomans occupied Belgrade. The Treaty of Belgrade of 1739 terminated all hopes for clergyman, educator, and politician Zosimas. At the time he addressed his letter to Emperor Karl VI he was only an ex-Archbishop, not Archbishop of the First Justinian Archepiscopate. He was, however, spokesman for his friend Archbishop Ioasaf. Zosimas helped elevate him to that position by influencing the other bishops.

Zosimas realized by then that Siatista's successful trade with Venice was coming to an end. Siatistian Nickolaos Hadje-Michael still exported goods to Fume in 1741[14]. In 1744, however, a report from the Venetian Consulate in Durres stated: Hungarian businessmen authorized "two Greeks from Siatista and two more from Ioannina to buy all wool at whatever prices and, as a result, many businessmen intending to ship their wool to Venice sold it to these people at much higher price." The century-old (1650 to 1750) extensive trade with Venice slowed down if not diminished. By the time Zosimas died (in 1746), his success was thorough. Siatista, Kastoria, and Moschopolis were the only towns administrative officials for the Archepiscopate in Achris could be selected from[15]. His sixty-year service to the

---
[13]George Laios, *Siatista and Its Commercial Houses Hadje-Michael and Manouses*, p. 38
[14]George Laios, *Siatista and Its Commercial Houses Hadje-Michael and Manouses*, p. 17
[15]Anastasios N. Dardas, "Nikeforos of Achris's Episcopal Service in Siatista," *Siatistina*, 3/1990, p. 28, note 34

same community enhanced the area's spiritual development, social progress, and national awakening[16]. New markets with equally great opportunities were in prospect up north. Siatistian children carried Zosimas's spirit of Hellenism to these lands. They traveled to Balkan and Central European cities, determined the needs for Macedonian goods, and—with maturity, prudence, and courage—established their business outlets. Their honesty and fairness met the locals' favorable response.

---

[16]Anastasios N. Dardas, "Zosimas's Episcopal Service in Siatista," *Siatistina*, 2/1989, p. 69

Chapter 12
The Explosion

Greek merchants trading in central European countries operated since Roman times. Their numbers grew during the Byzantine period. Marriages at the royal level improved considerably their relationships and activities[1]. Ottoman-Turks' presence in the Balkans and subsequent Greek element dispersal brought many Greeks to foreign armies' service. In 1526, a soldier from Macedonia named Nickolaos became known in the struggles of Croats and Hungarians for capturing the Hungarian crown. Troops guarding Buda(pest) against the Ottomans in 1541 included over one thousand Greeks, mostly Macedonians[2].

Siatistian traders, properly trained during Zosimas's era or thereafter, traveled north seeking business opportunities. Their trade with Venice enriched their knowledge and experience. Their move and settlement in northern communities became more palatable through their Hellenic values and behavior. Upper Macedonians moved freely throughout the Balkan areas as did all Greeks. No one has yet researched the official records and dates; but Stogiannis or Stogianovitz, born in Vlaste in 1692, moved in 1726 to the Semendria district[3]. In 1756, Greek businessmen operated in the following communities of Transylvania and Moravia (parts of Rumania): Albocoralina, Szasz-Regen, Nagy-Enyved, Thorenburg, Kolos Bistritz, Szamos-Uswar, Medlitz, Schassburg, Vasarheln, Radnoth, Nagy Sink, Axona, Coroncas, Nagy-Varanz, and Bungard[4]. Many Siatistians settled in Novi-Sad, Serbia. Settlers there formed their own Hellenic community[5]. The Serbian society eventually assimilated most of them into the local population[6]. Other communities chosen for settlement were Newsatz, Ujvidek,

[1]George Laios, *Siatista and Its Commercial Houses Hadje-Michael and Manouses*, p. 40
[2]John A. Papadrianos, *The Greek Settlers of Semlin*, p. 33
[3]Michael Ath. Kalinderis, *Life in the Community of Vlaste During the Turkish Occupation*, p. 62
[4]Panagiotes N. Lioufes, *History of Kozane*, p. 338
[5]John A. Papadrianos, *The Greek Settlers of Semlin*, p. 31
[6]John Apostolou, *The History of Siatista*, p. 16

Temesvar, Arad, Szentes, Debrecen, Tokaj, Miscolc, Eger, Vac, Buda, Pest, Panchova, Orsova, and Mehadia. Macedonians from Moschopolis settled in Miscolc while Kecskemet settlers hailed mostly from Siatista and Kozane[7]. Twenty-six Kecskemet settlers engaged in transport trade in 1708 formed their own association. Pecet Kecskemet Grece Compania's purpose was to organize their safety on the road. They emphasized their mutual assistance and obedience. In 1719, they elected Siatistian Demos Kaplanes to the presidency[8]. Their association received recognition from local authorities and the ruler Franciscus Racoczy II. The association's constitution included specific rules and regulations regarding the members' caravan travel. In 1721, they negotiated an agreement/contract with the city stipulating the following provisions, which were advantageous for the Greeks:

> 1) Permanent residency for Greek traders requesting it.
> 2) Establishment and operation of twenty stores for the association members' use with additional warehouses for safe storage of their imports.
> 3) Election of the association's own judge and jurors to resolve trade differences among its members.
> 4) Civic offenses of members would be turned over to the city's judicial authorities.
> 5) Differences between city residents and association members would be judged by city authorities with right of appeal to the prince or baron.
> 6) Consideration by the city for construction of stone-built warehouses for rental at reasonable fee to association members in order to control warehousing activities and minimize residential area deterioration.
> 7) Allow visiting Greek merchants a three-day stay in the city to sell their goods (extended stay compelled them to join the association and pay their obligations).

[7]George Laios, *Siatista and Its Commercial Houses Hadje-Michael and Manouses,* p. 43
[8]George Laios, *Siatista and Its Commercial Houses Hadje-Michael and Manouses,* p. 48

8) Wine barrels would not be owned nor maintained by Greeks, but they would procure wine supplies from public winery (apparently Siatistians, accustomed to producing their own wine back home, continued their practice, inviting the authorities' ruling).
9) The association would pay the city an annual fixed fee of 350 gold fiorins regardless of membership fluctuation. This fee would cover all members' Albanian guards and assistants. This provision documents the fact that Greeks relied on trusted Albanians for their safety at a fixed cost.
10) Greeks, members or not, refusing to follow the above terms or disobeying the association's judging committee's decisions could request assistance from the city judge.
11) All association members were responsible to obey the above terms and to respect the city and regional authorities. In case of disobedience, a fine of one hundred fiorins per violation would be imposed.

The above code-of-ethics contract provided the basis for organization of Kecskemet's Greek community later on. The association's elected officials and religious leaders guided every new arrival and fulfilled their spiritual, moral, religious, and educational needs. The contract promoted responsibility and appropriate behavior of all merchants. It served the interests of both parties. They renewed it in 1753 and again in 1775, fifty-four years from its original drafting. The following Siatistians served as association presidents after Demos Kaplanes: Christos Peyos in 1721, Demetrios Lazarou in 1724, George Misios in 1750, twenty-year-old John Papageorgiou in 1758, Theodore Diamantes in 1762, Pavlos Poulios in 1765, and Demetrios Drollios in 1774[9]. Kecskemet's Greek Association controlled and supervised the community priest's behavior contrary to Siatista's regime where Zosimas controlled all committees.

[9]George Laios, *Siatista and Its Commercial Houses Hadje-Michael and Manouses*, p. 52

Priests from Elasson's Monastery of the Virgin Mary and from churches back home served their needs.

The Austrians, in an effort to promote trade and ensure abundance of Eastern raw materials, wool, cotton, and skins much needed by their industries, included in the Passarowitz Pact of 1718 a privileged-for-Ottoman-subjects provision. This provision benefited the Greek merchants who traveled freely as Ottoman subjects. Upper Macedonians, in closer proximity to the Austrian Empire, covered every region of the country. The name Gorok (Greek) meant merchant and a generally well-off person[10]. Viennese Greeks established an Orthodox Church in 1723[11]. Saint George's Church functioned under the Metropolis of Karlowac. It served Greeks, Serbs, and all Eastern Orthodox Christians living in the area. Siatistians George and John Konstantinou and Demetrios Hadges served on its board of directors between 1746 and 1752. An elected eighteen-member board formulated its policy and governed the church. Siatistians Lazarus Michael, Demos Hadje-Kotse, and Nickolaos Demetriou were three of its members. The subsequent elections reduced the board members to twelve but kept three Siatistians. Konstantinos Koiou replaced Lazarus Michael.

The number of Greek merchants trading in Vienna in 1766 increased substantially. Out of 134 Ottoman subjects, 82 were Greeks mostly from Upper Macedonia. The remaining included 21 Armenians, 18 Jews, and 13 Turks[12]. Konstantinos Filippides von Gaya, a Greek from the city of Achris and adviser to Maria Theresia, conducted a census of Vienna traders in 1767. The census recorded the following Siatistians:

1. Hadje-Ioannou, Konstantinos, age twenty-nine, born in 1738, entered the country in 1753. He had a partnership with his father John Konstantinou and his brother-in-law George Manouses. Both were in Siatista. Hadje-Ioannou sold imported goods in Vienna, Regenburg and Meinningen in Germany.
2. Doucas, Michael, age twenty-six, born in 1741, entered the country in 1758. He lived with his wife and

[10]George Laios, *Siatista and Its Commercial Houses Hadje-Michael and Manouses*, p. 63
[11]George Laios, *Siatista and Its Commercial Houses Hadje-Michael and Manouses*, p. 71
[12]John A. Papadrianos, *The Greek Settlers of Semlin*, p. 48

children in Vienna. He sold his imports in Vienna and Regenburg.
3. Psaras, Metsos, age twenty-four, born in 1743, entered the country in 1759. Single, he rented two warehouses, one in his residence and one in Rossau. His brothers/partners were Nerantzes and Theodore in Siatista, John in Serres, and Pantos Manos in Semlin. He sold his imports in Vienna.
4. Liotas, Polyzos, age thirty-two, born in 1735, entered the country in 1749. He traveled to Siatista to visit his wife and children regularly. He sold his imports in Vienna and in Leipzig. He exported printed yard goods and miscellaneous items.
5. Lazarou, Nickolaos, age thirty-six, born in 1731, entered the country in 1748. He lived with his wife and children in Vienna. He and his partners Nickolaos and Pavlos Hadje-Michael and Theodore Konstantinou Manouses had four warehouses. They sold their imports worth one hundred thousand fiorins in Vienna and Amsterdam. They exported yard goods and cleaning chemicals valued at twenty thousand fiorins.
6. Hapsas, Demos, of Alexandros, age fifty, born in 1717, entered Austria in 1734. He imported through "Kostas Papadopoulos and Lazaros Yankowic" and maintained two warehouses.
7. Mavroudes, Demos, age fifty-seven, born in 1710, entered the country in 1727. His partner/brother Konstantinos was in Siatista. They imported goods valued eight thousand fiorins and exported to Ottoman markets printed yard goods and embroidered items. His family in Siatista continued to trade with Venice.
8. Hadje-Kotsios, Demetrios, age forty-eight, born in 1719, entered the country in 1737. His partner/brother Pavlos was in Siatista. Their firm "Demos Hadje-Kotsios" imported goods valued at ten thousand fiorins annually.
9. Rousses, John, age twenty-nine, born in 1738, lived in Vienna with his wife and children. He managed

Konstantinou's business residing in Siatista. The firm imported goods valued at fifty thousand fiorins annually.

10. Konstantinou, George, age fifty-eight, born in 1709, entered the country in 1729. He was married, living in Vienna with his wife and children. Previously he lived in Leipzig and Linz. He sold his imports valued at three thousand fiorins per year in Vienna and Linz.

11. Lazarou, George, age twenty-seven, born in 1740, entered the country in 1759. He lived in Leipzig prior to his moving to Vienna. He was in partnership with his brother John in Vienna and his father Nickolaos, who lived in Siatista. They imported goods valued at sixty thousand fiorins annually. They exported yard goods from Amsterdam and miscellaneous items from Leipzig. They stored their merchandise in Michael Lazarou's warehouse. Michael Ioannou, Lazarou's employee, ran his business when he was in Siatista.

12. Demetriou, Markos, age thirty-five, born in 1732, entered the country in 1751. He was partner with his brother Nickolaos who was in Siatista. He imported goods valued at five thousand fiorins annually. He exported to the Balkans goods produced in Nuremberg and Styre[13].

A similar census held in Kecskemet in 1769 found twenty Siatistians listed out of ninety-one Ottoman subject merchants.

Name	Age	Born	Entered the Country
1. Argyres, Konstantinos	38	1730	1768
2. Diamantes, Theodore	58	1710	1769
3. Theodore, Diamantes	27	1742	1757
4. Toulios, Konstantinos	26	1743	1752
5. Goumilas, Markos	24	1745	1760
6. Stefanou, Nickolaos-Miskoltzis	18	1751	1764
7. Konstantinou, Georgios	20	1749	1763
8. Hadje-Nickolas, Konstantinos	19	1750	1761

[13]George Laios, *Siatista and Its Commercial Houses Hadje-Michael and Manouses*, pp. 74-83

Name	Age	Born	Entered the Country
9. Pramatias, Anastasios	24	1745	1764
10. Drochlias, George	23	1746	1761
11. Drochlias, Theodore	32	1737	1768
12. Drochlias, Pavlos	20	1749	1764
13. Konstantinou, George	17	1752	1768
14. Drochlias, Nickolaos	30	1739	1753
15. Andranovic, Thomas	20	1749	1765
16. Poulios, Pavlos	42	1727	1764
17. Drochlia, Pavlos	26	1743	1757
18. Hadje-Michael, Nickolaos	22	1747	1760
19. Georgiou, Anastasios	44	1725	1737
20. Diamantis, Nickolaos	50	1719	1767

In addition to the above statistics, Siatistians Hamzas, Kozmas, and Miskolcje in 1728 and Harsi Janos (Hadje-Giannes), Pulyo Gyorgy (Poulios, George), and Demetrios (last name unknown) in 1737 rented warehouses in Kecskemet[14]. George Poulios had traded there since 1724. In 1738 he traded in Vienna. In twenty years he became a first-class merchant. John and George Konstantinou brothers traded in Kislly-Szallas. All traders imported Macedonian wool, skins, furs, red-dyed thread, wine, crocus, wax, and Thessalian cotton. Macedonian caravans carried north other products as well, i.e., figs, raisins, spices, coffee, and camel wool. They brought back to Ottoman lands jewelry, printed yard goods, Bohemian porcelainware, crystals, glass items, household utensils, and metal instruments[15]. The Passarowitz Pact forbade retail trade by Ottoman subjects in Austria. Siatistians overcame this by becoming Austrian citizens. Their level of education attained at Zosimas's Siatistian schools enabled them not only to become citizens, but elevated to barons. In 1787, twenty-one Greek merchants in Vienna, among them Siatistian George Manouses, Nickolaos Demetriou, Demetrios Tsetires, and Michael Vretta Zoupan, in order to promote ethical practices, financed an investigation to uncover possible improprieties. Eleven Austrian citizens and ten

[14]George Laios, *Siatista and Its Commercial Houses Hadje-Michael and Manouses*, p. 55
[15]George Laios, *Siatista and Its Commercial Houses Hadje-Michael and Manouses*, p. 84

Ottoman subjects signed the proposal. They quickly achieved restoration of their business respect.

The above censuses indicate 53 percent of the merchants from Siatista entered the country just sixteen years old or under. Only 15 percent were thirty years old or over. Most had a partner in Siatista, headquarters of their operation. Seven Siatistians of the twelve listed on Vienna's census of 1767 served on the church board of directors. Two of them served as chairmen.

Upper Macedonians were obedient to the local laws and customs of their adopted countries. Their devotion to their trade benefited the communities they lived in and their birthplaces. They all sent tremendous sums of money to Siatista to marry off their daughters and sisters. The approximately thirty traditional mansions existing today in Siatista are proof of their allegiance. Prudent handling by archons and public officials of donations/grants of expatriates for community projects enhanced Siatista's living standards. The donors derived immense satisfaction and enjoyed recognition and respect by the population. Competition to that end existed among expatriate returnees. W. M. Leake wrote in his book *Travels In Northern Greece in 1805*: "Almost every family in Siatista has one of its members residing as a merchant in Italy, Hungary, Austria, or other parts of Germany. Very few of the elders did not spend ten or twelve years of their lives in one of these countries. German is of course very generally spoken and Italian almost as much[16]." Nowadays Siatistians are dispersed in all European countries, Russia, America, and Australia. Their annual pilgrimage to Siatista renews their spirit of Hellenism.

---

[16] W. M. Leake, *Travels in Northern Greece in 1805, Siatista Memoirs*, p. A68

PART C
Chapter 13
Local Autonomy

Proper spiritual guidance and socially acceptable commercial orientation displayed by the Bishop assured successful operation of the community of Siatista. Zosimas automatically presided and directed the organization and operation of every committee. Committees' actions exercised firm control through their acceptance by the public. Residents' representation in the committees served best the newly established towns of Macedonia[1]. In a system called Demogerontia (from Demos meaning people and geron meaning elder), where the elders decided with logic and prudence, the people elected worthy individuals, all men, for their representatives. Demogerontia played an important role as go-betweens on behalf of area or local Ottoman authorities and the Ecumenical Patriarchate.

The locally elected archons ruled. Most men elected to Demogerontia were wealthy property owners. They filtered the feelings and complaints of the population and acted instantly on matters requiring immediate attention. They dealt with local problems of taxation, education, judicial administration, and civic law[2]. They performed for the account of the Ottoman authorities these unwelcome responsibilities. The elders assessed owned land and other property values, and imposed taxes on that basis. They administered the town's assets and properties. They judged all differences between and among individuals, worked out and imposed compromises, and appointed salaried community employees. Elected town employees and archons protected the rights of the town and its citizens. They guarded their vineyards, fields, animals, and other interests[3]. The elders' deliberations and decisions, approved by the bishop, impacted every citizen. They signed the recorded decision on the Metropolitan register as witnesses, and

---
[1] George E. Daskalakis, *The Ages-Long Development of Hellenism in Macedonia*, p. 41
[2] George E. Daskalakis, *The Ages-Long Development of Hellenism in Macedonia*, p. 46
[3] George E. Daskalakis, *The Ages-Long Development of Hellenism in Macedonia*, p. 47

implemented it as final and irrevocable. In one case appearing in Zosimas's "Metropolis of Sisani and Siatista Register" the Archbishop states: "Georgia, the daughter of Segouna Kotze, requests her share from her father's estate. She files suit against the children Demetrios and John because her brothers are dead. The judicial committee members Theodore Nerantzes, Hadje-Markos and the priest Demetrios represented the boys due to their minor age. Georgia authorized her husband to represent her. The four men figured out the estate of Kotze Segouna. Georgia receives another four hundred aslania, Turkish monetary unit, on April 13, 1697. Archbishop of Achris Zosimas confirms." The signatures of Georgia's husband and representative Michael Nikolaos and four other witnesses appear on the bottom.

The elders usually met in school, or in the bishop's or an elder's residence. Their spokesman gave an account of the year's actions and developments. They presented the collection status of imposed taxes to date and the residents' reactions. They discussed all matters pertaining to the community's operation. Continuation in office depended on whether their actions met the approval of the residents or not. Most of the time they shaped public opinion. In the case of election of new archons, all of them together proceeded to the appropriate Ottoman authorities for introduction, formal recognition, payment of respect[4], and acknowledgment of subservience.

Siatista's Most Respectable Men, as known to the populace[5], served their terms without any compensation[6]. Archbishop Zosimas's register recorded 102 decisions, 59 of which occurred during his last fifty years in office. Analyzing the register one can observe the first ten years he recorded 3.3 decisions per year. The following fifty years the rate dropped to only 1.1 decisions per year. This probably happened due to Zosimas's preoccupation with other, much more important matters. It is possible, however, he neglected to record decisions taken. It could also mean, and

---

[4]Panagiotes N. Lioufes, *History of Kozane*, p. 67
[5]Miltiades Strakales, *The Development of the Mayor's Office in Siatista*, Siatista Memoirs, p. A-57
[6]Michael Ath. Kalinderis, *Metropolis of Sisani and Siatista Register (1686-1746)*, p. 126

this is more probable, the prosperity of Siatistians brought by Zosimas's leadership reduced friction considerably.

Zosimas had firm control of Siatista's archons. He ensured continuation of his policy after his death by selecting Nikeforos from Achris in 1743 to succeed him[7]. The following three years until Zosimas's death in 1746, Nikeforos, an educated cleric, familiarized himself with Zosimas's thinking necessary to smoothly carry on his work. He subsequently served twenty-three years until 1769 and died in 1770. Nikeforos constructed several churches during his administration. He dedicated St. Athanasios in Vlaste in 1755[8], St. Georgios in Siatista in 1760[9], St. Chrysostom in Bogatsiko in 1760[10], and Virgin Mary in Eratyra in 1763[11]. Nikeforos, together with four other bishops in 1767, requested the Ecumenical Patriarchate of Constantinople to place their episcopates under its jurisdiction[12]. This meant the bishops of Kastoria's Efthymios, Bodenon (Edessa)'s Germanos, Stromnitza's Ananias, and Grevena's Gregory severed ties with the Justinian Archepiscopate of Achris. The Ecumenical Patriarchate accepted their request. The Archbishop of Achris submitted his resignation to the Ecumenical Patriarchate. The First Justinian Autocefalus Eastern Orthodox Patriarchate of Achris terminated its existence. It served the region for over twelve centuries. Its episcopates became Metropoles. Achris's episcopate joined the one of Prespa to form the Metropolis of Achris and Prespa[13]. Siatista's chief clergy became Metropolitan. No recorded objection on the part of the elders exists. It may mean the termination of Achris's Archepiscopate was a prudent act. This development possibly resulted from Sultan's learning of Zosimas's negotiations with the Austrians thirty years earlier.

[7]Anastasios N. Dardas, "Zosimas's Episcopate Service in Siatista," *Siatistina*, 2/1989, p. 83
[8]Michael Ath. Kalinderis, *Life in Community of Vlaste During the Turkish Occupation*, p. 93
[9]Committee of M. Dainavas, A. Dardas, D. Batzios, G. Bodas, D. Siasios, *Siatista, Acquaintance Invitation*, p. 18
[10]Parmenion N. Tzifras, *Brief History of Bogatsiko*, p. 75
[11]Committee of N. Liamades, D. Makres, A. Bellos, L. Papaioannou, K. Siabanopoulos, *Aquaintance with Kozane Prefecture*, p. 267
[12]Anastasios N. Dardas, "Nikeforos of Achris' Episcopal Service in Siatista," *Siatistina*, 3/1990, p. 9
[13]Anastasios N. Dardas, "Metropolitan of Prespa and Achris Anthimos," *Siatistina*, 11/1994, p. 47

Could it be the Ottomans, through the Ecumenical Patriarchate, advised the bishops to proceed in this direction? The archons had no alternatives.

Metropolitans and archons demonstrated remarkable cooperation. Vasilike Nikolaou, a Siatistian residing in Iasi, Romania, in 1817 donated to Siatista a substantial sum of money for construction and operation of an educational institution. The Greeks' revolutionary activities taking place in the years following her action prevented utilization of these funds by the elder's committee on education. A bank in Constantinople lent these funds to several Metropoles. In 1830, Metropolitan Ioannikios of Sisani and Siatista reminded his constituents of this inheritance. He stressed the advisability to proceed with the donor's provisions since the revolutionary war ended. The elders and the school committee collected the interest and the school became a reality[14]. In another instance, Ioannikios suggested to his constituents to discharge their financial obligation to the church, pending since 1824. These were exceptionally difficult years for Siatistians. Both Ottoman authorities and the revolting Greeks fighting for independence pressed for financial assistance. The much-treasured wealth, accumulated from the expatriates' gifts the previous century, came in handy. Siatistian intellectuals, keeping in mind Pericles of ancient Athens, who listed the removable gold ornaments of goddess Athena's statue in Acropolis (equalling to 1050 kilos) as an item to be used to finance his war preparations (Thucydides book 2), used the church's gold and silver items without hesitation. In an effort to help the revolutionary effort and yet stay in good terms with the Ottomans, they borrowed their churches' gold and silver[15]. They satisfied both requirements. The debt was still outstanding by 1834. The Metropolitan recommended repayment of the debt with promissory notes. Their principal equaled the value of the loan. The interest collected by the school committee at the rate of 10 percent per year resulted in the operation of the school. The implemented

---

[14]Anastasios Ch. Megas, "School and Church in Siatista (1817-1850)," *Siatistina*, 1/1989, p. 31

[15]Anastasios Ch. Megas, "School and Church in Siatista (1817-1850)," *Siatistina*, 1/1989, p. 20

plan produced the desired results in four years. Zosimas successfully used a similar plan a century earlier during his reign.

In 1839, during Metropolitan Leontios's tenure, a team of six most honorable and conscious citizens tried all commercial and civic differences of Siatistians. Ottoman authorities sanctioned this committee of six. Its renewal took place every six months[16]. A five-member drafting committee[17], presided over by the Metropolitan, drew all rules and regulations.

In 1860 the Ecumenical Patriarchate, with the approval of the Ottoman government, prepared and recommended to all Greek communities its General Regulations. The guidelines called for a uniform system of management. The Metropolitan approved all Respectable Citizens elected under constitutional rules drawn up by members of each community[18]. In Siatista, all men over twenty-one registered. Every neighborhood elected its own representative through a secret ballot. The Most Respectable Men were at least thirty years old, as stipulated by the ancient Athenians' Attica legislation[19]. They could serve for forty or fifty years if reelected. They organized themselves in three groups: 1) Demogerontia, made up of four persons, oversaw/administered justice to local citizens. They observed local customs, decided on forced participation without compensation of citizens on public projects and collected money for these projects. 2) School committees, one for each part of Siatista (Chora and Geraneia) served for two years. These five-member committees met every other week under the presidency of the Metropolitan. The committees appointed teachers, paid salaries, visited classrooms to evaluate the teachers' performance, and supervised the final examinations. 3) Church committee, made up of seven members: four from Chora and three from Geraneia. The committee appointed church assistants, ran the candle store, and managed the community treasury. The committee paid the Metropolitan's allowance.

[16]Michael Ath. Kalinderis, *Metropolis of Sisani and Siatista Register (1686-1746)*, p. 126
[17]George Th. Ganoules, "The Administrative Organization of Siatista During the Turkish Occupation," *Siatista Memoirs*, p. A-78
[18]Stephan J. Papadopoulos, *Educational and Social Activities of Macedonian Hellenism During the Last Century of the Turkish Occupation*, p. 12
[19]Konstantinos A. Plevris, *Socrates Facing His Death*, p. 102

The authorities communicated with the population through priests' announcements at the churches. Additionally, public callers went around central locations and screamed off their announcements with all their might. On special occasions families used these persons to invite the community to marriages, etc.

The system of "Demogerontia" appropriately served all towns of Upper Macedonia, Kastoria, Kleisoura, Nymfaio, Monastere, and Vlaste[20]. It cultivated cooperation, respect for the authorities and for fellow citizens, human dignity, and promotion of national unity.

---

[20]Fotes Vittes, *Stachyologemata (Collection of Short Stories), Demogerontia*, p. 53

Chapter 14
Homes and Mansions

The structures found in many small villages in mainland Greece as late as 1950 consisted of an upper level serving as family quarters and the lower ground floor. The lower level dirt floor accommodated the animal shelter, or was used for the storage of family supplies and equipment. Such houses never existed in Siatista. Prolonged hard winter days could only be met with well-built, low-lying facilities. Such ground-level housing limited its exposure to strong, cold winds and snowstorms, usual phenomena in the area. Stones found in abundance in the area permitted construction of solid structures. Their living quarters consisted mainly of a winter room and an extra utility room. The utility room accommodated all kitchen and hygiene functions. A small hall separated the two rooms. The entrance from outside into it and quick closing of its door allowed the cold air to be absorbed and prevent it from entering the rooms. The small hall allowed access to both rooms. A third door opposite the outside main entrance led to an adjacent storage room used for warehouse of supplies, tools, and equipment. Fairly good-sized families of Siatista with relatively better financial means almost always necessitated additional space. An inside ladder from the small hall led upstairs to a reception space with two adjacent rooms on either end. The upper level handled all social gatherings and festivities performed, weather permitting. Families with improved financial capabilities built fireplaces in the upper-level rooms.

Prosperous families expanded their homes according to their needs. Adjacent to the structure described above, a ground-level, rather spacious kitchen handled all summer activities except sleeping. Over it, an enclosed equally spacious upper level provided additional storage. This multipurpose room space sheltered fireplace wood supplies procured early fall to last all winter. The stables accommodating horses and mules were adjacent to the summer kitchen and its upper-level storage at the opposite end of the living quarters. The corresponding overhead storage facility existed for storage of animal provisions of hay and barley. The animals performed all transportation and moving tasks. High and thick stone walls around all premises provided protection from thieves and intruders, especially during restless, unsafe political situations and uprisings. All areas, front yard, rear of the structure spaces, and small garden plots wherever they existed, were within the protecting wall. A ten-foot ladder had to be used to climb over it. Water wells as much as sixty feet deep, dug within the compound, provided water for cleaning purposes. They alleviated the chronic water shortage problem. Drinking water had to be carried from distant fountains and springs. Ovens built inside the protected areas but outside the living quarters, baked the housewives' bread and pies. Lavatories, often placed at the center part of the entire premises where the summer kitchen was, accommodated their needs. In many instances they communicated with the living quarters. These arrangements allowed performance of all family functions safely within the compound.

Successful merchants built extensive warehouses to store wheat and other grains bought during harvest time. They sold them later at higher, off-season, prices. Caravan operators had excessive facilities to accommodate not only their own animals, but additional ones hired to supplement their strength on extra occasions. Shepherds protected their sheep and goats in covered huts, four to five feet high, big enough to handle the entire herd. All shepherds located their facilities at close-by mountain sites on the outskirts of town.

Increased trade with Venice and central European cities brought significant changes to Upper Macedonians and particularly to Siatistians. Their new life-style increased their housing requirements. The impact received from experiences exposed to in the civilized centers was profound. The enormous wealth they brought home originally from Venice and, subsequently, from Balkan, central European cities improved their lives considerably. Byzantine-oriented mansions found in ancient Macedonian cities of Veroia and Kastoria[1] were built[2]. Publishing house Melissa of Athens published in English and

[1] Panos Gr. Tsolakes, *The Boats of Kastoria*, p. 35
[2] Despoina Beikou, D. N. Rizos, "Siatista Architecture" p. 15

Greek, a brilliant study of Siatista mansions. Many colored photos picturing the mansions support the excellent commentaries written by architects Despina Beikou and Danae Nomikou-Rizou. The first mansion, Voidomates's, most likely was built in 1669 while Naoum Nerantzes's was built in 1710. This last one did not survive the Second World War. Several, however, did survive and function to this date. Most are still occupied by heirs of original owners or sold to other Siatistians. The National Archaeological Agency of Greece purchased some of them for maintenance and protection. The dates of construction of the ones that survived are as follows: Tzouras's in 1725, Sanoukos's in 1742, Hadje-Michael's and Manouses's in 1746, Poulkos's in 1752, Nerantzopoulou's in 1754, Gerechtes's in 1755, Tzonos's in 1756, Alexiou's and Maliogas's in 1759, and Kotoulas's in 1760. Dates of construction for others are not known. Most went up at the end of or following Zosimas's golden years.

Skilled technicians and laborers working under a single contractor's supervision built the mansions. Close-by communities in Epirus, Konitsa in particular, had several such contractors. These teams visited several Balkan towns and built many mansions. Construction could only be done during favorable weather, usually May through September. The five-month construction periods forced organization of efforts and teamwork cooperation. Larger structures required larger number of technicians, specialists, and assistants. In order to prevent supply shortages and delays, lumber and stone supplies contracted for earlier, arrived on time, prior to technicians' engagement. These technicians developed an advanced architecture, having no similarity to any European architecture. Solid, defense-oriented construction greatly contributed to Siatista's protection. The structure was, and still is, impressive and imposing. Its artistic decor and beauty are immediately noticeable. Efficiency is attained through two distinct horizontal levels.

The lower level of the structure includes an enclosed yard, cellar, several stores, and its first floor. These are the areas the families live in most of the time. It is built with thick, stone, outside walls. Wooden logs were placed in the wall horizontally from ground up at about three feet intervals. This technique was repeated on both the inside and outside sides of the walls for the entire perimeter of the structure. For added strength the logs were nailed, bonded together at intervals with short logs as long as the wall's width, usually between two and three feet long. These logs support the cemented stones. The stones were shaped for uniformity and appearance. Building corners were made with large, squared stones to form strong columns and provide additional strength. Small windows were opened on strategic spots. At the time the mansions were built, they were useful in fighting off intruders and attackers. Strong metal bars were permanently installed on outside windows. They are fastened securely within the walls close to their outer side. The outer view is similar to defense posts when looked at from a distance. Thick wooden beams placed over the lower-level solid walls support the second floor and upper level. The ceiling of the first level and of the enclosed yard is nailed on these beams. There is a ceramic tile-covered roof. The outside wall surface of the upper level is plastered and decorated with various designs. The roof's lumber extends from the walls approximately two feet, and offers added protection from rain, hailstorms, and severe windstorms. The fireplaces are stone and the chimneys extend over the roof. The chimneys are decorated with designs and remind the observer of square, Greek island pigeon nest towers.

    The structure is designed to meet local requirements and customs. The main, lower-level entrance opens to a spacious yard inside the structure. It is usually paved with white marble or large flat stones. All secondary functions are performed around this enclosed yard. There are warehouses and small storage closets for wheat, meat, pickled vegetables, and other food items. Entrance to appropriate cellars with wine barrels is also made from this space. All these storage facilities and closets are either on ground level or below. Two solid stone-built ladders, one immediately to the left and one diagonally across, begin from this enclosed yard. The first one, immediately to the left of the main entrance of the house, has the second one diagonally across it. The second one takes you to the first floor and the inside balcony that surrounds the enclosed yard on its three sides. A meticulously carved wooden post fence blending harmoniously with all decorations of the first level protects the visitors and residents from falling. Four winter-oriented rooms, one in each corner, are built on this floor, which is part of the structure's first level. All four rooms are entered from the interior balcony. Among the two rooms on the north side is an open, room-sized, space. Three outside windows allow the sunrays to enter this space. Metal, densely designed, sturdy iron bars are permanently installed in these windows. This space is named sunny room and is used by all visitors in the winter. It is the best decorated space on this otherwise austere first floor. Wooden panels, decorated with many colorful designs, cover the sunny room walls. They are artistically joined on their top with the wholly or partially carved and colorfully decorated ceiling. The sunny room's side to the balcony is identified with several wooden columns appropriately designed and carved. Fireplaces providing heating and cooking functions are built in all four rooms. The size of the family determines their use. At least one is used for kitchen. Wooden, built-in closets are used for partitions of each room with the inside balcony. Their width is approximately three feet. Floor covers, blankets, flokati rugs, comforters, linen items, and pillows are stored in these closets. The occupants often used these spaces to hide precious stones and jewelry. The entrance to each room has two doors. One opens towards the balcony's side and the other opens towards the inside of the room. The space between the entrance doors serve as insulation, as do all closets. All door panels are carved and decorated. The walls are decorated with angels appearing in clouds, flower arrangements, and scenery of faraway cities in which the original owners lived prior to having these mansions built.

The left stone ladder leads to the central living room on the second floor or the second level. Both north and south sides of the living room are extended four to five feet outside and over the first level. This makes it considerably more spacious and accommodates a built-in sofa on its extensions. Additionally, it provides an overview of the surrounding area and in cases of emergency, serves as an observation and surveillance post. It simultaneously traps in more precious sunlight in the winter. Four sleeping rooms are also accommodated in the second-floor corners. The rooms have built-in sofas, one on each side. The two northern rooms never extend outside over the first level while the southern ones occasionally do, along with the living room part of that floor. An elevated room-sized space between the two northern rooms, as happens on the first floor with the sunny room, is reserved for dignitaries or honored guests at times of celebrations. When local band musicians are hired, they are placed there to permit use of remaining living room space for dancing. A corridor leading to the lavatory separates the two left rooms. This is usually extended over the first level. Directly across, between the two right rooms is a second corridor. It forms a walk-in closet essential for entertainment occasions, engagements, marriages, and baptisms. Glasses, trays, pitchers, and the like are stored there. This provides an easy access of these items on festive days and cuts down running up and down to lower level closets.

Contrary to the austerity of the lower level, the upper level has three to four windows in each sleeping or living room. Over each window a smaller one is located. The upper windows are permanently sealed with decorated, colorfully designed glass panels. The bottom windows are protected with wooden panels opening outside for light and ventilation. The lavishly decorated ceilings, windows, closet doors and walls, make this floor the most impressive one of the entire structure. Fireplaces are built in all sleeping rooms of this floor as well. Business associates and important personalities are accommodated on the second floor. The fireplaces are richly built on both floors. The upper-level ones, however, excel and dominate in appearance. Their platform is raised from the floor about five to eight inches. The platform's ends are made with marble on which designs are sculptured. The upper portions are built with either marble or stone. Several shelves exhibit solidly installed art pieces and statues, depicting flowers, birds, and hunting scenes. The wooden ceilings have their own decorative motives. Small squares inserted into larger ones and hexagonal or cyclical geometric figures, carved and painted, harmoniously appear on the ceilings[3]. The wall paintings, drawn by local, tradition-oriented artists, express the owners' own feelings and

[3]Despoina Deikou, D. N. Rizos, "Siatista Architecture" p. 26

experiences with scenery of Venice, Constantinople, and European cities. The mythological scenes portrayed in the drawings reflect the owners' devotion to the classical Hellenic spirit taught in Zosimas-era schools. Poetic expressions of love to the masters and their women are written on walls and windows. The teacher Michael Papageorgiou composed the following poem, appearing on a wall of Hadje-Yiannis Nerantzopoulou's mansion:

> *"Come over, spectator, look at this beautiful home,*
> *That brightens Siatista like the sun (does),*
> *For the indescribable fame of famous Yiannis (John),*
> *We hope the master of universe, protects it forever...."*

Multicolored imported glass panels of exceptionally fine art are installed on the second-floor windows. Outside decorations on the second floor blend harmoniously with wooden window panels when opened. The arrangement presented a beautiful sight to visitors entertained in the open yard.

The yard was carefully planned. Huge, meticulously clean, flat stones cover the ground. Flowers able to withstand local climatic conditions are planted in landscaped areas. Auxiliary facilities, including a fire wood oven, are built in the back. Top marble structures cover the water wells dug mostly in the center of the yard. An overhead or nearby kiosk, covered with ceramic tile, provides rain and sun protection. The usual stone wall, thick and high, built around the mansion's perimeter, has one main entrance and a smaller, secondary one. Two-panel doors constructed from heavy, solid wood block entry to the main entrance. Their surface, reinforced with large-head metallic nails, provides greater strength and resistance. Only one of the panels would open during the day. The second would stay closed. On festive days, or whenever loaded horses and mules needed to pass through, both panels opened. A thick, heavy log stored into an appropriate hole built lengthwise in the thick wall slides out during the night and blocks both panels. It slides into a similar space/hole on the opposite door-side for added fortification. This makes the door impregnable. A metal rod hung on the left panel of the door serves as ring bell. Its lower end shaped like a hammer hits the metal plate installed at the point it hits. The noise sends the message. Overhead, second-floor extensions are used to survey the area and the space in front of the main gate door. In case forced entry somehow occurred, the heavily reinforced windows and strategic openings on the building proper are used to repel the aggressors. Secretly covered underground canals, entered by mansion occupants in an emergency from an enclosed yard storeroom underpass, lead to an escape exit. Underpasses connect the underground canals used for drainage and sewer system. Such sophisticated provisions added to Siatista's efficient housing and security. Most houses' underground sewer connections washed rain away downstream. The project was a vanguard innovation in Greece. Conceived and financed as well by expatriate Siatistians, it served the community for nearly two centuries.

Manouses's mansion in Upper Siatista.
Photo by G. Logdanides

Poulkos's mansion in Geraneia, Lower Siatista.
Photo by G. Logdanides

Chapter 15
The Enlightenment

Siatistian society of the seventeenth century reached relatively high standards in commerce and education. Previous chapters discussed the emphasis Siatistian Bishop Zosimas placed on education. Padova University of Italy was the choice of many Siatistians. One of them, George Papadopoulos, in 1678 copied in Padova clergyman and teacher George Sougdoures's book *The Way To Write a Speech*[1]. Zosimas's son George Rouses, a graduate of Padova University and philosopher, returned home in 1710. He taught in Siatistian schools under his father's guidance and support. Details didn't survive but his curriculum included courses in Greek, Latin, and Italian. His broad education, added to his father's keen judgment, proved extremely valuable. The two searched for, identified, and invited the best talent available to teach Siatista's children. Their education was of paramount importance. By 1715 Siatista operated the Hellenic Courses Institute[2]. In it educators taught, in addition to ordinary courses, all Hellenic classics and Latin achievements. One of its most important teachers was Methodius Anthrakites from Ioannina.

Highly educated Methodius Anthrakites taught from 1721 to 1723. A contemporary of George Rouses known to him from his Padova days, Anthrakites was a student of George Sougdoures at Ioannina. He became a priest and served the Greek community's Eastern Orthodox Church of Saint Georgios in Venice from 1697 to 1708. His book *Christian Theories and Psychiatric Approaches*, written in Venice and published in 1699, helped his parishioners and Diaspora Greeks. He returned to Ioannina and in 1710, at about the same time Rouses returned to Siatista, Anthrakites accepted an appointment to teach at George Kyritzes's school in Kastoria. His teachings followed Malebranche and Cartesius's philosophical doctrines deviating from Aristotle's philosophical lines. Kastoria's conservative

[1]George Laios, *Siatista and Its Commercial Houses Hadje-Michael and Manouses*, p. 21
[2]Demetrios G. Siasios, "The School of Zosimas," *Siatistina*, 7/1992, p. 16

elements denounced his liberalism. In his debate with his opponents, he enjoyed the support of Kastoria's archons. He resigned, however, and accepted Siatistians', and Zosimas's, offer to teach Siatistian children. He taught physics, mathematics, and theology in addition to philosophy. His supporters and students Balanos Vasilopoulos from Ioannina, Sevastos Leontiades from Kastoria, and others, impressed with his theories, followed him to Siatista[3].

Anthrakites's efforts, upon his departure, continued in Siatista by clergyman Chrysanthos from Zitsa, Epirus, from 1725 to 1728. Chrysanthos repatriated earlier from Transylvania, bringing his own experiences and talent. Nickolaos Scholarios from Ioannina, who later became Bishop, taught in Siatista for ten years from 1732 to 1742. The last six years served with Scholarios as schoolmaster, brilliant Paisos Demaros[4]. Working hard under Zosimas's supervision, they taught Siatistian children from 1736 to 1742. In 1744, philosophers Solon, Plato, Plutarch, Aristotle, Thoukydides, and Sibylla's portraits decorated the walls of Prophet Elias's church along with other saints' icons. Upon Demaros's departure to a new teaching position in Ioannina, fifteen-year-old student Michael Papageorgiou followed him. At Ioannina, Papageorgiou was fortunate to have another brilliant teacher, Evgenios Voulgaris. Clergyman/scholar Voulgaris led many intellectuals to Hellenism's revival and, eventually, the Greek revolution of 1821 and rebirth of modern Greece. His contribution to Greek enlightenment is considered the most successful in terms of performance and results.

Voulgaris was born in the island of Corfu in 1716. His teachers were Antonios Kateforos (1685–1763) and Vincent Damados (1679–1752)[5]. He continued his studies at Padova University. Like Anthrakites before him, Voulgaris became a clergyman in 1737. He served as priest in Venice's Saint Georgios Eastern Orthodox Church for five years. Anxious to assist his countrymen he returned to Ioannina. He became a schoolmaster, replacing conservative Balanos. The opposition to his liberal views forced him to accept a new position in Kozane[6] in 1745[7]. Ecumenical Patriarch Serafeim

[3]George Laios, *Siatista and Its Commercial Houses Hadje-Michael and Manouses*, p. 26
[4]Anastasios N. Dardas, "The Education in Siatista," *Elimeiaka*, 16-19/1987, p. 37
[5]Demetres Fotiades, *The Revolution of 1821*, Vol. I, p. 161
[6]Panagiotes N. Lioufes, *History of Kozane*, p. 183
[7]Ch. G. Patrinellis, "The First Teachers of Kozane's School,"*Elimeiaka*, 36/1996, p. 86

noticed his bright record and experience. In 1752 the Patriarch invited Voulgaris to organize the Athonian Academy at the Holy Community of Mt. Athos. Voulgaris spent his six most productive years there. In 1758 he moved to Constantinople.

Voulgaris's twenty-year priest and scholar experience expanded his Ecumenical concept. His next stop was Leipzig, Germany, to publish the many books he wrote. He highly respected German philosopher Leibniz (1646–1716), founder of Berlin's Academy of Sciences, and British philosopher Locke (1632–1704), author of *An Essay Concerning Human Understanding*[8]. In Leipzig, he met Theodore Orlof, a Russian general. Orlof liked the Greek clergyman and scholar, and perhaps with the concurrence of Siatistian George Papazoles, who knew Voulgaris from his teaching in Kozane, recommended him to Ekaterine the Great, the Russian ruler. Russia's war of 1768 against the Ottoman Empire necessitated the coordination of all Orthodox elements. Voulgaris accepted Ekaterine's invitation and went to Russia in 1772. In 1776, Petroupolis's Academy of Scientists honored him with membership[9]. He worked and lived there until his death in 1806. His devotion to his position elevated him to Russia's top ecclesiastical position. He became Archbishop of Slavinia and Herson in Ukraine[10]. Voulgaris wrote and/or translated seventy-five books. Among the books he wrote are his *Logic* and *Vosporomachia* (Battle in the Strait of Vosporus). His translations included Voltaire's *Memnon*, the first translation into Greek, contrary to the Ecumenical Patriarchate's position. He covered all fields of knowledge: physics, mathematics, philosophy, literature, history, and the arts. Voulgaris was among the greatest promoters of Hellenism and its classical writings. In 1794, jointly with Russian poet and translator N. A. Lvof, they translated from Ancient Greek into Russian and Modern Greek, Anacreon's (ancient Greek writer) works. His student I. I. Martinof published translations from Homer, Herodotus, Sophocles, Pindaros and others. These formed the basis of Zukovski and Giredits's translations of Homer's *Iliad* and *Odyssey*. Voulgaris's efforts to assist the Greek

---

[8]Demetres Fotiades, *The Revolution of 1821*, Vol. I, p. 161
[9]G. L. Arch, *Greek Intellectuals and Merchants in Russia, Benefactors of National Education in the 18th and 19th Century*, International Chamber of Commerce, p. 172
[10]Demetres Fotiades, *The Revolution of 1821*, Vol. I, pp. 161-162

nation through promotion of Russia's Orthodox Church was a tremendous success. Ekaterine and subsequent rulers of Russia adopted a doctrine of Eastern Orthodox protectionism. It served Russian interests well in its relations with Ottoman Empire. Pan-Slavism replaced the doctrine in 1856 following the Crimean War. The new doctrine encouraged Slavs' establishment of an outlet into the Aegean Sea[11].

Siatista's schools continued their impressive progress. Michael Papageorgiou returned home from Ioannina. He taught in Siatista and nearby Eratyra. At the same time, intellectual Nickolaos Barkozes from Ioannina taught six years along with Siatistian priest Michael. Priest Michael later left for Venice where he died[12]. Barkozes's contribution to Siatista's schools impressed Eugenios Voulgaris, director in Kozane's school. In 1749, he invited him to teach in Kozane. Upon Voulgaris's leaving Kozane, Barkozes stayed on for another six years and probably took over its direction[13]. Barkozes's younger brother Kallinikos followed his brother's steps. He taught in Siatista and Kozane's schools. Their graduates moved to schools established in European cities and communities under Ottoman rule. They taught the expatriates' children. Graduates of other Greek schools followed the same road. Paraskevas Amphilochios from Ioannina served as priest at Kecskemet's church from 1754 to 1757. He wrote in Greek and published in Vienna, his books *Logic*, *Mirror of Philosophy* and *Basics of Rhetoric*. Kallinikos Barkozes's student in Siatista, Anthimos, working for spiritual enhancement, wrote his books *Prayers of Virgin Mary* and *Ecclesiastical Ethics* in everyday, commonly spoken language[14].

Siatistian Michael Papageorgiou made a significant contribution to Upper Macedonian Greek expatriates. A descendant of a long-standing family of priests, Papageorgiou concentrated his efforts on education. He followed his friends and neighbors on their great wave north. He strengthened his high-caliber education in Germany by further studying German, Latin, philosophy, and medicine. He joined the faculty of Santa Barbara College and taught Greek subjects to theology students. He

[11] Konstantinos Metsakis, *Macedonia Throughout the Centuries*, p. 48
[12] George Zaviras, "Siatistian Intellectuals (NEA HELLAS)," *Siatista Memoirs*, p. G8
[13] Anastasios N. Dardas, "The Education in Siatista," *Elimeiaka*, 16-19/1987, p. 38
[14] George Laios, *Siatista and Its Commercial Houses Hadje-Michael and Manouses*, p. 53

continued his contribution by teaching Ancient and Modern Greek, philosophy, rhetoric and poetry in Buda(Pest) and Miscolc Greek community schools prior to settling in Vienna. His purpose was enlightenment of Greeks in Diaspora. He quickly realized the need among the Greeks to learn German, and wrote his book *Introduction to German Language*, published in Vienna in 1764. He also wrote the first book of its kind ever published in Greek, *The Basics of the Greek Language* (Vienna, 1771), reprinted in Pest in 1788. In 1772, he published in Vienna his *Easy German for Greeks* with its second edition appearing in 1792. In 1773, he published Emmanuel Moschopoulos's books *Biography* and *Grammar*. Papageorgiou's book *Greek for Beginners*, published in Vienna in 1783, included sentences and dialogues to help those associating with Greeks. A detailed *German Grammar*, as well as tens of articles, letters, poems, and speeches, found among his belongings upon his death, never saw publication. After a brilliant career in central European cities, he returned home in Siatista and died in 1776 at the age of sixty-nine[15].

Michael Papageorgiou's contemporary in Siatista, Nerantzis Metrapezopoulos, who received an equally fine education, preferred to stay home. His family was better off financially and socially. He served as archon of Siatista for many years. He translated into Modern Greek Mohammedanism's sacred book, the *Koran*.

George Papazoles, Metrapezopoulos's schoolmate, however, followed his own principles. Son of a trading merchant, he received equally fine education and training at home. It is not known if he attended Kozane's school where Voulgaris taught in 1745. He was then twenty years old. Siatistian young men entered trading activities at a much younger age. His family, reacting to Turks' desire to abduct him, helped him escape through underground canals. He traveled to Russia's city port of Odessa. There, he met Gregory Orlof, brother of Theodore, officer in the Russian army. His ambition and initiative impressed Orlof, who suggested his enlistment in the Russian army. Papazoles joined the Imperial Guard under Orlof's command. Russia's ruler Ekaterine, promoting Russia's Eastern

---

[15] George Zaviras, "Siatistian Intellectuals (NEA HELLAS)," *Siatista Memoirs*, p. G13

Orthodox Protectionism doctrine, appointed Papazoles as Special Ambassador. His specific orders were to organize the enslaved Greeks for revolution. Papazoles supplied with necessary funds and strong determination to enlighten his countrymen, wrote and published in 1765 his book *Introduction to War Tactics*. In an effort to pass its highly appropriate knowledge to restless Greeks, he went to Greece. He first visited his parents in Siatista, dressed as a Turk clergyman and proceeded to Epirus. He met with archons and armed gang leaders operating in the mountains. Their disillusionment at Western powers' indifference already oriented them to their brothers-in-religion Russians. Papazoles encouraged them and promoted his plans to distribute his book. His activities brought the suspicion of the Ottomans. To prevent his arrest, he escaped to Venice. On his way back to Greece, pirates captured his boat. He ended up as prisoner in Albania. He won his freedom with the assistance of the Austrian Consul of Trieste where he promoted his revolutionary spirit to the city's fairly large Greek Community[16]. His fluency in Turkish helped him return to Epirus under the name of Hadje-Murat.

Papazoles traveled throughout Greece and drummed up his plans for the Greek revolution. Greek's enthusiasm skyrocketed. Their optimism traveled to Russia's high command. Russia's chief-of-staff sent six officers to Malta to gather intelligence data for the forthcoming activities. When the Russo-Ottoman war of 1768 started, Papazoles returned to Russia and briefed Ekaterine about the situation. In February 1770 the Russian fleet, under Gregory Orlof's brothers Alexander and Theodore Orlof, arrived at the shores of Peloponnese. The Greeks immediately responded and revolted. Upper Macedonia already had seventeen armed groups operating in the mountains[17], maintaining pressure. Chief Ziakas near Grevena, Zedros and Lazos in Mt. Olympus, Vlahavas in the Chasia region, and old man Farmakes in Vlaste challenged the Ottoman authority. Military revolutionary activities lasted several months. The attack in Peloponnese to capture Tripolis, its capital, from the Ottomans failed. In June, the Russians withdrew. The Ottomans

---

[16]George M. Bodas, "Siatistian George Papazoles," *Elimeiaka*, 27/1991, p. 139-141
[17]Parmenion Tzifras, *Brief History of Bogatsiko*, p. 12-13

punished the Greeks severely. In Upper Macedonia Albanian irregulars, stirred up by Ottoman troops, attacked Kozane[18]. Siatista, assisted by her mountainous terrain, repelled the attackers. The assistance of neighboring towns of Galatine[19] and Vlaste again proved valuable. Hundreds of villages around Siatista, Grevena, Kastoria, and Florina suffered extensive hardships. Thousands ran away. Many lost their lives. Eugenios Voulgaris personally presented the Greeks' plight to Russian Empress Ekaterine in 1772[20]. George Papazoles failed to see his dream realized. He died in 1775. At least two cities recognized and honored his services. Siatista and Salonica named one of their streets after him[21]. Siatistians and other intellectual Greeks continued their efforts to enlighten settlers residing in Europe's big cities and in Diaspora.

Zosimas's achievements and Hellenic values, promoted by Eugenios Voulgaris, cultivated most Siatistian youth. Demetrios Karakases, born in Siatista in 1734, studied mathematics, physics, philosophy, and theology under clergyman Michael. He continued his schooling in Kozane[22] under Eugenios Voulgaris. Most likely at his suggestion at seventeen, he accepted an offer to serve as secretary to Siatistian Metropolitan of Grevena Gregory. In 1752 he left for Hungary with other Siatistians. He mastered both Latin and German and studied Luther's aspects on religion. In Halle, Germany, he studied medicine. He continued his philosophical studies in Vienna. Anxious to be of assistance to his countrymen, he followed his merchant friend Nikolaos Kakavas to Larisa, Thessaly. He gained broad respect by Greeks and Ottomans for practicing his medicine. He returned to Siatista at the invitation of its archons. He married a girl from Kozane and they relocated to Craiova. He gained fame as a successful scientist in Bucharest, their new residence. He excelled as director of St. Panteleimon Hospital. His book *About Arteroctomy*, published in Vienna in 1760[23], and several more medical analyses, translated into Latin, benefited many medical students.

[18]Panagiotes N. Lioufes, *History of Kozane*, p. 60
[19]Nikolaos K. Gadonas, *Galatine*, p. 35
[20]G. L. Arch, "Greek Intellectuals and Merchants in Russia, Benefactors of National Education in the 18th and 19th Century,"International Chamber of Commerce, p. 173
[21]George M. Bodas, "Siatistian George Papazoles," *Elimeiaka*, 27/1991, p. 144
[22]Panagiotes N. Lioufes, *History of Kozane*, p. 185
[23]George Zaviras, "Siatistian Intellectuals (NEA HELLAS)," *Siatista Memoirs*, p. G11

The list of bright scientists produced during Siatista's golden years grew impressively. Thomas Demetriou settled and traded in Vienna. Fluent in German and Italian, he wrote his *Grammar of Italian Language*, published in 1779. To assist the Greek merchants he wrote two more books: *Commercial Behavior* and *Basic Accounting* in 1793 and 1794, respectively. He published all of his books in Vienna[24]. Demetrios Demetriou surpassed Thomas's contribution. His parents Theodore and Afrate settled in Zagreb in 1790. He and his four sisters—Elizabeth, Maria, Alexandra, and Rosa—received a truly Siatistian, Hellenic education. They spoke Greek (their mother tongue) at home[25]. Family friend and poet Mantzouranic learned Greek from his association with them. The family enjoyed very high respect from Zagreb residents. Elizabeth married Nickolaos Nicolic, real estate owner and prominent Zagreb citizen. Maria married A. Demtsos, successful merchant in Bucharest. Alexandra married attorney Ivan Mantzouranic. Her second marriage was with poet and governor of Croatia Jentzins. Rosa remained single.

Demetrios, born in Zagreb, at the age of sixteen in 1827, wrote his first play, *Virginia*, in Modern Greek. He attended Zagreb schools, studying philosophy and medicine. He continued graduate studies at Gratz and Vienna schools but chose to receive his doctorate from Padova University in 1836. He practiced medicine in Zagreb until 1841, but his love for literature and the theater prevailed. He wrote several works in Croatian. They appeared in *Almanac Iskra* magazine. These writings reflected Pushkin's strong influence while Lord Byron influenced his book *Grobnicko Polze*. In it he idealized Croats' victories in their wars against Franks and Tatars. His book *Teute* presents the Illyrian queen's struggles over the Romans. Poetry dominated his works in the newspaper *Danica* and *Narodne Novine*. He became drama director at Zagreb's National Theater. Demetrios worked closely with his friend Ludovikos Guy, the Illyrian movement leader, to unite all Yugoslavs. *Enciklopedia Yugoslavije* recognized his great contribution[26] by listing his achievements. Demetrios invested all of his family's estate to the

---

[24]George Zaviras, "Siatistian Intellectuals (NEA HELLAS)," *Siatista Memoirs*, p. G7
[25]Demetrios K. Chadjes, *Ioannis M. Trampatzes*, p. 19-20
[26]John A. Papadrianos, "Demetrios Demetriou," *Siatista Memoirs* p. G28

spiritual enhancement of Croatian people. He promoted use of Croatian language in the theater and literature[27]. His name appears second on Zagreb's National Theater commemorative plaque. A bust of him decorates the theater's open grounds.

Siatista's most outstanding personality among the expatriates and champion of Zosimas's spirit was Michael Papageorgiou's nephew (his sister's son), George Zaviras. Born in 1744, he started his training with his uncle at the age of four. Priest Michael and Nickolaos Barkozes taught him their knowledge. Zaviras entered trading activity and moved north to Hungary in 1760 at the age of sixteen. His ever-growing hunger for learning brought him in touch with Latin philosophers. He invested most of his business income plus considerable time and effort into his library of respectable size and volume. He studied and mastered Latin, German, Hungarian, French, Italian, and Serbian[28]. Zaviras's work *New Hellas*, published by George Kremos in Athens in 1872, sixty-eight years after Zaviras's death in 1804, is an excellent and reliable source of information regarding Greeks' spirit and enlightenment effort. Zaviras wrote fifteen books. He covered theology, history, geography, physics, astronomy, medicine, commerce, and education. His nineteen translations into Greek and Hungarian languages assisted appreciably the Greeks' enhancement and success in the Austrian-Hungarian society. The Greek community, estimated to number, then about four hundred thousand[29], operated twenty-six schools for their children's education[30].

Zaviras published in (Buda)Pest in 1787 three books: 1) *Medical Advices*, discussing most common diseases and their therapy, translated from Hungarian; 2) *Botanology*, published in Greek, Latin, German, and Hungarian; and 3) *History of Old and New Testament* for young readers and beginners. The last one saw three more publications in Vienna and (Buda)Pest the following twelve years. His translation into Greek of *Worth-Mentioning Events of Kantakouzenos and Vragavanon*, written in German by Demetrios Kantemer, ruler of Moldavia, was published in 1795 at the printing shop of Vienna's Siatistian Pouliou brothers.

[27]John Apostolou, *History of Siatista*, p. 65
[28]George Laios, *Siatista and Its Commercial Houses Hadje-Michael and Manouses*, pp. 66-67
[29]Charilaos Kanatsoules, *Theochares Tourountzias*, p.8
[30]George Laios, *Siatista and Its Commercial Houses Hadje-Michael and Manouses*, p.63

Zaviras's brother Konstantinos financed *Medical Advices* and *Botanology*. (Buda)Pest's Greek school's financial director, in recognition of Zaviras's leaving his valuable library to the school upon his death, financed in 1815 the publication of Zaviras's translation *Method of Star Studying*[31].

Zaviras lived in Hungarian cities of Rackeve, Kalocsa, Kunszentmiklos, Dunavecse, and Szabadszallas, where he died. He visited his mother's two other brothers, uncles John and Konstantinos Papageorgiou in Kecskemet repeatedly. They died in 1818 and 1823, at the age of eighty and ninety-one, respectively[32]. Zaviras's cousin, George Papp (Papageorgiou), taught at Kecskemet school. He, too, like his uncle Michael Papageorgiou and cousin Zaviras, in 1844 prepared a beginner's book to make learning Hungarian easy. Zaviras adored his uncle Michael Papageorgiou, his respected teacher of his childhood years. He visited him regularly in Vienna. While there Zaviras enjoyed his long discussions with much younger Anthimos Gazes, community priest and spiritual leader of the Greek Orthodox Church. Zaviras traveled extensively, visiting most Greek communities. He visited Prussia, Bohemia, Saxony, and Moravia. He stayed at Prague, Dresden, Berlin, Leipzig, Halle, and others, always promoting Hellenic values. His enjoyment and satisfaction was learning of Greeks' activities and their progress.

Diaspora Siatistians always reflected their birthplace's culture and advancement. Michael Douka Hadje-Michael, student of Michael Papageorgiou in Siatista, continued his philosophical studies in Vienna. The social movements of materialism and naturalism that swept Vienna impressed him. He mastered his Latin, German, and French. He translated from French into Greek, and published in Vienna in 1783 in two volumes his *Persian King Cyrus' Ethical Behavior*, *Vellisarios's* (Roman emperor Justinian's General) *History*, and *Mythological, Ethics of Pelpa* (Indian Philosopher)[33]. Michael's brother[34] Konstantine Doukas wrote and published in Vienna in 1820 his two volumes of *Practical Arithmetic*.

[31]George Laios, *Siatista and Its Commercial Houses Hadje-Michael and Manouses*, p. 70
[32]George Laios, *Siatista and Its Commercial Houses Hadje-Michael and Manouses*, p. 64
[33]George Zaviras, "Siatistian Intellectuals (NES HELLAS)," *Siatista Memoirs*, p.G18
[34]George Laios, *Siatista and Its Commercial Houses Hadje-Michael and Manouses*, p. 121

Siatistian Stephan Miskolsky translated from Greek into Hungarian the *True Faith Confessions* of Russian Archbishop Petro Mogila. His desire was to promote its teachings to Greek children of mixed marriages in cases where their mother was not Greek. Stephan's son Nickolaos published the book in (Buda)Pest in 1791, ten years from his father's death in 1781[35].

In addition to Siatistians, many more Upper Macedonian authors contributed their talent to Greeks' betterment and enlightenment. Konstantine Theodore Zoupan, descendant of a prominent Moschopolitan family, studied medicine in Vienna and Halle. In 1760, he published in Vienna in Latin, his book *About Blood Pressure*. He returned home to practice medicine. Following his father's death he succeeded him as archon of Moschopolis. He served as personal doctor to the Ottoman-area governor at Monastere. He simultaneously provided his services to the people free of charge[36]. His son Naoum married Helen, daughter of a prominent Siatistian family of Demetrios John Moraites.

Kleisoura, a thriving community located at Mt. Pindus mountain range north of Siatista near Kastoria made an outstanding contribution to Greek expatriates' enlightenment. Its residents spoke mostly Wallach, a Latinized version of the Greek language. Their strong Hellenic background and culture were towering. Many moved north. They settled in various Balkan cities. The family of Nickolaos and Octavia Darvares chose Semlin. In 1769, their sons, John and Demetrios, followed. Demetrios, a bright student, was twelve years old. He spent fourteen more years studying. In Semlin, he mastered his German and Serb within two years. He studied additional Slav languages at Latino-Slav school in nearby Ruma for two years. He mastered his Ancient Greek under George Leontiou at Novi-Sad for four years. He attended Hellenic classics at Bucharest's Authentic Academy for another three years. His instructors at the Academy, Theodore Silistrianos and Manasses Iliades did their best. His three-year post-graduate studies between 1780

[35]George Laios, *Siatista and Its Commercial Houses Hadje-Michael and Manouses*, p. 64
[36]Anastasios Ch. Megas, "Archives of Zoupan-Moraites-Perikleous," *Siatista Memoirs*, pp. A90-99

and 1783 at Halle and Leipzig of Saxony enhanced his literature and philosophy capability[37].

Broadly trained Demetrios N. Darvares or Dimitrijem Nikolajevicem Darvar privately taught Orthodox children in Semlin and Vienna. He wrote several books with the intent to promote Hellenic values and Eastern Orthodoxy. His efforts assisted Greek merchants and financiers operating throughout the empire. His simple language made comprehensible by all social levels all topics presented. In addition to his own writings, he translated many Hellenic classics into German, Russian, Serb, and other Slav languages. In order to assist Greek and Serb students attending Semlin's Orthodox school with the German language he wrote *German Grammar*, published in 1785 in Vienna. German was essential for business, scientific, and social activities. Darvares translated and published in 1786 from ancient Greek to Slavic, *Christoethia* or Christian behavior, of Antonios Byzantiou. In introducing the Vienna publication he wrote: "When I came across *Christoethia* I considered it very necessary and beneficial for the Slavo-Serb youth. For this reason, now that my faculties still permit it, I translated it for the benefit and use by Slavo-Serbs, to promote their logical behavior and to improve their ethical characteristics[38]." Fifty years later, Rajno Popovic translated *Christoethia* into Bulgarian, consulting Darvar's translation.

For the benefit of all Greek and Wallach children, Darvaris published in 1791 his *Small Catechism*. It provided religious instruction as per the Holy Synod of Orthodox Bishops at Karlovac instructions of 1774. The book saw repeated publications the following seventy years, the last one in Corfu Island in 1844. Darvaris translated and published in 1795 the ancient Hellenic classic Theophrastus's *Ethical Characters*. His brother John financed both of the above publications in Vienna[39]. For the benefit of Eastern Orthodoxy at large, he translated from Ancient Hellenic into Slavo-Serb language the classics *Golden Rules* by Kevin of Thebes and *Guide* of philosopher Epiktitis. (Buda)Pest's Royal University in 1799 printed both volumes

---

[37] John A. Papadrianos, *The Greek Settlers of Semlin*, p. 123-124
[38] John A. Papadrianos, *The Greek Settlers of Semlin*, p. 182
[39] John A. Papadrianos, *The Greek Settlers of Semlin*, pp. 184-185

under the title *Kevita Tivjejskago Ikona* (Books of Ethical Behavior). Their translations into Greek benefited all Greeks of Diaspora not familiar with Slavic languages. Introducing this work Darvaris stated: "It teaches proper ethics and is dedicated solely to you, young people. Not only it is a good teacher but simultaneously creates and encourages within you the desire to love all things that provide happiness. Accept, therefore, dear youth, this small book with pleasure in your heart and read it with understanding." Darvaris settled and died in Vienna in 1823. He willed his library to Greek schools operating throughout the empire[40].

George (Papazachariou) Zachariades's or Georgijem Zacharijevic's publications were outstanding and undoubtedly of great benefit to the public. He arrived in Semlin in 1799 from Tyrnavo, Thessaly, at the age of twenty-one. His educational training led to his appointment to teach at Semlin's Helleno-Museum school. In 1806 he turned over his position to Siatistian John Tourountzias[41] for four years, returning to his job in 1810 to serve for another ten years. His thorough knowledge of both Ancient and Modern Greek as well as old Slavic languages served not only Greeks, but also all Slavs[42]. His first work in 1803 was his *Dictionary of Greek and Slavic* or *Recnik Grecesco-Slavenkij*. The Greek Educational brotherhood financed this publication. It included Greek grammar for nouns and verbs. Its ten dialogues provided examples for conversation. It mainly assisted the Slavo-Serb students to improve their Greek. Zachariades's objective was to assist, improve, and enhance life through education. He translated from Ancient Greek into Slavo-Serb language and published in 1807 two Hellenic classics: Plutarch's *About Upbringing of Children* and Isocrates's *Advice to Domenikos*. Schools in all Balkan countries widely taught these classics because they contained instructions on family behavior. Merchant Stergios Poulios absorbed all costs for both of these publications while a year later in 1808 another Greek merchant, Mark Ioannou, absorbed the cost of Zachariades's important translation, Plutarch's *Marriage Counseling*. Both (Buda)Pest

[40]John A. Papadrianos, *The Greek Settlers of Semlin*, p. 126
[41]John A. Papadrianos, *The Greek Settlers of Semlin*, p. 153
[42]John A. Papadrianos, *The Greek Settlers of Semlin*, p.p. 186-195

publications written in Greek and Slavo-Serb languages promoted harmonious living between couples in marriages between Greeks and Slavs. His *Greek Grammar*, a detailed 425-page Vienna publication of 1816 included translations of certain parts in both German and Slavic. It assisted German- and Slav-speaking students with improving their Greek. Zachariades wrote in 1824 and published in Buda in 1832 another valuable tool, his *Slavenska Grammatica*. His contribution to understanding between Greeks and Slavs, living and working together, included several other works.

Many more authors effectively used their talent and effort for the Greeks' enlightenment. Nickolaos Barkozes, who taught in Siatista around 1750, translated into Modern Greek from Latin Frederick Ch. Baumeister's *Logic and Metaphysics*. He published it in Vienna in 1795 with the financial assistance of Siatistian Athanasios G. Manouses[43]. Considerably helpful were George Rousiades's works. Rousiades from Kozane, evading the Turk's attempt to capture him, left for Trikala, Thessaly, and in 1802 went to Hungary. He entered trading activities in (Buda)Pest and relocated to Vienna. In 1806 he moved to Trieste. He went to Bucharest and again back to Trieste and Vienna. He mastered his French, German, and Italian. He translated from Ancient into Modern Greek Homer's *Iliad* and published it in Vienna in 1817. His translation from French into Greek of I. A. Venetis's book *Parga City* saw publication in (Buda)Pest in 1822. His two-volume translation of *Discovery of America* from German into Greek appeared in Vienna.

Rousiades's devotion to education and his failure to pay his commercial debts landed him in jail. He eagerly invested his idle time in learning. Upon his discharge from jail he registered at Vienna's Academy, studying philosophy for three years. As an Academy graduate he taught privately and wrote his *German-Greek Grammar* published in Vienna in 1834, the same year he joined the faculty of the Academy. He simultaneously taught Greek at Vienna University. He was a regular contributor to Vienna's Greek magazines *Kalliope* and *Telegraphos*. Four years later in 1838 he translated from Italian into Greek and published in Vienna his *Themistocles at the Persians*. His translation from

[43]Committee Presentation on *Siatista Memoirs*, p. 4

Ancient to Modern Greek of Homer's *Odyssey's* A, B, C, and D portions waited publication until 1848 in Athens. Rousiades's restless, ambitious, and explosive character continued. He added to his list the following works: 1. *Training of Children*, 2. *Two Diaries*, 3. *Turkey's Road Map*, 4. *Greek Literature History Synopsis*, 5. *Review of Italian and German Works from Antiquity to Constantinople's Fall*, 6. *About Greek Dialects*, especially those of Homer, 7. *Psychological Experiences*, 8. *Greek-German Dictionary*, 9. *Greek Language Composition*, 10. *Short Catechism* for young children, and 11. *Arithmetic, Algebra, and Geometry Basics*. His death in 1854 interrupted the following projects: *Synopsis of Greek Grammar*, *Synopsis of Ethics, Philosophy, Physics and Geometry* and translation from German into Greek of *Esthetics*[44].

Promotion of Hellenism continued at every opportunity.

---

[44]Panagiotes N. Lioufes, *History of Kozane*, pp. 218-22

Wall painting in prophet Elias Church in Siatista with philosophers Plato, Thoucydides, and Sivylla worshipped as saints.

Chapter 16
Social Development

Upper Macedonian traders, especially the ones from Siatista, traveling north carried with them their Hellenic virtues and culture. They respected their fellow men, their families, their properties, and customs. They even shared their goals and often their aspirations. They adjusted successfully in their adopted lands. They became important in financial and local political circles. Their contributions to local developments were significant. Entre Horvath wrote in his 1940 Budapest *Hungarian Hellenic Bibliography*, p. 56: Greeks' translations into Slavo-Serbian and Rumanian "are proofs of the civilizing role the Greeks played among the Balkan peoples." The Greeks played a leading role in Hungarian capitalism's birth and development[1]. Siatista's Zosimas and his handpicked successor Nikeforos (translated victory carrier) guided Siatistians' destiny for eighty-three years. These were very crucial years for Siatistians and Greeks in general.

Kecskemet's Greek community, with strong Siatistian and Kozanitan[2] presence, employed a priest since 1710[3]. Their public library operated since 1742. The community's, highly Zosimas-oriented, school offered languages and commercial courses long before 1750. The community officers, strongly determined to help the churches back home, solicited donations for assistance. The churches' elders displayed two collection boxes during church services. One accepted donations for the benefit of Holy Trinity church in Siatista. The other intended to assist Kozane's Saint Nickolaos church. Christians of twenty surrounding communities attended Kecskemet's Eastern Orthodox Church and offered their donations. The Ecumenical Patriarchate, following the abolishment in 1767 of the First Justinian Archepiscopate of Achris, extended its services to the entire region[4]. Maria Theresia's

---
[1]George Laios, *Siatista and Its Commercial Houses Hadje-Michael and Manouses*, p. 62
[2]George Laios, *Siatista and Its Commercial Houses Hadje-Michael and Manouses*, p. 43
[3]George Laios, *Siatista and Its Commercial Houses Hadje-Michael and Manouses*, p. 53
[4]Konstantinos Babouskos, *Ecclesiastical Relations of Serbs and Ecumenical Patriarchate the 19th Century, Helleno-Serbian Symposium*, p. 264

decision in 1776 to grant Saint Georgios church of Vienna independence from Karlowac's Serbian bishop[5] impacted favorably to Kecskemet parishioners. Emperor Joseph II's declaration on church's autonomy in 1781 enhanced the situation. Kecskemet parishioners in 1791, led by Bishop Dionysios Popovic of Buda, collected over ten thousand fiorins for construction of a new church. The new church, located in the center of Kecskemet and dedicated to Holy Trinity, required at least 14,222 fiorins for completion.

Siatistian Michael Papageorgiou's teaching performance elevated the idea of universal brotherhood. Miscolc's Greek community established, in addition to a church, its own hospital and old-age home. In its institutions it accepted patients indiscriminately on the basis of need, irrespective of nationality or religion[6]. Similar mentality prevailed in most of the over one hundred Greek communities existing and prospering in Hungary.

(Buda)Pest's Greek community members worshipped with Serbs as per existing directives. In 1780, following the authorities' favorable rulings stated above, about two hundred Greek families responded to their elder's call for establishment of their own church. Their drive collected over fifty thousand fiorins. Bishop Dionysios Popovic dedicated the Virgin Mary church in 1792. The community constructed a rental income building close to it. Rents collected supplemented the annual dues, special gifts, donations, and inheritance grants willed by church members. This way they easily defrayed the church operational costs plus all school, library, hospital, old-age home, and community offices[7]. Siatistian merchants' presence in the community, with the initiative of educator Michael Papageorgiou who taught there for a while and his nephew George Zaviras, promoted Zosimas's spirit of Hellenism.

In Vienna, Siatistians George Konstantinou and Pavlos Hadje-Michael with Konstantinos Zebovekis and Demetrios Savvas in 1760 negotiated with Serb bishop at Karlowac all problems that appeared between Serbs and Greeks regarding their joint management of the church. Siatistian businessmen, participating

[5]George Laios, *Siatista and Its Commercial Houses Hadje-Michael and Manouses*, p. 73
[6]George Laios, *Siatista and Its Commercial Houses Hadje-Michael and Manouses*, p. 63
[7]George Laios, *Siatista and Its Commercial Houses Hadje-Michael and Manouses*, p. 65

in the mostly Upper Macedonian twelve-member Board-of-Directors, provided initiative and guidance.

Siatistians maintained similar representation in the five-member Vienna Trade Commissioners Board. The commission "Waren sen salen" established in 1770 monitored the quality and price of imported goods into Vienna from the Orient. The commissioners' income was 1 percent of sales, paid by the seller. They logged all names of sellers and buyers, dates and prices for each transaction. Special registers recorded Macedonian wool imports, because of their importance[8]. Siatistian George Poulios, an Austrian citizen and ex-Internal Revenue Service employee, served in this strategic position. He enjoyed personal dignity because of his multilingual capability and knowledge of the market. For his appointment he presented certificates procured from the Wholesaler's Association and the Boards of Directors of both Greek communities confirming his virtues. Austrian citizen Greek merchants broke away from the first community in 1787 and formed a new one. The new community established its own Eastern Orthodox Church dedicated to "Holy Trinity." Siatistians George Theohares and John Manouses served the all-important position of Trade Commissioners later on[9].

Empress Maria Theresia strengthened her administrative system in areas bordering with the Ottoman Empire. Greeks, mainly Upper Macedonians, controlled most commercial activities. Out of 120 major Viennese firms trading with East, 115 were Greeks. They maintained operation of warehouses as well as retail stores. Their repeated exhibitions promoted their wares to the public. Their distribution networks employing trusted representatives served distant communities. To push their imports, they formed loan agencies and finance institutions that quickly developed into banks. They established leather processing and textile product manufacturing plants. They employed many Austrian youth as apprentices working next to experienced Greek hands. These trainees formed the basis for Austro-Hungarian industry and commerce. Establishment of School of Commerce, the higher business institution of learning in the country, followed much later.

[8] George Laios, *Siatista and Its Commercial Houses Hadje-Michael and Manouses*, p. 85
[9] George Laios, *Siatista and Its Commercial Houses Hadje-Michael and Manouses*, p. 158

Siatistian traders carrying Zosimas's spirit of Hellenism continued to play a dominant role. Theodoros George Moustafa extended his fur business from Siatista to Leipzig and Vienna. Anastasios Doudoumes and brothers Demetrios and Adames Tseteres with their sister Ekaterine also prospered in these cities[10]. However, Joseph Nakos's descendants married into the Royal family. Austrian prince Graf Naco became Senator in Vienna[11].

Details from the family history of Hadje-Michael Nikou from Dryovouno, a village close to Siatista, provide an interesting case. Michael Nikou, following a visit to the Holy Lands, picked up the honorary title "Hadje" conferred to visiting devoted Christian. Hadje-Michael relocated to Siatista around 1700 for business purposes[12]. His wife Kyrano and children followed for safety reasons. Zosimas's administration improved both aspects of these areas. Hadje-Michael with his three sons Nickolaos, Doukas, and Pavlos traded with Venice. The plethora of Siatistian merchants trading with Venice strengthened their position. Upon father Michael's death in 1734, the three brothers continued shipping goods to Venice as well as to Trieste and Fume. Pavlos explored Vienna in 1740 seeking possible opportunities. In 1742 their shipment of eighty parcels of Macedonian wool went to Venice. Most probably older brother Nickolaos, headquartered in Siatista, had the overall management. His likely training at schools away from Siatista enabled him to maintain records of transactions since 1733.

Hadje-Michael brothers' partnership continued trading with Venice and Vienna even after their mother's death in 1743. In 1750, they established their subsidiary in Vienna. Pavlos assumed management of the new branch. Brother Doukas supervised all shipments to Vienna, indicating the importance they placed on this operation. They shipped from Macedonia wool, cotton, crocus, semi-processed skins, and other goods totaling one hundred thousand fiorins annually. They sold these products in Vienna, Buda(Pest), Leipzig, Amsterdam, and their surrounding markets. From these markets they bought silk

---

[10] John Apostolou, *The History of Siatista,* pp. 15,17
[11] John Apostolou, *The History of Siatista,* p. 64
[12] George Laios, *Siatista and Its Commercial Houses Hadje-Michael and Manouses,* pp. 102-149

products, women's apparel, jewelry, household items, decorative objects and other industrial goods destined for Macedonia and the greater trading area. Their value exceeded twenty thousand fiorins per year. They shipped goods to most major Balkan trading centers, Constantinople, and Izmir (Smyrne) in Asia Minor. Their representatives in Belgrade, Nis, Velessa, Durres, Elbasan, Serres, Salonica, Larisa, Lamia, and elsewhere coordinated their efforts through Siatista. In 1760, brother Doukas withdrew from their partnership, forming his own firm in Vienna. His two sons, Michael and Konstantinos, although they devoted considerable interest and energy in education, kept it going until 1796. Nickolaos and Pavlos continued operating their own Vienna firm. In 1785, Pavlos's efforts concentrated in more ambitious plans. These plans will be reviewed in the chapter on Barons, Bankers, and Benefactors.

Nickolaos Hadje-Michael in 1754 married in Siatista Anastasia Charisiou from Kozane. Anastasia brought from her parents an impressive dowry in cash, 183,120 aspra (Turkish monetary unit) as it appears from a contract confirmed by Zosimas's successor Bishop Nikeforos. Nickolaos invested part of it to build his mansion in Siatista in 1757. The mansion was necessary to accommodate and entertain all commercial visitors arriving in Siatista from many Balkan regions. The couple had nine daughters and one son, Demetrios. One of the daughters, Soultana, married Siatistian John Georgiou Tourountzias, merchant and teacher at Semlin's Greek school. Another daughter married Michael (last name unknown), who, when widowed, turned a clergyman. His education and abilities elevated him to Metropolitan of Pelagonia, adopting the name Meletios. All remaining seven daughters married sons of prominent families. They all received appropriate dowries as per Siatista's customs. In 1786, following Nickolaos's death in Siatista, they all received their inheritance share from their father's estate. Brother Demetrios distributed equally all liquidation proceeds from their Vienna firm.

The following year, in 1787, Demetrios married Agnes Georgiou Manouses, a neighborhood girl living next door in another mansion. The cash dowry he received, 508,000 aspra, exceeded by far the impressive amount his father received. The young couple lived in the Hadje-Michael family mansion. Demetrios traveled to Vienna regularly. He continued his business on his own until 1798. Demetrios, a prominent and respectable citizen in Siatista, participated in all deliberations of Siatista's public affairs. His advice during the critical revolutionary war of 1821 weighted heavily. He remained active until 1839 at an advanced age. His granddaughter Agnes married[13] Athanasios Konstantinou Kanatsoules from Kozane, a Vienna doctor in 1856. Agnes and doctor Kanatsoules returned to Siatista and lived in Hadje-Michael's mansion. Agnes's son, born after his father's death in 1859, received his father's name. Young Athanasios's relatives in Constantinople stepped in. They brought him up and educated him properly. They sent him to High School in Galatsi, Rumania. He studied law at Athens University and returned to Siatista. He taught at Siatista's schools. Upon functioning of Siatista's Trapantzeion Gymnasium in 1888, he taught history and French for forty years. Among his many works he researched and recorded his family's historical lineage and its activities.

The Siatistian family of Markos Poulios's contribution to Hellenism is equally outstanding. Markos, a Zosimas-era youth product, traded in Leipzig in 1763. He settled in Vienna in 1776. His two sons Poulios and George learned their German, Latin, and Italian languages. Parallel to their linguistic and academic knowledge they picked up commercial courses. For their career they chose employment at F. Ch. Baumeister's printing shop. Poulios, like his brother, became an Austrian citizen. In 1790, both brothers requested permission from Austrian authorities to publish a Greek language daily newspaper. Efemeris, the first Greek daily ever to be published[14] anywhere, appeared in Vienna on December 31, 1790. Poulios and George Poulios became newsmen, printers, and publishers. Their achievements are detailed in Liberalism and Revolutions chapter.

Back in Siatista, Demetrios J. Moraites's operations are typical of progress made under Archbishop Zosimas's administration. Moraites's representatives network covered most Balkan regions. Merchants of Ioannina, Preveza,

---
[13]Vasilike Siasiou, *Educational and Cultural Society of Siatista Calendar 1997*, presentation
[14]Demetres Fotiades, *The Revolution of 1821*, Vol. I, p. 179

Ambelakia, Larisa, Elassona, Tyrnavos, Tsaritsane, Grevena, Katerine, Kolindros, Salonica, Serres, Smyrne, Constantinople, Sofia, Semlin, Belgrade, Monastere, Perlepe, Moschopolis, Korytsa, Kastoria, Berate, Trieste, Leipzig, Budapest, and Vienna experienced his dealings as it appears from Zoupan-Moraites-Perikles archives[15]. Records indicate transactions involved close-proximity areas of Kozane, Edessa, Veroia, Vlaste, Megarovo, Mavrovo, Vrontos, Vidin, Dortali, Velessa, Avdella, Souli, Arta, Koboti, Lamia, and Navpaktos. Rumania's cities Bucharest, Iasi, and Rosiava are also mentioned on available documents. In 1788, D. J. Moraites's representative in Sofia, Theodore (last name unknown), recommended Siatistians expand to Urdi (?). Existing opportunities in this area attracted many Kleisoura and Bogatsiko merchants already. In 1799, Moraites's associate from Vienna ordered goods for delivery to Semlin's merchant Konstantinos Zygoures. Demetrios Nickolaou Hadje-Michael, in a spirit of Siatistian cooperation and solidarity, wrote to Moraites. He advised him of higher than prevailing market prices, paid by Moraites's partner Nickolaos Zoupan from Moschopolis, for goods ordered in Leipzig for Semlin delivery. In 1800, D. J. Moraites and Nickolaos Zoupan financed a joint venture. They procured a loan from Konstantinos Ch. Koutentakes of Serres. They arranged its repayment through commercial notes to Stergios John Batrinos in Kastoria. In 1801, Nickolaos Zoupan closed another deal in Ioannina. The brothers John and Konstantinos Tzotza bought goods stored in Serres for delivery at Perlepe's annual fair.

Profits seemed to be expected from all deals. Vienna firms financed all of these operations. Many transactions involved Veli Pasha, a Turk and Ottoman official. In 1805 Moraites's employees prepared a statement of account involving these transactions. They utilized Turkish numerals to emphasize Pasha's attention. Pasha Veli owed D. J. Moraites and Nickolaos Zoupan a substantial sum for goods received. Other Greek merchants in Tsaritsane and Smyrne received similar credit as well. In 1806, John Hadje-Konsta of Ambelakia, Thessaly, sent an order for merchandise. Transaction shipments of yard goods and crocus to

[15] Anastasios Ch. Megas, "Archives of Zoupan-Moraites-Perikleous," *Siatista Memoirs*, pp. A89-A128

Athanasios Klokones in Smyrne followed the next year. Prevailing prices and market conditions, however, were depressed. Unfavorable terms binding Moraites-Zoupan's operations with Vienna's Swartz Company aggravated the situation. The partnership's business failure became unavoidable. Moraites's death prompted their catastrophe. In 1807, Naoum K. Iatrou, son-in-law of D. J. Moraites through his daughter Helen, wrote from Ioannina to Siatista's archon Demetrios Hadje-Michael. He offered assistance to prevent collapse of his father-in-law's operations. Naoum, an employee and assistant of Ottoman officials and Pashas, utilized his position of power to assist his mother-in-law. Together, they collected debts from Greek merchants and Turkish pashas. In 1819, Naoum K. Iatrou was still in the service of Ottoman officials. He held the position of Veiz Aga's secretary.

Naoum Demetriades Moraites, D. J. Moraites's son, trying hard to regain his father's business, settled in Semlin in 1812. Informed about Greek revolutionary activities against the Ottomans in 1821, he wrote to his sister Helen in 1822 offering assistance. Helen lived in Siatista taking care of her family and their mother. D. J. Moraites's widow Maria, Helen and Naoum's mother, died in 1833. She outlived her husband by twenty-seven years. Four years later in 1837 Helen's husband, Naoum K. Iatrou, died. Helen with her five children accepted brother (and uncle) Naoum's condolences from Semlin, the permanent residence of Naoum Demetriades Moraites. Semlin, the town Naoum and other Siatistians lived and prospered in, was a model community in the Balkans.

Chapter 17
Model Community

The city of Semlin proved a heaven for Greek merchants, especially from Upper Macedonia. Semlin is located opposite Belgrade, where the Danube River and its tributary Savo meet. It is approximately halfway on the overland route from Constantinople or Salonica to Vienna. Ottoman armies occupied the area in 1521[1]. Continued use of Belgrade as an administrative and commercial center kept Semlin a small, neighboring community. Austrian troops captured the area in 1688 for two short years. In 1690, the Ottomans regained its control[2] and kept it until 1717 when the Austrians recaptured it. The Passarowitz Pact of 1718 between Austria and the Ottomans included favorable trading terms to Ottoman subjects importing Oriental goods into Austria. Semlin population grew from fifteen hundred inhabitants in 1720 to two thousand in 1739 when Austria returned Belgrade to Ottoman authority under the terms of the Belgrade Treaty[3]. Semlin, however, remained under Austrian control. Its strategic location opposite Ottoman-occupied Belgrade weighted heavily with Austrian's policy makers. Semlin quickly became a privileged border town.

The Austro-Hungarian Empire encouraged Semlin's development. Ambitious young men moved in steadily, seeking trade or employment opportunities. Most of them were Serbs but Greeks followed. Many arrived from Upper Macedonia. In 1736 about one hundred Greeks lived and traded in Semlin. They spoke Greek but also Wallach, the Latinized mountainous region dialect. They organized their "Community of Romans and Macedo-Wallachs[4]." Their religious life closely resembled that of other Orthodox people, mainly the Serbs[5]. The Eastern Orthodox community established its own church in 1740. Their liturgies

---
[1] John A. Papadrianos, *The Greek Settlers of Semlin*, p. 27
[2] John A. Papadrianos, *The Greek Settlers of Semlin*, p. 34
[3] John A. Papadrianos, *The Greek Settlers of Semlin*, p. 41
[4] John A. Papadrianos, *The Greek Settlers of Semlin*, p. 31
[5] John A. Papadrianos, *The Greek Settlers of Semlin*, p. 99

took place in a small, wooden structure. The rebuilt church, dedicated to Saint Nickolaos in 1752, serviced 262 Eastern Orthodox Semlin families. Ninety-six Catholic families had their own congregation. Saint Nickolaos's priests Moschos and Stergiades, well-versed in Slav and Greek languages, indiscriminately performed all services. They alternated their liturgies in Slav and Greek languages. In its school Theodore Stergiades taught Serbian to Serb children and Greek to Greek children from 1740 to 1754[6]. George Spidas from Moschopolis taught Greek on a private basis from 1754 to 1776.

The Austrian government in 1749 instituted semiautonomous administration for Semlin. Its citizens elected its own City Council in 1751. It was purely an administrative agency, separate and independent from military authority. Elite citizens composed the Magistrate. Many Greek residents, Macedonians and Siatistians, achieved the distinction of elite citizenry. Political freedom and trading opportunities brought prosperity and growth to Semlin. The number of families increased from 358 to 632 within five years. About four out of five, or 499 families, owned homes. In addition to above, another thirty-two gypsy and nineteen Jewish families lived with them and owned their homes. Among Orthodox families thirteen were traders and thirty-four storekeepers. Small workshops producing various products at home provided employment to 168 families. Vineyards and wine making provided work to fifty-five families, while another thirty-nine families chose farming. In 1755, ordinary laborers were only thirty-one families. Transit trade was mainly in the hands of Macedonian Greeks. The families of Spidas, Nastos, and Panayiotou from Moschopolis, Darvaris from Kleisoura, Sollaros from Katranitsa, Andreas Demetriou and Poulios Margarites from Argyrokastro, and John Georgiou thrived and prospered. Semlin had 1635 Orthodox residents in 1764. They arrived from Wallachia, Hungary, Croatia, Herzegovina, Bulgaria, and other areas. Serbs came from Belgrade, Valjevo, Kragujevac, Palez, Kumodraz, Visnjica, Slamac, and Groeka. Approximately 15 percent of the Orthodox population came mostly from Macedonia. Theodore Apostolou

[6]John A. Papadrianos, *The Greek Settlers of Semlin*, p. 122

from Salonica arrived in Semlin in 1765[7]. Theodore Kostits from Vlaste arrived in 1766[8].

Semlin was a stopover and adjustment point on their way north to many settlers. Fifty-six percent of the 333 Orthodox settlers in Croatia and Slovenia between 1720 and 1776 passed through Semlin. Seventy-five percent of the eighty-two Greek merchants operating in Vienna tried their luck in Semlin first. Ten Greek commercial firms of Vienna maintained a branch in Semlin[9]. The Russo-Ottoman hostilities of 1768–1774 and Ottoman pressures to nationals of occupied lands for assistance led many escapees to Semlin. Moschopolitans hurriedly abandoned their city in 1769. Twenty-eight families found refuge in Semlin. Another thirty from Upper Macedonia made the same choice. Vlaste sent five additional families[10]. The failure of Siatistian George Papazoles and Russian General Orlof in the uprising of 1770 sent waves of Greeks up north. Semlin accommodated another eighteen families. The seventy-five Semlin Greek families of 1770 doubled to 150 in 1775[11]. A year later, in 1776, eight Serbs and Greeks donated their homes to have a second Eastern Orthodox Church built[12]. The new church dedicated to the Virgin Mary functioned in 1780. Personal contributions and service fees of church members paid the Orthodox priests' allowances, contrary to Catholic priests whose salaries were part of the city's budget[13].

More Greeks arrived in Semlin during the period. George Perros, Michael Zekos, Nasos Kaissorou and Nickolaos Rouses came from Moschopolis, from Tepeleni Mark Tepelen-lis, from Monastere Athanasios Konstantinou, from Ostrovo (Arnissa) Christos Ostrovan-lis, from Sipischa Theodore Stova, from Gabrovo John Sirokas, from Kastoria George Konstantinou Pop and from Vlaste Bayios Demetrievitz with his brother Nickolaos, Kostas Zefkou, Andreas Ignatiou, John Randits, Pavlos

[7] John A. Papadrianos, *The Greek Settlers of Semlin*, p. 47
[8] Michael Ath. Kalinderis, *Life in the Community of Vlaste During the Turkish Occupation*, p. 63
[9] John A. Papadrianos, *The Greek Settlers of Semlin*, p. 48
[10] Michael Ath. Kanlinderis, *Life in the Community of Vlaste During the Turkish Occupation*, p. 62
[11] John A. Papadrianos, *The Greek Settlers of Semlin*, p. 56
[12] John A. Papadrianos, *The Greek Settlers of Semlin*, p. 101
[13] John A. Papadrianos, *The Greek Settlers of Semlin*, p. 110

Noumkovatz, and Yangos (John) Matits. Among Vlaste's expatriates first was George Zaglas (details in the following chapter). Theodore Kostits developed a successful silk goods trade. His descendant Kostas N. Kostits served Serbia as foreign minister. Other Semlin settlers included: from Katranitsa, Christos Skyvrou Hadje-Meletiou; from Servia, brothers Fotis and Kostas Tagaras; from Tsaritsane, Thessaly, Panayiotes Evaggelou; and from Tyrnavo, Thessaly, Demetrios Konstas and Athanasios Margarites. Origin of Kostas Bratoglou, John Poulios, George Christou, Kostas Georgiou, John Paikos, and Demetrios and Naoum Doursou is not identified.

Vienna's Imperial War Council worried about increased southerner's migration into Semlin. In 1782, it issued an order through Slovenia's General Command to Semlin's City Council. The order directed the city to institute incentives in order to attract German craftsmen and entrepreneurs[14]. Greek settlers continued to invite their relatives and friends, however. Michael Pop from Kastoria with Stergios Demou and Zafeires Theodorou arrived in 1783. Michael Voulkos and Emmanouel Slavones from Katranitsa and Demos Popovics from Edessa followed. In 1787, Semlin's population reached 4468 inhabitants. With 86 Jewish and one Evangellian persons lived 896 Catholics and 3485 Eastern Orthodox[15]. The need for additional Orthodox churches was obvious. Theodore Apostolou's presence in Semlin completed its twentieth year in 1785. His financial success in addition to comforts and respect from Semlin's citizens elevated him to the presidency of the Soap Manufacturer's Association. In 1786, he built the church of Archaggelon at his own expense. Apostolou's son Nickolaos or Nicole Apostolovica (1766–1827) became an artist. Completely absorbed by the prevailing wave of Europe's liberalism in 1804 he assisted the Serbian revolution. Apostolou's first daughter married Dragasevic, whose son Jovan Dragasevic became a general in the Serbian army. Apostolou's second daughter married Rukavina. Their son J. Rukavina became a Baron, utilizing the family's financial means and social status.

[14] John A. Papadrianos, *The Greek Settlers of Semlin*, p. 57
[15] John A. Papadrianos, *The Greek Settlers of Semlin*, p. 59

The Russo-Ottoman war in 1787 brought additional pressures on populations under the Ottoman's control for assistance in their war effort. Ottoman authorities in 1788 executed two remaining archons of Moschopolis who chose to forget the city's tragic experience of 1769. The death of Theodore Vretta Zoupan, whose grandson Naoum Konstantinos Zoupan married Siatistian D. J. Moraites's daughter Helen, and Naoum Goustas caused a new exodus by Moschopolis' residents. Semlin accepted escapees John Zafeires, Andrew Boubouroniou, Naoum Peschares, and Gioza Vretta from the new exodus. Angellis Tsiames, Kostas Tzekou, and brothers Markos and Vassilios Boukouvallas from Kleisoura brought additional talent to Semlin. From Vlaste arrived Theodore Liotits and Kostas Boukouvalas. Other newcomers were George Athanasiou from Eratyra, George Antoniou from Meleniko, Michael Andreou from Sipischa, and the Ignatiou family from Velesniko. The ones above and George Mantzarles's arrival strengthened competition with established merchants. Theophylactos Nikolaou and Stavros Ioannou were two important arrivals from Ioannina. Stavros Ioannou's son George utilized his family's estate and his own ingenuity. In 1841, he established the internationally present National Bank of Greece.

Promotion of fair trade practices and education by Upper Macedonians performed miracles. Their efforts concentrated in equality and mutual respect. Greeks earned their acceptance wherever they settled. The Serbs were their neighbors, associates, employees, friends, customers, and spiritual brothers. They worked and worshipped together. Their common spiritual source, drawn from the same priest, resulted in close social relationship. Mixed marriages in predominantly Serb Orthodox communities increased. In an effort to get close to their hearts and pocketbooks, Greeks added Slav suffixes to their names[16]. George Zachariades became Georgije Zaharijevic, Demetrios Darvares was known as Dimitrije Darvar, and so on. Greeks' financial success ensured their elevation to Semlin's social order. Their participation in community affairs was firm. They were restless, however, due to their absence from the decision-making process. They advanced to their authorities their desire to audit

[16] John A. Papadrianos, *The Greek Settlers of Semlin*, p. 36

the church's financial records. The community Orthodox school's funding relied completely on self-generated funds, to a considerable degree on their efforts, since its inception. In 1778, city authorities picked up the salaries of two teachers, one each for Orthodox and Catholic instruction. The German language, so necessary in Semlin's society and a requirement for higher education, was not part of the school's curriculum. This was detrimental to Orthodox children's advancement. Absence of Greek courses was noticeably disturbing. The same situation prevailed for fifteen years. In 1793, the Greek merchants petitioned the City Council. They requested permission to teach Greek at the Orthodox school along with Serbian. A Greek teacher would supplement the two Serbs on the faculty[17]. The City Council favored this solution, but Serb opposition surfaced. Their only alternative was establishment of a Greek school.

Semlin Siatistians enriched with Zosimas's spirit of Hellenism anxiously waited. They always practiced their Siatistian customs. They remembered and honored all Christian names annually on a given date. Such was the occasion on December 6, 1793. Nickolaos Rouses (unknown if he was a descendant of Zosimas's family whose last name was also Rouses) held an open house on Saint Nickolaos day. Fellow Siatistians, friends, and associates all came to pay their respects. Siatistian John Tourountzias, merchant-turned-teacher in the under establishment school; Theodore Liotas Hadje-Theodorou, probably from Siatista; and Athanasios Hadje-Bakes (1763–1812), from Vlaste, the benefactor of the poor and destitute as per magazine *Telegraphos* of Vienna (1820 issue 6 column 47), were there and ready. In a festive and euphoric atmosphere, with plenty of Siatistian wine and delicious snacks, they deliberated and acted. They decided to establish an Educational Brotherhood and a Greek school. The school's name, Helleno-Museum, emphasized their intent and expectations. Donations poured in. An elected three-member committee reported a total of 6650 fiorins on hand in less than a month. The school opened its doors within one year. Available merchants/educators served as instructors. In September 1794, George Avxentiades from Pentalofos, a village west of Siatista, directed its operation. His love and devotion to education plus his recognition of Siatistians' proper behavior led him to will his books

---

[17]John A. Papadrianos, *The Greek Settlers of Semlin*, pp. 127, 128

to Siatista's school after his death in 1813[18]. This donation formed the nucleus of today's rich Manouseios Public Library operating in Siatista. Others followed his example. Demetrios Argyriou from Thrace taught in Helleno-Museum in 1796. Demetrios Sklavakes added his efforts in 1798 and 1799. The same year brought brilliant George Zachariades from Tyrnavo, Thessaly, for a seven-year career. Siatistian John Tourountzias replaced him for a three-year period from 1806 to 1809[19]. Tourountzias, deeply influenced by his brother's execution in 1798 (along with the Greek revolutionary war martyr Regas), promoted human rights and taught religion, emphasizing refinement of personal behavior. Helleno-Museum's curriculum excelled in quality. It instituted Hellenic studies and commercial-oriented courses. Many non-Greek Semlin families recognized the Greek teachers' humble devotion. Children of Serbs, Hungarians, and Germans took advantage of Helleno-Museum's positive contribution. The Austrian authorities accredited the school in 1816 and validated its constitution[20].

Semlin's population reached 6760 in 1799[21]. Orthodox Christians were 5362, Catholic 1218, Jewish 156, and Protestants only 24 individuals. Greeks numbered seven hundred persons. Most wholesale trading in town and a good number of taverns and coffeehouses were in Greek hands. Demetrios Poulios from Vlaste, brother of the head priest back home, brought over his two nephews and trained them in business[22]. All Greeks in addition to the original founders of the school (i.e., the families of Darvares, Sollaros, Peschares, George Kyriakes, Konstantine Hatias, John Poulios, and Doukas Konstantinou) supported morally and financially the school and benefited from the school's existence. Their children received the education the parents preferred.

The Serb revolution of 1804 caused many Belgrade residents to move to Semlin for safety. About one hundred of them were

---
[18]John A. Papadrianos, *The Greek Settlers of Semlin*, p. 150
[19]John A. Papadrianos, *The Greek Settlers of Semlin*, p. 157
[20]John A. Papadrianos, *The Greek Settlers of Semlin*, p.133
[21]John A. Papadrianos, *The Greek Settlers of Semlin*, p.66
[22]Michael Ath. Kalinderis, *Life in the Community of Vlaste During the Turkish Occupation*, p. 63

Greeks. The Greek element in Semlin increased in relation to Serbs. Additionally, many Serbs returned to their hometowns probably to join their brothers in the revolution. Siatistian Naoum Demetriades Moraites arrived in Semlin in 1812[23] most likely to take advantage of prevailing war conditions and trade opportunities offered. Suppression of the revolution in 1813 flooded Semlin with Serbs. The same phenomenon occurred in 1815, when again the Serbs left to assist with their second revolution[24].

In 1823, after the Greek revolution broke out, Semlin's population grew to about nine thousand. The Greeks numbered about one thousand. Newcomers from Upper Macedonia were George Agoras and Konstantinos Barthalames from Kozane, Petros Nedelkovic and Konstantinos John Anthoula from Kleisoura, Konstantinos Stergiou Doumtza from Grammousta, John Thomas from Veroia, John Hadje-Thomas from Meleniko, and Nickolaos and Stefanos Georgiou. They all labored hard and contributed to the community's well-being. Younger John Anthoulas's efforts ended in the establishment of Serbia's National Bank. Death records for the first third of nineteenth century reveal the extent to which Upper Macedonians lived and prospered in Semlin. Out of 318 deaths recorded, 79 hailed from Kleisoura, 21 from Vlaste, 20 from Moschopolis, 12 from Meleniko, 8 from Siatista, 6 from Kastoria, 4 each from Serres and Katranitsa, and the remaining (half of total) from other Balkan locations and Greece[25]. Most Siatistians, perhaps with better financial means, repatriated to Siatista.

Eventually, the Hellenic community of Semlin lost its numbers and strength substantially. Many relocated to liberated Greece. Some discovered locations with greater business opportunities. Most, however, succumbed to the local population assimilation. Mixed marriages, mainly with Serb spouses, almost always produced Serbian children. George Kyriakou, born by a Serb mother in 1784, became Kirjakovic, Serbian version of Kyriakou, and at the age of fifty wrote to Vuk

---

[23]Anastasios Ch. Megas, "Archives of Zoupan-Moraites-Perikleous," *Siatista Memoirs*, p. A113

[24]John A. Papadrianos, *The Greek Settlers of Semlin*, p. 71

[25]John A. Papadrianos, *The Greek Settlers of Semlin*, p. 73. *The Greek Settlers at the Yugoslav Countries*, p. 44

Karadjic: "I am a pure Serb and I will die like a Serb. I only wish I had ten souls to sacrifice for my country[26]." Many wealthy families with strong and solid Hellenic education and background continued their culture and tradition in Semlin.

---

[26] John A. Papadrianos, *The Greek Settlers of Semlin*, p. 75.

Chapter 18
Liberalism and Revolutions

Trade and unrestricted travel encouraged by Austrians and Ottomans increased understanding and developed opportunities on both sides. Intermingling of religions and social organizations cultivated mutual respect.

Russia implemented her policy of Orthodox protectionism during the Russo-Ottoman war of 1768–1774[1]. It encouraged all Orthodox nationalities to help her effort. Greeks got another boost for their national aspirations. However, failure of Russia's initiative in 1770 in the case of the Greek insurrection under General Orlof and Siatistian George Papazoles caused reassessment of their position. Greek intellectuals and merchants strengthened their determination. They worked harder and harder both on financial achievement and on education. Their efforts turned to their Orthodox brothers. They used for this purpose their improved financial positions and influence. The European political trends and decisiveness influenced their thinking. The American Revolution and the French that followed in 1789 provided them with courage. They endorsed its principle of taxation with representation. The renewal of fighting in the Russo-Ottoman war of 1787–1792[2] strengthened their hopes. The French revolutionaries' slogan—Equality, Liberty and Justice—moved them. They added it to their objective. Their freedom had to include these human values. It could only be materialized in a free society.

Austria's opposition to the French Revolution in 1791 disappointed many minorities of the empire[3]. Greek intellectuals and merchants, convinced of their noble ideas, remained firm. They endangered their prosperity and sacrificed their lives for dignity and self-respect. They gave Greece's national independence top priority. Ordinary people and the middle class as well idealized the French liberalism[4]. Simultaneously they preached Greek nationalism

---
[1] A. Lily Macrakis, "Introduction: 1000 Years of Hellenism and Russia," *International Chamber of Commerce*, p. 17
[2] John A. Papadrianos, *The Greek Settlers of Semlin*. p. 66
[3] John A. Papadrianos, *The Greek Settlers of Semlin*. p. 64
[4] Apostolos E. Vacalopoulos, *The History of Thessalonike*, p. 98

enthusiastically and energetically. They hoped the French revolutionaries' victorious advance signaled the liberation of Greece[5]. The Greek communities in central European cities as well as in Danubian principalities of Moldavia and Wallachia welcomed this development. Educated Greeks[6], appointed by the Ottoman Empire, administered both Moldavia and Wallachia. Today they are parts of Rumania, independent since 1878.

Vienna's printing shop of Baumeister where Siatistian brothers Poulios and George Poulios worked provided an ideal revolutionary facility. Christodulos Kirkland's book *School of Delicate Lovers* brought the revolutionaries together. Kirkland (later baron von Langenfeld) and Regas Fereos brought from Bucharest the book's Greek translation by Regas for printing. Regas stayed with the Poulios brothers for six months[7] working on the book. The Poulios brothers' and Regas's political views coincided. They shared liberal ideas and aspirations. Their prolonged meetings cemented their cooperation. They decided the time was ripe for action. The opportunity was not late in coming. Baumeister, the printing shop owner, in 1792 joined the Emperor's staff as child counselor. This appointment resulted in turning over the operation of the printing shop completely to the Poulios brothers. The Poulios brothers published their own daily newspaper, *Efemeris*, since December 31, 1790. They also printed books, calendars, programs, brochures, and other items. Due to their maturity and responsible behavior, they gained absolute freedom of action. In full cooperation with Regas, they published revolutionary leaflets, articles, and magazines with political contents. *The Military Guide of von Kheven Huller* translated from German and *Constitution* translated from French were among them. They published the works of Regas Fereos and his comrade Koronios, *Constitution of the Greek Democracy, New Civilian Government*[8] and the *Ethical Tripod*. In 1794 they printed in Greek the book written in French, and translated by Nikeforos Theotokes, challenging Voltaire's *Bible*.

[5]George Laios, *Siatista and Its Commercial Houses Hadje-Michael and Manouses*, p. 95
[6]George G. Arnakis, *Americans in the Greek Revolution*, p. 3
[7]George Laios, *Siatista and Its Commercial Houses Hadje-Michael and Manouses*, p. 90
[8]George Laios, *Siatista and Its Commercial Houses Hadje-Michael and Manouses*, p. 95

The Poulios brothers concealed their sympathy with the French revolutionaries and their willingness to assist any effort to restore freedom and justice to Greece and its people. Regas's return to Vienna in 1796, however, revealed their revolutionary zeal. Regas and the Poulios brothers met and worked out their plans. In December 1796, Poulios Poulios traveled to Wallachia with the stated purpose of selling French books. His real objective was to promote revolution. His plan, however, leaked out. The Austrian consul in Wallachia, Merkelius, intervened. The authorities confiscated all of Poulios Poulios's materials and books[9]. Poulios in 1797 joined a group of Polish volunteers on their way to join Napoleon's French army. His brother George took complete control of the printing shop. George continued to publish their newspaper *Efemeris* and worked closer and closer with Regas.

Regas's call to freedom found many supporters. Siatistians Konstantinos Doukas, Athanasios George Manouses—who two years earlier financed F. Ch. Baumeister's book *Logic*—Theohares George Tourountzias, and medical student Konstantinos Karakases (son of author and philosopher Demetrios) followed the Poulios brothers. The Kastorian[10] brothers John and Panagiotes Emmanouel—whose mother was Siatistian—and medical student George Konstantinou Sakellariou[11] joined in. The doctors Demetrios Nikolides and Kyritsos Polyzos from Ioannina, trader Antonios Koronios (coauthor with Regas), wholesale trader from Chios Island Efstratios Argentes, and John Karatzas from Cyprus Island followed. They all worked with Regas. So did the Vienna Hellenic community. Followers met regularly at night alternately at the Argentes, Poulios, and Theohares homes. They exchanged news and ideas on how to recruit others to join them. Austrian government servants suspected their moves. Austrian consul in Bucharest Merkelius and Ambassador in Constantinople Herbert Rathkeal notified their government of the suspicious movements of Regas and Poulios. Baumeister, however, covered Poulios and their activities. It is uncertain if he was aware of what was going on.

[9]George Laios, *Siatista and Its Commercial Houses Hadje-Michael and Manouses*, p. 92
[10]John Apostolou, *History of Siatista,* p. 21
[11]George Laios, *Siatista and Its Commercial Houses Hadje-Michael and Manouses,* p. 93

In 1797, Regas circulated a new map of Greece. It presented as Greek the region of Asia Minor and substantial Balkan areas held by the Ottomans. In December, on his way to Greece and ready for action, Regas went to Trieste. Prior to his leaving, he shipped revolutionary pamphlets and circulars to Koronios's representative in Trieste. Koronios's representative, however, was away. Demetrios Economou, entirely unfamiliar with the case, received all materials and instructions in Koronios's absence and notified the authorities. The Austrian police arrested sixteen persons. Authorities proclaimed guilt on Regas, Antonios Koronios, Efstratios Argentes, Demetrios Nikolides, John Karatzas, Theohares Tourountzias, and brothers Panagiotes and John Emmanouel. In May 1798 they turned them over to the Ottomans. A month later, in June 1798, their bodies were thrown in the Danube River from Belgrade's Neboisa tower prison. George Poulios and Konstantinos Doukas—Austrian and Russian citizens, respectively—got away with only expulsion orders from the country. The same thing happened to George Theohares, Konstantinos Toullios, Philip Petrovitz, and Kaspar Peters. The business operations of Efstratios Argentes and Athanasios Manouses continued as usual. The authorities prevented disruption of Vienna's commercial activity. The Poulios brothers' Greek daily newspaper, *Efemeris*, ceased to be published[12].

Anthimos Gazes, Vienna's Saint Georgios priest since October 1797, rekindled the revolutionary spirit. We can assume with certainty that Gazes's acquaintance and friendship with the much older and brilliant Siatistian intellectual George Zaviras strengthened his spirit of Hellenism[13] through their prolonged discussions on Hellenic values and current events. Gazes published his translation of Benjamin Martin's *Grammar of Philosophical Sciences* in 1799. In 1800, he circulated his map of Greece. He framed it with exactly the same decorations the original Regas map had. Regas's *Freedom Proclamation* called on all Balkan peoples to revolt. His poem's 128 verses included the following:

---
[12]George Laios, *Siatista and Its Commercial Houses Hadje-Michael and Manouses*, p. 97
[13]George Laios, *Siatista and Its Commercial Houses Hadje-Michael and Manouses*, p. 97

"East, West, South and North (all of us),
Should have one heart for our homeland,
Every one (to be) free to practice his own faith,
We should all run to the glory of war.
Bulgarians, Albanians, Armenians and Romans
(Greeks),
Black and white. With a common thrust,
Let us grasp our swords for our freedom."

In another part it stated:

"To light a fire in all of Ottoman Empire,
To run from Bosnia all the way to Arabia[14]."

In 1804, the Serbs revolted. Geortze Karadgeordzevic[15] led them from victory to victory. In a spirit of brotherhood many Greeks fought against the Ottomans on the Serb revolutionaries' side[16]. Nicole Apostolovica, thirty-eight-year-old son of Semlin soap manufacturer Theodore Apostolou, an artist, painted many paintings portraying the Serbs' struggle[17]. Militarily, Upper Macedonian Georgakes Olympios, married to a Serbian woman, was among the Serbs' most precious supporters. Head of Wallachia's National Guard (Wallachia and Moldavia were demilitarized regions between Russia and Ottoman Empire), Olympios displayed his gallantry in the Serbian and Greek revolutions. When Serb leader George Karadgeordzevic revolted, Olympios with a contingent of seven men[18] reported to Karadgeordgevic's chief-of-staff Velco Petrovitz[19]. Two of these men, George Zaglas and John Farmakes, were from Vlaste. George Zaglas's three brothers, Demetrios, Pavlos, and Theodore, settled earlier in Serbia's Smederovo. Zaglas's commander Vouitsa Voulitsevic commissioned him an officer for his heroic actions. His discharge from the military accompanied him with a war veteran's

---

[14]Demetres Fotiades, *The Revolution of 1821*, Vol. I, p. 201—author's translation
[15]Demetres Fotiades, *The Revolution of 1821*, Vol. I, p. 268
[16]Konstantinos Metsakis, *Macedonia Throughout the Centuries*, p. 43
[17]John A. Papadrianos, *The Greek Settlers of Semlin*, p. 109
[18]Michael Ath. Kalinderis, *Life in the Community of Vlaste During the Turkish Occupation*, p. 152
[19]Spyros D. Loukatos, *Serbs, Montenegrans and Bosnian Fighters of the Greek Revolutionary War*, Helleno-Serb Symposium, p. 101

pension[20]. Zaglas's comrade under Olympios John Stergiou Farmakes lost his brother George in a battle near Belgrade fighting with the Serbs[21]. The Farmakes brothers, sons of a prominent Vlaste family, took part in armed resistance to Ottoman authority from an early age, assisting their father. Farmakes joined Olympios in a life-long friendship and comradeship. They both fought heroically and with determination on the Serbs' side. Exactly the same resolution possessed Greek rebel chieftain Nikotsaras and his armed band operating in Macedonia. They left their base and moved north[22].

In 1806, the Serbs and the Ottomans negotiated their war. Upper Macedonians again stood by the Serbs. Petro Itzko from Katranitsa turned from a successful merchant to an effective diplomat. He negotiated with the Ottomans and gained partial autonomy for the Serbs. The treaty prohibited residence of Turks in Serbia. An Ottoman official in Belgrade had limited authority and ensured collection of an annual tributary fee[23]. In 1807, Triantafyllos Doukas from Kastoria, a Semlin-based successful merchant[24], wrote his book *History of Slaveno-Serbians*[25] in Greek, although he knew Serbian well[26]. In his 124-page poem, Doukas presented with considerable details all Serbian suffering. He described the revolution from its inception in 1804 to its termination in 1806. Poet Sima Milutinovic-Sarailia translated *History of Slaveno-Serbians* into Slavo-Serb twenty years later. Sarailia, at the time of the Serb revolution, was a student of Siatistian John G. Tourountzias at Semlin Helleno-Museum school[27]. In writing his book-length poem, Doukas attempted to not only make known the Serbs' glorious revolt but mainly to inform the Greeks of the Serbs' valor and achievements.

[20]Michael Ath. Kalinderis, *Life in the Community of Vlaste During the Turkish Occupation*, p. 159
[21]Michael Ath. Kalinderis, *Life in the Community of Vlaste During the Turkish Occupation*, p. 149
[22]Spyros D. Loukatos, *Serbs, Montenegrans and Bosnian Fighters of the Greek Revolutionary War*, Helleno-Serb Symposium, p. 101
[23]John A. Papadrianos, *The Greek Settlers of Semlin*, p. 200
[24]John A. Papadrianos, *The Greek Settlers of Semlin*, p. 67
[25]John A. Papadrianos, *The Greek Settlers of Semlin*, p. 197
[26]John A. Papadrianos, *The History of the Slaveno-Serbs by Triantafyllos Doukas from Kastoria and Its Significance*, Helleno-Serb Symposium, p. 279
[27]John A. Papadrianos, *The Greek Settlers of Semlin*, p. 201

Undoubtedly, he hoped to stir up Greek nationalism by presenting their gallantry.

The war-like instability continued throughout the Balkan Peninsula. In Mt. Olympus, priest Efthimios Vlahavas arranged in early 1808 a conference of all area rebel leaders. Russian experts attached to Serb revolutionaries were present. They planned to coordinate their action for May 1808[28]. Up to that time, armed groups acted independently in most Greek mountains. In 1812, many of these bands clashed with Ottoman troops in an effort to relieve pressure on the Serbs[29]. The same year Theodore Kyritsas, younger son of Semlin ex-mayor John Kyritsas from Bogatsiko from 1803 to 1807, attempted to flee to Bucharest. He intended to join the Russian army. The Austrian authorities, informed of his plans, arrested him and threw him in jail[30]. The Ottomans finally were able to put down the Serbian revolt in 1813. The Serbs' main suppliers of food and ammunition were Semlin-based Greek wholesale merchants Vomvas, Hadje-Bakis, Dimitrievitch, Konstantinos Hadios[31], and Wallachia-based Greek merchant Hadje-Giannouses from Epirus. Wallachia's governor Konstantinos Ipsilantis, whose son Alexander accepted leadership of the Greek revolutionaries in 1820, did everything possible to help the Serbians. The burden, however, fell heavily on the Serbian people and the responsibility exclusively on their leadership.

The new Serbian leader Milos Obrenovic looked for diplomatic assistance from John Kapodistrias, a Greek hailing from Corfu Island[32] serving as Russian Foreign Minister for European affairs. Kapodistrias supported the independence of all small occupied countries, especially in the Balkans, contrary to the foreign ministers of England and Austria, Castelreagh and Metternich, respectively. Obrenovic utilized in his service another Greek from Zagori, Epirus. George Popovic Celes (Greek

[28]Michael Ath. Kalinderis, *Life in the Community of Vlaste During the Turkish Occupation*, p. 153
[29]Konstantinos Metsakis, *Macedonia Throughout the Centuries*, p. 44
[30]John A. Papadrianos, *The Greek Settlers of Semlin*, p. 92
[31]Slavko Gavrilovic, *The Greek and Koutsovlach Natives of Macedonia and Merchants of Semlin*, Helleno-Serb Symposium, p. 266
[32]Spyros D. Loucatos, *Serbs, Montenegrans and Bosnian Fighters of the Greek Revolutionary War*, Helleno-Serb Symposium, p. 102

name George Papazoglou) originally settled in Wallachia working for his hometown friend, an earlier settler. In 1814, assisting his boss in animal trading he went to Vanato. His brother Mathew and a married sister lived in close-by Panchevo. Papazoglou left his friend and went to work for Retzep-agha, at Antakale (Orsovo). Retzep-agha detecting Papazoglou's capabilities, sent him on a mission to Milos Obrenovic. He was to detect how Obrenovic felt about a possible alliance with him for the purpose of fighting the central Ottoman government. Obrenovic disagreed with the idea presented but, impressed by Papazoglou, offered him employment. Papazoglou's education back home prepared him for key positions most educated Greeks enjoyed in the service of Ottoman and other European powers. They served as secretaries, teachers, doctors, and advisers at all governmental levels. From these positions they assisted the Greek revolutionary effort.

Papazoglou's knowledge of Serbian, Albanian, Greek, and Turkish languages was put to good use by Obrenovic, who appointed Papazoglou a member of his government in 1815[33]. The Serbs' second revolution had just broken out. With its termination the Serbs won another important concession from the Ottomans. A national advisory body established in Belgrade handled all taxation and judicial matters. Papazoglou filled the multilingual civil servant position requirement. Multitalented Papazoglou was also familiar with the Turkish mentality. Milos Obrenovic respected Papazoglou's honesty, devotion, and integrity. He kept him as personal friend and adviser. In 1816, Obrenovic appointed Papazoglou as interpreter and member of the negotiating committee sent to Constantinople to negotiate financial and taxation matters. In 1817 Papazoglou administered the Belgrade Treasury. His appointment in 1820 as leader of the fourth delegation to Constantinople, however, solidified his success. Papazoglou's assistants were Paul Stetenovic and Savvas Liotits. Their objective was to request appointment of an Ottoman commissioner empowered to evaluate Serbian feelings. The delegation requested in writing freedom in administering its domestic affairs, expansion of its border jurisdiction, and

---

[33]George Voures, *George Papazoglou from Epirus at the Service of Serbia's Ruler Milos Obrenovic,* Helleno-Serb Symposium, pp. 253-260

establishment of a flat, specific annual payment to the Sultan's government. They compromised in the appointment of the Ottoman representative. Greater autonomy and border jurisdiction had to wait. Commissioner of Serbia Mehmed Essad accompanied the delegation back to Belgrade.

Papazoglou, and Itzkos in 1806, Greek merchants-turned-diplomats, served Serbia's interests well. Their contributions were in accordance with Regas Fereos's revolutionary spirit of reducing Ottoman authority. Serbia gained her independence with the Russian-Ottoman war of 1878[34]. Serbs' pressures benefited the Greek revolutionary cause. Serbia prevented total confrontation with the Ottomans by accepting partial gains. A contrary development could have caused complete reorganization of the Ottoman forces. The Serbs' revolutions enhanced the maturity of the Balkan peoples. Greek revolutionaries could count on Serbian people's assistance. Papazoglou, who maintained constant touch with the Greek revolutionaries, married John Farmakes's widow Alexandra, in his second marriage. A drunken Turk mistakenly killed him in 1825. Obrenovic and the Serbian people respectfully honored Papazoglou's services to Serbia. The Serbian and Greek leaders once again realized the necessity of Balkan cooperation preached by most intellectuals and Regas Fereos.

---

[34] Demetres Fotiades, *The Revolution of 1821*, Vol. IV, p. 272

Bronze presentation of Alexander the Great published be Regas Fereos to remind Hellenes of their ancestor's glory.
Photo from *Kathemerine* newspaper, March 21, 1998.

Decorations around Regas Fereo's map of Greece in 1797 prior to Greece's war for Independence of 1821.

Photo from *Kathermerine* newspaper, May 14, 1995.

PART D
Chapter 19
Greek Revolution

Adamantios Koraes, a Greek from Chian parents living in the city of Smyrne in Asia Minor (presently Turkey's Izmir) and an admirer of French poet and philosopher Voltaire, took up the torch of freedom. Koraes studied at Montpellier, France, and became a doctor. He settled in Paris in 1787 and died there in 1833. He witnessed the French revolutionaries' struggles and received from them a lasting impression. Enthused by Fereos's teachings and shocked by the loss of lives in Belgrade in 1798, he wrote in 1800 his *Call to War*, addressing all Greeks to fight the barbarian tyrants of Greece[1]. Koraes's correspondence with Greek intellectuals at home and in Diaspora reminded them of the achievements attained by Hellenes prior to Ottoman and Roman periods. He successfully led the reorientation of Greek thought towards ancient Greece. The names of ancient Hellenic generals and heroes like Hercules, Agamemnon, Achilles, Aristides, and Themistocles often replaced the family Christian names in children. The same thing happened with the names of almost all Greek merchant marine vessels that instantly turned into warships as soon as the revolution broke out in 1821[2].

Greeks and Philhellenes formed social clubs and associations to promote their revolutionary spirit. Siatistians relocated their efforts from Vienna to Paris. Siatistian Gregory Zalikes, brainchild of Zosimas's spirit of Hellenism[3] through his parents, responded to Koraes's *Call to War* and to a speech Koraes delivered in January 1803 in Paris. The two men reinforced each other's views. They lived in the same Greek community. Zalikes's translation into Modern Greek of Jean-Jacques Rousseau's (1712–1778) *Contract with Society* certainly met Koraes's approval. With Zalikes's initiative, several intellectuals formed the "Greek Language Hotel" club in Paris in 1809. The club's purpose was liberation of Greece. Thoroughly familiar

---
[1]Demetres Fotiades, *The Revolution of 1821*, Vol. IV, p. 304
[2]Demetres Fotiades, *The Revolution of 1821*, Vol. II, p. 182
[3]Demetres Fotiades, *The Revolution of 1821*, Vol. I, p. 236

with Vienna's events a few years earlier where his hometown Siatistians lost their lives along with their leader Regas, Zalikes and his four friends formed the organizing committee. They adopted secret procedures in order to protect the club's members. One member of the organizing committee was Athanasios Tsakalof[4], the cofounder five years later of the most effective secret revolutionary organization of Diaspora's Greeks. Many of these secretive procedures became part of Filike Etaireia (Friendly Society). The members of the "Greek Language Hotel," both Greek and prominent French personalities, gathered every Sunday in various hotel rooms to discuss politics. French archaeologist and diplomat Choiseul-Gouffier presided over this movement. Apparently the French government approved its activities. This prevented its expansion to international levels.

In 1810, Eastern Orthodox Metropolitan Ignatios of Bucharest established the Philological Society[5]. The Hellenic spirit of the community found an outlet and dared play its role for further progress. Bucharest's thriving Greek community gave it its unconditional support. Ignatios's effort, although it remained localized, encouraged Anthimos Gazes[6], Vienna's priest and spiritual leader, to carry it further. In 1811, guided by Vienna's events and Siatistian intellectual George Zaviras's enthusiasm, he organized and published in Vienna his magazine *Logios Hermes*. Its first issue included a report of the Greek school "Lyceum of Bucharest" graduation exercises of that year. Metropolitan Ignatios's presentation of the achievement awards to top performers strengthened the students' respect and devotion. The thirteen-year-old Siatistian student Thomas received the top award[7] for his excellence in physics and the Russian language. His Siatistian friend, student Demetrios Pavlou, shared his happiness. *Logios Hermes* continued publication even after Gazes's departure from Vienna. Theokletos Farmakides and Konstantinos Kokkinakes successfully promoted its objectives. Kokkinakes steadfastly carried it through its last two years (1819 to 1821).

[4]Demetres Fotiades, *The Revolution of 1821*, Vol. I, p. 244. Tsakalof's father, a furrier from Ioannina, resided in Moscow and sent his son to Paris to attend its University.
[5]George Laios, *Siatista and Its Commercial Houses Hadje-Michael and Manouses,* p. 98
[6]George Laios, *Siatista and Its Commercial Houses Hadje-Michael and Manouses,* p. 97
[7]George Laios, *Siatista and Its Commercial Houses Hadje-Michael and Manouses,* p. 98

All above efforts failed to enthuse the great masses to the extent Regas Fereos did fifteen years ago. In 1814, Athanasios Tsakalof of Paris's "Greek Language Hotel" club met Nickolaos Skoufas and Emmanuel Xanthos in Odessa, Russia. The three discussed his involvement in the Paris club and its secretive procedures. Xanthos volunteered to Tsakalof and Skoufas the secrecy procedures he acquainted himself with as a Mason[8]. The three evaluated the situation and quickly concluded freedom could only be attained with God's blessing, but only by the Greeks' own efforts. A massive organization encompassing all influential Greeks in Diaspora was necessary. They formed "Filike Etaireia," a Masonic-type secret brotherhood society. Their call to fellow Greeks brought immediate results. Store owners and clerks, wholesale merchants, ship owners, teachers, clergy, military officers serving with other nations' armed forces, armed band leaders operating in Greek mountains, and local archons of occupied Greece responded. Their common denominator was absolute devotion to their cause of freedom. They joined and swore to God to take their secret to their grave. Extremely few recruits became unworthy of their oath. Some contributed more than others. Many donated all of their wealth. Many more gave their lives. Anthimos Gazes joined the governing body of the Filike Etaireia[9]. Demetrios Vatikiotis, a Greek officer in the Russian army with a capability to command fourteen thousand Bulgarians, joined in 1817[10]. Filike Etaireia officers approached fighters Georgakes Olympios and John Farmakes and revealed to them their plan[11]. They enthusiastically joined. Olympios revealed their action to their brother-in-arms Serb legendary revolutionist Geordge Karadgeordgevic. He instantly agreed to organize all Serbs and revolt against the Ottomans' rule in conjunction with the Greeks' revolt. Karadgeordgevic took the Filike Etaireia oath at the home of Konstantinos Ipsilantis, in the presence of Georgakes Olympios[12].

[8]Demetres Fotiades, *The Revolution of 1821*, Vol. I, p. 239. Establishment of "Filike Etaireia" was Xanthou's idea.
[9]Demetres Fotiades, *The Revolution of 1821*, Vol. IV, p. 295
[10]Demetres Fotiades, *The Revolution of 1821*, Vol. I, p. 268
[11]Michael Ath. Kalinderis, *Life in the Community of Vlaste During the Turkish Occupation*, p. 154
[12]Demetres Fotiades, *The Revolution of 1821*, Vol. I, p. 269. Konstantinos Ipsilantis was a governor of Wallachia and Moldavia. In the Russian-Ottoman was of 1806, he sided with Russia and at the end of the war he settled in Kiev.

They all concurred the revolution should begin in Serbia and Peloponnese simultaneously.

Recruitment of important personalities continued. John Farmakes's attempt in 1818 to enlist the membership of Ecumenical Patriarch Gregory V failed. The Patriarch, living in exile at the Mt. Athos Holy Community, hoped to return to his throne in Constantinople. He managed to return three years later, but the Ottomans hanged him at the Patriarchate's door when the revolution broke out. The Patriarch's answer to Farmakes was, "My membership should be taken for granted. Either way I am in[13]." The original three cofounders of Filike Etaireia sought a capable and influential individual for its top position. John Kapodistrias, Russia's Foreign Minister, perhaps after a thorough evaluation, thought he could best serve the cause by declining the offer[14]. He turned down Emmanuel Xanthos's offer in 1820[15]. Alexander Ipsilantis, Russian Army officer and a Mason since 1810[16], accepted the offer[17]. He was one of four brothers, sons of Wallachia governor Konstantinos Ipsilantis, all Russian army officers. Alexander was a graduate of Russia's Military Academy class of 1810[18] and was idealistic and brave. He already suffered the loss of his right arm fighting France's general Napoleon. Alexander Ipsilantis took over and directed the revolution until 1821.

Volunteers from all Balkan nationalities responded to Ipsilantis's call. A force of sixty-five hundred troops gathered by March 31, 1821. Only two thousand of them were Greeks. The remaining included Albanians, Bulgarians, Kozacs, Moldavians, Serbs, Wallachs, and others[19]. About one-fourth of them were unarmed. Among their leaders were Georgakes Olympios and John Farmakes. Serb general Mladen served under Kantakouzenos's command in Wallachia[20]. Ipsilantis with his advisers, his own

[13] Asemakes A. Kardases, *Demetsana*, p. 44
[14] Helen Koukkou, John Kapodistrias, "One Thousand Years of Hellenism in Russia," International Chamber of Commerce, p. 207. One of his assignments was to look into Brazil's acquisition of Uruguay, contrary to USA and England's desires.
[15] Demetres Fotiades, *The Revolution of 1821*, Vol. I, p. 300
[16] Demetres Fotiades, *The Revolution of 1821*, Vol. I, p. 302
[17] Demetres Fotiades, *The Revolution of 1821*, Vol. I, p. 307
[18] Demetres Fotiades, *The Revolution of 1821*, Vol. I, p. 310
[19] Demetres Fotiades, *The Revolution of 1821*, Vol. I, p. 413
[20] Demetres Fotiades, *The Revolution of 1821*, Vol. I, p. 438. George Kantakouzenos was battalion commander in the Russian army and friend of Ipsilantis.

brothers George and Nickolaos, Dr. George Typaldos, and George Lassanes from Kozane, made their decision in February 1821. Twenty-four-year-old Lassanes was a teacher in Odessa's Hellenic Commercial School[21]. His parents and grandparents implanted in him Zosimas's and Voulgaris's Hellenic values and liberal views. He wrote many patriotic and inspiring plays while serving his teaching position. He joined Filike Etaireia and promoted its cause[22].

Georgakes Olympios, who—as chief of Wallachia's governor's Guard—helped Theodore Vladimiresku rise to power, convinced him to join them in the revolt. Vladimiresku joined and entered Craiova, capital of Small Wallachia, on March 1. He met Olympios and Farmakes, whose troops advanced and entered Bucharest. Ipsilantis reorganized his troops. He appointed George Lassanes second-in-command and Athanasios Tsakalof[23] his liaison for the Holy battalion, just formed mainly from untrained college students. In Vessaravia Montenegrins, Serbs and others formed an All-Balkan brigade. Karadgeordgevic's ex-guard commander Anastase Dimitrevic commanded 105 Serbs[24]. Serb Stephan Zivkovic, who in his youth worked for an Upper Macedonian fur family in Belgrade, learned the skilled craftsmanship and the Greek language, mentality, and culture. He fought in the Serbian revolutions under Karadgeordgevic and Obrenovic. In 1821, he joined the Greek Revolutionaries[25]. Greek George Kontopoulos's unit in Moldavia-Wallachia included twenty-five Serbs. In May 1821, authorities at Galatsi, Moldavia, killed about one hundred Greeks and two hundred Moldavians who favored the revolution[26].

The first major battle of Ipsilantis's army took place at Dragatsani, north of the River Danube and the town of Craiova.

[21]Konstantinos K. Papoulides, "The Greeks of Russia in the 19th and Beginning of 20th Century", International Chamber of Commerce, p. 230
[22]Demetres Fotiades, *The Revolution of 1821*, Vol. I, p. 415
[23]Anthanasios Tsakalof was the only one of the three founding Filike Etaireia members who actually fought in the war.
[24]Spyros D. Loucatos, *Serbs, Montenegrans and Bosnian Fighter of the Greek Revolutionary War*, Helleno-Serb Symposium, p. 103
[25]Anthanasios E. Karathanases, *Stefan Zivkovic and the Greek Family Douzes*, Helleno-Serb Symposium, p. 247
[26]Demetres Fotiades, *The Revolution of 1821*, Vol. IV. p. 325

It was June 7, 1821, less than four months from the beginning of hostilities. Ipsilantis's small force suffered a devastating defeat. Bravery under no circumstances can overcome lack of discipline[27]. The Holy Battalion, or remnants of it, dispersed left and right. Swiss volunteer Verntie fell along with most of the young students-turned-soldiers. Ipsilantis with his two brothers, George Lassanes, Polish battalion commander Ventsel Hornofski, Gerasimos Orfanos, and Kavaleropoulos, Ipsilantis's personal attendant, sought refuge in Austria. On July 14, 1821, the Austrian authorities changed heart, captured them, and sent them to jail[28]. They stayed in prison for six years. Their release on November 22, 1827[29], stipulated requirement for permission to leave Austria. Ipsilantis, demolished physically and mentally, died on January 31, 1828. Ipsilantis's Serb General Mladen, who commanded Kozacs and others in the battle, left his comrades for Serbia. His performance disappointed Serbian ruler Obrenovic, who killed him[30].

Olympios and Farmakes survived the calamity at Dragatsani. Chased by Ottoman forces they kept on fighting. After three months' struggle, they secured themselves at Seku's monastery. The odds were against them. They fought valiantly, however, to achieve two objectives. First they hoped to engage the Ottoman forces as long as possible, causing them extensive losses, and second they wanted to give a chance to other revolutionary forces in the Greek mainland to organize. They succeeded. Olympios and his comrades finally blew themselves up on September 8, 1821, by setting fire in the powder supply depot of Seku Monastery, their stronghold[31]. The Ottomans butchered to death most of the remaining defenders.

---

[27]Demetres Fotiades, *The Revolution of 1821*, Vol. I, p. 426. Contrary to specific orders by Ipsilantis and Olympios, V. Karavias prompted the battle while he was drunk.

[28]Demetres Fotiades, *The Revolution of 1821*, Vol. I, p. 430. Austria ignored the false docu ments given to Ipsilantis by Transylvania permitting their travel to America.

[29]Demetres Fotiades, *The Revolution of 1821*, Vol. I, p. 433. Ipsilantis's remains are presently interred in the park grounds of a small church located close to the lower end of Alexandras's Avenue in Athens.

[30]Demetres Fotiades, *The Revolution of 1821*, Vol. I, p. 445

[31]Demetres Fotiades, *The Revolution of 1821*, Vol. I, p. 447. The defenders surrendered at Austrian Wolf's mediation but Ottoman promises for safety were not kept. They sent Farmakes to Sultan for his execution.

Fighting the Ottoman troops in Wallachia all summer of 1821 gave a breathing spell to the revolutionaries everywhere else. Ali Pasha[32], the Ottoman Governor of Epirus at Ioannina, continued his defiance of Sultan's central government. Ipsilantis's envoys, visiting other regions within the empire and many European cities, brought positive results. John Kolokotrones's forces, supported by Siatistians Sachines and Sfekas at his side, defended their position at Nochetu[33] monastery in Wallachia. His cousin Theodore Kolokotronis, one thousand miles away at Valtetsi, Peloponnese, defeated the Ottoman forces in May. In September, the day Olympios blew up Seku's monastery, killing himself and his comrades, Theodore Kolokotronis captured the fort of Tripolis, Peloponnese's capital. Serb commander Hadje-Christos Dagovic and his unit, made up of Serb and Bulgarian salaried volunteers in the service of Hoursit Pasha, defended the fort. Kolokotronis's persuasive powers made Hadje-Christos switch allegiance and become an invaluable ally of the Greek Revolutionaries[34]. Hadje-Christos Dagovic turned over to the revolutionaries approximately twelve thousand much-needed rifles, swords, pistols, and thirteen big containers with all precious items the Turks of Tripolis accumulated for centuries. The revolutionaries' morale skyrocketed.

Expatriate Greeks within and outside the Ottoman Empire intermingled with all Balkan nationalities in time of peace. Wartime conditions had the same effect, only with greater devotion and determination. Greeks fought under non-Greek leaders and officers and vice-versa. Ipsilantis's brother Demetrios, taking leave from the Russian army, was able to leave Kiev and reach Greece. He continued his brother's mission. He repeatedly led his troops to battle. Kontopoulos's force with his Serb volunteers moved south from Moldavia and fought in the mainland, defending Messolonghi. Serb leader Stephan Nivitsa led a formidable unit of 250 men composed of all nationalities, including Greeks[35]. Nivista operated under the French Philhellene officer Fabvier who

---

[32] Ali Pasha was trying to form his own state.
[33] Demetres Fotiades, *The Revolution of 1821*, Vol. I, p. 422. Family names Sachines and Sfekas are found in Siatista even today.
[34] Spyros D. Loucatos, *Serb, Montenegran and Bosnian Fighters of the Greek Revolutionary War*, p. 105
[35] Spyros D. Loucatos, *Serb, Montenegran and Bosnian Fighters of the Greek Revolutionary War*, p. 107

provided his troops' logistic support also. Fabvier's "Crusaders" had their own flag. Vasos Mavrovouniotes (translated Montenegrin)[36] with his brothers and relatives, living at the time in Asia Minor, formed their own group and arrived to join the revolutionaries. Their successes in the island of Evvoia were significant.

Hadje-Christos Dagovic[37], Mavrovouniotes, and most Albanians, Bulgarians, Montenegrins, Serbs, and other fighters carried the spirit of Hellenism. They felt 100 percent Greek. The first two became generals of Greece's tactical forces. Stephan and Anastase Dimitrevic[38] each led one-thousand-man units. Several others commanded smaller fighting units. Hadje-Christos led his troops in the all-important battle of Dervenakia[39] in July 1822 under Theodore Kolokotronis. He did the same seven years later in June 1829 with his cavalry near Thebes. His compatriot at home wholeheartedly approved his activities. Serb author Jovan Sterija Popovic, son of a Greek father and Serb mother, published in 1825 his collection of Regas Fereos's and Adamantios Koraes's poetry, plus other freedom-loving works entitled *Sevenfold Flower to Fighting Greeks*[40].

The Greeks' enormous sacrifices, stamina, and heroic struggle attracted worldwide attention and interest. Dr. Epites, Ipsilantis's personal envoy to Germany, met Theirsius in Munich[41]. Theirsius wrote in the widely circulated newspaper of the city of Augsburg. The German public opinion's response was prompt and favorable. Philhellene Germans formed a committee in Stuttgart for assistance of the Greeks. Recruitment by their Philhellenic committee of volunteers followed. Within a short time, in the fall of 1821, about two hundred German soldiers landed near Argos in Peloponnese. They participated in Nafplion's blockade. Philhellene committees also formed in

---

[36]Spyros D. Loucatos, *Serb, Montenegran and Bosnian Fighters of the Greek Revolutionary War*, p. 104
[37]Hadje-Christos dropped his last name Dagovic utilizing only Hadje-Christos.
[38]Spyros D. Loucatos, *Serb, Montenegran and Bosnian Fighters of the Greek Revolutionary War*, p. 108
[39]Demetres Fotiades, *The Revolution of 1821*, Vol. II, p. 261. Demetrios Ipsilantis troops participated in this battle.
[40]Vasilije Krestic, *On Some Echoes of Greek Instructions in Serbian Literature*, Helleno-Serb Symposium, p. 268
[41]Demetres Fotiades, *The Revolution of 1821*, Vol. II, p. 176. The German people resisted Austrian Metternich's efforts against their national unity.

Dresden, Dusseldorf, Hamburg, and other cities. Dr. Epites's efforts met with an enthusiastic response in France as well. Its public opinion forced unfriendly-to-the-cause Sautauvriant, minister of foreign affairs, to switch sides. He became a staunch supporter of the Greek revolutionaries. A strong Philhellene movement, "Le Reveil du Philhellenisme," prevailed in France. British public opinion led by important personalities forced a similar change in the attitude of the British government. British Foreign Minister Lord Castlereach, an enemy of the revolutionaries, committed suicide. The Ottomans' destruction of Chios Island and the atrocities incurred in many sites of Greece caused foreign observers to sympathize with the Greek people. The government of Haiti was the first to recognize the Greek nation in January 1822[42]. The U.S. Senate rejected Daniel Webster's proposal for recognition in December 1823, but the United States of America became the second country to recognize the Greek revolution. President James Monroe declared strict neutrality. He sympathized with the Greeks' revolution; however, in order to keep out European intervention in America, he would not intervene in European affairs[43].

British Lord Byron adored Hellenism from his Cambridge University days. Years earlier in 1812, his poem "Child Harold" elevated ancient Spartan Leonidas and his three hundred men for their gallant stand against the Persians at Thermopylae. Byron mourned the status of the Greek nation at the time, eloquently expressing his feelings about Greece in several poems, among them "Maid of Athens," "Age of Bronze," "Unhappy Greece," and "Curse of Minerva." The last verses of his poem "Don Zouan" state:

> *"The Moslem Orphan (Greece) went with her protector,*
> *For she was homeless, houseless, helpless: all*
> *Her friends, like the sad family of Hector,*
> *Had perished in the field or by the wall:*
> *Her very place of birth was but a spectre*
> *Of what it had been; there—the muezzin's call*
> *To prayer was heard no more. – And Juan wept,*
> *And made a vow to shield her, which he kept*[44]*."*

---
[42]Demetres Fotiades, *The Revolution of 1821,* Vol. II, p. 179. Haiti had just won her independence from Spain.
[43]Demetres Fotiades, *The Revolution of 1821,* Vol. II, p. 172
[44]J. W. Lake, *The Works of Lord Byron,* Vol. II, p. 430

In July 1823, George Gordon Byron left Genoa for Greece. He had with him Edward Trelawney, Prince Pietro Gamba, his personal assistant Fletcher, and money[45]. He lent half of his money to the Greek government. His destination was blockaded Messologhi, arriving there the day before Christmas[46]. He formed at his own expense a military force of 225 men, made up from Souliotes, a region of mountainous Epirus, and foreigners. His associate Pietro Gamba published in Italian, German, French, and English the newspaper *Telegrapho Greco*. Byron strengthened his unit with a rocket expert, William Pary, and his eight English technicians and four officers, sent to him by London's Philhellene Committee. Two of the officers were English, one German and one Swede[47]. Byron did not live, however, to enjoy the results of his efforts. In April 1824, after a short illness and less than four months in the battlefield, he died[48] of pneumonia. Greeks honored Byron, and they continue to honor him even today. Philhellenes honored him by following his example. It was the best and most effective way to offset the presence of Western officers employed by Ottoman forces[49].

Ordinary men and officers poured into Greece to help. Several were employed by the government. The majority came voluntarily, guided by their own conscience. Among the Italian volunteers, Joseph Kiappe published his own newspaper in Hydra Island. Battalion commander Tarella took over command in April 1822. Giusti served as intelligence officer, informing the Greek government in February 1824 from Alexandria, Egypt, about Mohammed Ali's preparations to invade Greece[50]. Army Engineer Ratzieri sacrificed his life in Messolonghi attempting to reinforce its defenses. Danish Philhellene prince Kanelen and Prussian Eunemast were killed at the battle of Epate[51]. English artillery

---

[45] Demetres Fotiades, *The Revolution of 1821*, Vol. II, p. 354. Lord Byron, liberal intellectual in conservative England, traveled to Malta and Greece since 1809. He worked for Iraly's independence since 1816 prior to arriving to Greece.
[46] Demetres Fotiades, *The Revolution of 1821*, Vol. IV, p. 357
[47] Demetres Fotiades, *The Revolution of 1821*, Vol. IV, p. 358
[48] Demetres Fotiades, *The Revolution of 1821*, Vol. II, p. 381. Byron refused Samuel Burt's offer to have him recuperate at Zakynthos Island. He felt obligated to stay by his comrades at blockaded Messolonghi.
[49] Demetres Fotiades, *The Revolution of 1821*, Vol. IV, p. 120
[50] Demetres Fotiades, *The Revolution of 1821*, Vol. IV, p. 359
[51] Demetres Fotiades, *The Revolution of 1821*, Vol. IV, p. 339

officer Fenton, author Edward Trellowney, nineteen-year-old Whitcombe, battalion commander Urquhart, and Ch. Fallen did their best. Admiral Frangiscus Abney Hastings also fought in Messolonghi[52]. All Philhellene volunteers honored Greece, themselves, and Lord Byron. Swiss doctor John Mayer, who published his Greek daily Hellenic Chronicles in blockaded Messolonghi,[53] died assisting with Messolonghi's attempt to break the blockade. Hungarian cavalry training expert Kameron taught his techniques to fighter/leader Odysseus Androutsos. Swede officer Sass, sent to Lord Byron by London's Philhellenic Committee, fell from a Souliote soldier's bullet[54] for unknown reason. Their comradeship, however, prevailed. Frenchman Carol Fabvier, ex-officer of Napoleon's army, in 1823 added his own love for freedom to the Greek's all-out enthusiasm. In 1825 the Greek government authorized him to reorganize its tactical forces[55]. French volunteer general Dancelle and General Maison[56], chief commander of France's Expeditionary Force in Greece, brought their experience and liberalism from Napoleon's campaigns. They devoted themselves to the cause and fought for its success[57]. The German volunteers proved equally valuable. Experienced army engineers Stilltzberg and Delawney were essential for blockaded Messolonghi's defenses[58] while general Karol Norman and Johann B. Heise[59], a seaman from Hamburg, fell in the battle of Peta on July 16, 1822. Dr. Trieber, who served the needs of the revolution from 1822, settled permanently in Greece serving as chief surgeon of the armed forces[60].

The absence of coordination among the numerous local and Philhellene armed groups added to personal antitheses. The diversified ground forces with no central control became disobedient and engulfed the well-disciplined and experienced naval forces as well. As victory seemed near, the diplomacy of

[52]Demetres Fotiades, *The Revolution of 1821*, Vol. IV, p. 62
[53]Demetres Fotiades, *The Revolution of 1821*, Vol. II, p. 371
[54]Demetres Fotiades, *The Revolution of 1821*, Vol. II, p. 370
[55]Demetres Fotiades, *The Revolution of 1821*, Vol. III, p. 311
[56]Demetres Fotiades, *The Revolution of 1821*, Vol. IV, p. 101
[57]Demetres Fotiades, *The Revolution of 1821*, Vol. IV, p. 107. The French government promoted him to Chief Army Commander.
[58]Demetres Fotiades, *The Revolution of 1821*, Vol. III, p. 159
[59]George G. Arnakis, "Americans in the Greek Revolution," *George Jarvis*, p. 6
[60]Demetres Fotiades, *The Revolution of 1821*, Vol. II, p. 378, note 81

Europe's big powers, England, France, Austria, and Russia, compounded the problem. Many non-Greek officers took command of the Greek forces. Thomas Cochrane's appointment by the Greek parliament as "First Admiral of All Naval Forces of Greece" in March 1827 disappointed many patriot fighters[61]. English Richard Church, another ex-Napoleon officer known to Theodore Kolokotronis from his service during the British Reserve Battalion days in the Ionian Islands in 1809, was the second to receive a top post by the same body. The nation's representatives made him Chief Commander of all land forces in Greece in April 1827[62]. The provisional Greek parliament a day later elected John Kapodistrias to head the first government of Greece. Kapodistias's opponents within Greece and in Europe debated his Kapodistrian administration. Civil strife led to extremities and to Kapodistria's assassination in September 1831[63]. Portuguese officer Almeida[64] was guard commander at Nafplion at the time opposition killers gunned him down in front of Nafplion's Saint Spyridon church. Kapodistrias worked out a plan for implementation upon termination of hostilities in Greece. He forwarded it to Russia's Czar Nickolaos for consideration and hopefully, adoption. Russia completely ignored Kapodistrias's plan. She obviously favored the Ottomans' presence in the Balkans.

Kapodistrias' plan called for creation of five autonomous states under one central government. He earmarked Constantinople as its capital. Below are the five states he proposed:

1. Dacia, to include Moldavia and Wallachia.
2. Serbia, to include Serbia, Bosnia, Herzegovina, and Western Bulgaria.
3. Macedonia, to include Thrace and Macedonia.
4. Epirus, to include Epirus and Albania.
5. Hellas, to include all remaining areas the Ottomans occupied in Europe, including all Aegean Islands.

[61] Demetres Fotiades, *The Revolution of 1821*, Vol. III, p. 330
[62] Demetres Fotiades, *The Revolution of 1821*, Vol. IV, p. 398
[63] Demetres Fotiades, *The Revolution of 1821*, Vol. IV, p. 249
[64] Demetres Fotiades, *The Revolution of 1821*, Vol. IV, p. 257

Constantinople with Eastern Bulgaria would seat the Federation's central government[65]. Kapodistrias liked the U.S. geographical arrangements and political system in existence and attempted to duplicate it in the Balkans.

Foreign volunteers in the Greek revolution included many Americans. George G. Arnakis prepared a detailed account of George Jarvis's diary, published by the Institute of Balkan Studies in Salonica in 1965. Jarvis, the first known American volunteer, arrived in Greece on April 3, 1822. His diary reveals the impact the revolution had on the world's intellectuals and youth. J. P. Miller of Vermont arrived in Greece on November 26, 1824, after forty-five days of travel from Boston to Malta. Miller's account of George Jarvis is quoted below:

> "*George Jarvis is a son of Benjamin Jarvis of New York who held a situation under the United States government at the Hague. His son George was born in Germany and received his education there. Possessed of an uncommonly strong constitution and great energy of character, he engaged in the Greek struggle in 1822, since which time he has pushed himself forward as a guerrilla soldier to the rank of Brigadier-General. He has numerous friends among the Greeks, but few among the Philhellenes owing to his entering fully into all the prejudices of the Greeks. He has probably seen more fighting and undergone more hardships than any foreigner who has taken part in this contest, having been frequently sick and wounded*[66]."

J. P. Miller's own record is noteworthy. A commissioned colonel, Miller distinguished himself as a brave and efficient officer. He rendered every material service to the Greek people by securing several vessels laden with provisions and clothing, donated by U.S. citizens for the benefit of the destitute Greeks. Upon his return home in Montpelier, Vermont, Miller brought his adopted son, a Greek orphan found in the abandoned town of Laviadia soon after a battle had taken place within its streets[67]. Son Lucas Miltiades Miller, constantly reminded of his ancestry

---
[65]Demetres Fotiades, *The Revolution of 1821*, Vol. IV, p. 178
[66]Demetres Georgiades Arnakis, *Americans in the Greek Revolution*, p. XXIII
[67]George P. Perros, "The First Greek in Congress," *The Ahepan*, Fall 1998, p. 19

through his middle name (an army general in ancient Athens), became a U.S. citizen and studied law. In 1846 he settled in Oshkosh, Wisconsin, where Governor Dodge appointed him colonel. L. M. Miller entered politics and in 1853 won a seat in the Wisconsin legislature. He became a commissioner of the State Board of Public Works and served as chairman of the Winnebago County Board of Supervisors for ten years prior to his election to the U.S. Congress. He served in the House of Representatives, probably the first Greek American to do so, from 1891 to 1893 prior to his retirement. He died in 1902.

Swiss citizen Henry Fornezy published a list showing 319 volunteer Philhellenes that died on the side of the Greek revolutionaries. Johann Wolfgang von Goethe translated six Greek folk songs from the unpublished collection of Werner von Haxthausen[68]. The collection was a gift to Haxthausen from Siatistian Theodore Manouses who learned these songs from his grandmother Alexandra, a Zosimas-era Siatistian. Theodore Manouses's devotion to the Greek revolution landed him in jail. The Austrians forbade his exit from the country until 1826[69].

Siatistian intellectual Nickolaos Kasomoules, who was born in Kozane and lived in Diaspora for ten years, returned to Siatista as soon as the revolution broke out. Upon his return he gathered information from three different contacts, including Thessaly and Chalkidike, regarding fighting developments. Movements of Ottoman troops through Kozane and Siatista on their way to Ioannina to fight Ali-Pasha's dissension to his central government increased Siatistians' concern[70]. Prominent citizens Demetrios Hadje-Michael, George Nioplios[71], Naoum K. Iatrou from Moschopolis (Siatistian son-in-law)—who served as secretary and adviser to Ottoman officials in prior years—and others met under Metropolitan Ioannikios. The times were critical. Prudent decisions and delicate moves were necessary. They sought information from Siatistian Nickolaos Laspas[72], who at the time served as secretary and adviser to Souleiman Pasha

---
[68]Demetres Fotiades, *The Revolution of 1821*, Vol. II, p. 180
[69]George Laios, *Siatista and Its Commercial Houses Hadje-Michael and Manouses*, p. 100
[70]Nick Kasomoules, "Memoirs of the Greek Revolution 1821-1833," *Siatista Memoirs*, p. G-20
[71]John Apostolou, *The History of Siatista*, p. 32
[72]John Apostolou, *The History of Siatista*, p. 27

fighting Ali Pasha's troops at Ioannina. Laspas was a member of Filike Etaireia since 1819[73]. Siatistian clergyman (from nearby Eratyra) Theophanes[74] assisted Chalkidike's revolt leader Emmanuel Pappas. Siatista equipped and dispatched to the mountains its first contingent of twenty-five men. Twenty-four-year-old Kasomoules led them to Mt. Olympus to join Captain Diamantes's force of three hundred men[75]. Kasomoules's brothers George and Demetrios followed as soon as their contingents were ready. Father Konstantinos with remaining members of the family moved to Naousa, forty miles distant from Siatista, probably to evade unfriendly retaliatory steps. Ottoman troops attacked and destroyed Naousa in a few months. Father Kasomoules with the assistance of his fourth son John, wife, and daughters fought the attackers. The Kasomoules family killed eighteen enemy troops before being captured. The father's three wounds caused his death within four- or five-hours' time[76].

Nickolaos Kasomoules continued his fight with fantastic courage and determination. He found himself on the island of Psara. He led his troops, Siatistians and others, to many major battles under Nickolaos Stournares and George Karaiskakes. He entered the hard-pressed Messolonghi to assist with its three-and-a-half-year blockade. While there the command decided on an exodus to break the blockade. Kasomoules, ignoring all risks, carried the worked-out plan to all defending posts of the perimeter, encouraging the defenders and promoting their coordination[77]. His superiors promoted him to one-thousand-men unit commander. His troops and Lassanes's[78] fought side by side in Mavrovouni near Thebes. They both took part in the last battle of Petra[79] in September 1829, eight years from the day

---

[73] George Bodas, Nickolaos Laspas, Siatistian Member of Filike Etaireia," *Elimeiaka*, 35/1995, p. 169
[74] George Laios, *Siatista and Its Commercial Houses Hadje-Michael and Manouses*, p. 101. Theophanes previously served as Holy Synod Secretary and became Archimandrite.
[75] Nick Kasomoules, "Memoirs of the Greek Revolution 1821-1833," *Siatista Memoirs*, p. G-22
[76] Nick Kasomoules, "Memoirs of the Greek Revolution 1821-1833," *Siatista Memoirs*, p. G-24
[77] Demetres Fotiades, *The Revolution of 1821*, Vol. III, p. 212
[78] Demetres Fotiades, *The Revolution of 1821*, Vol. IV. p. 160
[79] Demetres Fotiades, *The Revolution of 1821*, Vol. I, p. 415

Kasomoules left for the mountains. Finally, the Ottoman Empire recognized Greece's independence in April 1830[80]. Kasomoules wrote his narrative of personal experiences *Memoirs of the Greek Revolution of 1821–1833*[81]. It remains one of Siatistian society's outstanding contributions to modern Greece's history. Kasomoules wrote, "Frantzes (another historian) attributes success of the Greek revolution to three classes of people: the clergy, the archons, and the people. We, in mainland Greece, and even in the islands, know better. Several of the armed mountainous bands and archons actually welcomed the outbreak of the revolution. Only a few bishops and priests did. Not only did they not take part in it, but they actually fought both revolutionaries and members of Felike Etaireia. On the contrary, merchants and traders and technicians of various skills who lived in foreign lands, Europe, Eastern and European Ottoman Empire, promoted the revolution. They knew the empire's strength and dared take up arms against it. Let any one who took part in the revolution examine the facts and will conclude expatriate intellectuals and merchants first dared and moved, carrying with them archons and mountain armed groups to seek independence[82]" (N. Kasomoules, Memoirs of the Greek Revolution of 1821–1833, Volume III, pp. 625–26).

The Ecumenical Patriarchate denounced the revolution. It sent appropriate directives, with instructions to be read by priests to parishes of all churches[83]. Compliance to Ottoman's orders by the Patriarchate could not and did not damage the revolutionaries' spirit and determination.

---

[80] Demetres Fotiades, *The Revolution of 1821*, Vol. IV, p. 422
[81] Demetres Fotiades, *The Revolution of 1821*, Vol. III, p. 150
[82] Demetres Fotiades, *The Revolution of 1821*, Vol. I, p. 281
[83] Panagiotes N. Liofes, *History of Kozane*, p. 86

Chapter 20
Barons, Bankers, Benefactors

The Austrian-Hungarian Empire awarded the title of Baron to persons whose actions benefited the country's security and development. Its citizens earned it through their commercial success, development of desolate lands, or extraordinary service to the country. Many Greeks attained this recognition. Many of them came from Upper Macedonia.

John A. Economou from Edessa first settled in Braila, Rumania, where his son Constantine was born in 1876. In 1877, the family moved to Trieste for business opportunities. The family attained remarkable success operating merchant marine ships, insurance companies, banks, and industrial manufacturing units. His son Constantine received Hellenic education and studied at Vienna University. Records of his impressive achievements in aeronautical engineering can be found at Vienna's War Archives. His postgraduate studies in medicine and medical research resulted in the discovery of encephalites lethargia. Dr. Constantine von Economo became famous. The Austrian government in 1976, at his one hundredth birthday anniversary, issued commemorative stamps in his honor[1]. Constantine von Economo's marble bust decorates Vienna University. The cities of Trieste and Vienna honored the Economos by naming one of their streets after them.

It is uncertain if the Siatistian family of Economou[2] mentioned by Metropolitan of Kozane in his letter to Zoe Reininghaus-Karajan in 1925 had any connections with Edessa's John Economou. The Karajan family came to Vienna from Kozane. Professor P. Lioufes from Kozane in his book *History of Kozane* (Athens, 1924) stated Stefanos Karagiannes was born in 1732 in Kozane and moved to Vienna in 1748. His son George was born in Vienna[3]. Polychrones K. Enepekides, professor at Vienna University, in his book *Macedonian Cities and Families*

---

[1]Polychrones K. Enepekides, *Macedonian Cities and Families*, 1750-1930, p. 309
[2]Polychrones K. Enepekides, *Macedonian Cities and Families*, 1750-1930, p. 253
[3]Panagiotes N. Lioufes, *History of Kozane*, p. 282

(Athens, 1984), sixty years after P. Lioufes's book, stated George Karajan was born in Kozane in 1743 and moved to Vienna in 1760[4].

George Karajan's record is impressive. George initially imported/traded mostly wool, cotton, and skins as did most of his compatriots. He married Peristera (meaning pigeon) Economou from Siatista. Peristera, endowed with Zosimas's spirit of Hellenism, became his associate and firm supporter. They expanded his operations by adding their own textile manufacturing unit in Chemnitz, Germany. George Karajan had the help of his two younger brothers, Theodore and John, whom he brought from Kozane. Their activities strengthened and expanded the local industry. Frederick Augustus of Saxony awarded him the title[5] of baron.

George Karajan's financial and social success could not be disputed when in 1799 his wife Peristera died. George von Karajan, unable to meet loneliness, returned to Vienna in 1800. His brother and partner Theodore operated in Vienna the commercial house they established together earlier. In 1802 George von Karajan donated his Vienna house to the Greek Church. In doing so he stated: "I, the undersigned, believing precisely that philanthropic actions are much more appreciated by men and blessed by God when done at the time donors are healthy and alive rather than after death, ordering others to perform their wishes, hereby voluntarily decided to donate my house in Vienna, No. 758, in its entirety, to our Holy Church of Saint Georgios which serves the local Greek merchants." As Karajan stated, Macedonian and generally Greek settlers moved north, not just to earn a living but to trade, accumulate wealth, and educate themselves. Construction of the church began shortly thereafter[6].

George von Karajan, fifty-nine, as soon as the three-year mourning period for the death of his wife Peristera ended as per Orthodox customs, remarried eighteen-year-old Zoe Domnandou from Constantinople. The two had seven children in seven years. Only three of them, Ekaterine, Demetrios, and

[4]Polychrones K. Enepekides, *Macedonian Cities and Families*, 1750-1930, p. 236
[5]Polychrones K. Enepekides, *Macedonian Cities and Families*, 1750-1930, p. 241
[6]Panagiotes N. Lioufes, *History of Kozane*, p. 283. George Karajan's death is placed by Lioufes at 1818 while Enepekides places it at 1813.

Theodore survived. Theodore was born in Vienna in 1810. A year later George and Zoe separated and divorced. George von Karajan again lived alone and died two years later at the age of seventy. Son Theodore von Karajan's education began at Vienna's Greek community and church elementary school. He studied philosophy and other courses required for enrollment in the University at the German High School. He had a natural inclination for literature and history. His first employment at the Ministry of Defense led to his transfer to the Finance Ministry. He married Julianne Voggenhuber from north Austria, a Catholic. They had six children. His family life and career had parallel advancement. Theodore became a director of the Financial Archives Office in Vienna. This all-important office held all financial records of area Greeks as well. His immediate access to the handwritten documents of Vienna's Imperial Library gave him an opportunity to research unknown sources of German literature. He became a politician and in 1848 became a representative to Frankfurt's parliament. He interrupted his term after only five months in office and accepted in 1849 an offer to become a professor of German literature at Vienna's University. A member of the Imperial Academy since 1853, he took over its presidency in 1866. He died in 1873. His six children, five boys and one girl, followed their mother in Catholicism. Max, the oldest, became a professor of Hellenic studies at Gratz University. Max's daughter, granddaughter of Theodore von Karajan, Zoe Reininghaus remembered and honored her grandfather[7]. She wrote to Kozane's Metropolitan Ioakeim inquiring about her ancestors. She followed up with her visit to Kozane and Siatista thus honoring the first wife of the first Karajan, the creator of Karajan family and estate. Max's brother, Ludovikos Theodore von Karajan, became a doctor. He practiced medicine in lower Austria. Ludovikos's son, Ernst von Karajan, followed his father in medicine and became director of Salzburg's hospital. Ernst's son, Herbert von Karajan, the world-renowned director of Vienna's Philharmonic Orchestra, devoted himself to promoting universal understanding through his talent in music.

[7]Polychrones K. Enepekides, *Macedonian Cities and Families*, 1750-1930, p. 252

Kozane produced more barons and benefactors. George Takatzes, successful in his trade of cotton, silk, and crocus among others, became a big landowner in the Dembertza region. He received the title for his successful land development. George and his brother Nickolaos sent generous sums to assist Kozane's library and school[8]. Another settler from Kozane, George Paikou Armenoules, traded in Pest. He received the title for his considerable contribution to Hungary's commercial activity[9]. Metropolitan Dionysios Popovic, however, earned his title for an entirely different reason.

Demetrios Papayiannouses or Dionysios Popovic (1750–1828) was born in the town of Servia. He moved to close-by Kozane in 1768 and studied under Kallinikos Barkozes from Ioannina. In 1770 he became a priest and a teacher. He married but after having a son, his wife died. Advancing his career he went to Constantinople. He became an Archimandrite in 1783, adopting the name Dionysos from Demetrios. In 1789, during the Austrian-Ottoman war, from his Belgrade position, he seized the opportunity and delivered the Ottoman-held Belgrade to Austrian General Laudon. He employed for this purpose seventeen compatriots from Kozane who lived in the area. The huge quantity of wine consumed by his helpers and the guards resulted in his friends having the keys. They unlocked the gate[10] for the troops to storm in. The Austrian government honored him for this service. He became the first Greek to be Eastern Orthodox Bishop of Buda(Pest) in 1790. His persistent efforts to have a Greek Academy established in Pest by the government produced a positive decision. Demetrios Darvares would head the Philosophy Department and Athanasios Psalidas, another brilliant intellectual, the Department of Theology[11]. This decision never materialized for unknown reasons. Popovic wrote several works and books. *Catechism*, published for his followers in Buda(Pest), proved immensely useful.

The town of Vlaste had its own influential barons in Diaspora. Konstantine D. Bellios was born in Vlaste in 1772. The Hellenic spirit and education promoted by Siatista's Zosimas touched Vlaste

[8]Panagiotes N. Lioufes, *History of Kozane*, pp. 302, 303
[9]John Korkas, "Details from the Liberation of Kozane," *Elimeiaka* , p. 165
[10]Panagiotes N. Lioufes, *History of Kozane*, p. 192
[11]George Laios, *Siatista and Its Commercial Houses Hadje-Michael and Manouses*, p. 66

as well. Bellios's parents Demetrios and Despina moved to Constantinople. The family eventually joined the thriving Greek community of Bucharest. Bellios's parents are buried at Ramdo Boda Monastery[12]. The three boys, Stephan, Konstantin, and John, continued their education in their adopted lands. Stephan became an adviser to Wallachia's governor John Karatzas and served as Justice Commissioner. Stephan's son Alexander married Wallachia's ruler Barbu Vakarescu's daughter[13] and became a police director in Bucharest. Their four sons studied under Siatistian Demetrios Argyriades at the recommendation of Alexander's Uncle Konstantin[14].

Uncle Konstantine followed his own plans. At the age of twenty, he translated from German into Modern Greek the book *Young Robinson's Behavior*, published in Vienna in 1792. Siatistian brothers Adam and Demetrios Konstantinou Tzeteres of Vienna[15] financed this publication. Konstantin D. Bellios like everyone else engaged in business. His success expanded into land development and banking. In his huge estate in Wallachia at the Pereto of Teleorman district lived and worked over 650 families[16]. His progress exceeded all expectations. His valuable contribution in land cultivation and extensive banking services to the country prompted Emperor Frankiskus I in 1817 to award Konstantin Freiheir von Bellio the title of baron[17].

Konstantin followed very closely the Greek revolution. He discreetly assisted the activities approved by Austrian authorities. In 1827, he donated two hundred silver fiorins to help homeless refugees in Greece. He simultaneously published the permission given by Higher Police Commissioner in Vienna to collect funds for women and children suffering and for freeing slaves. Upon establishment of a free Greece, he invested heavily by purchasing several properties in Athens to stimulate its economy. Bellios donated all these properties to newly established Athens' City Hospital "Elpis" for its construction. He donated a big, heavy steel safe to handle Greece's infant Treasury

[12]Michael Ath. Kalinderis, *Baron Konstantin E. Bellios, 1772-1838*, p. 19
[13]Michael Ath. Kalinderis, *Baron Konstantin E. Bellios, 1772-1838*, p. 22
[14]Panagiotes N. Lioufes, *History of Kozane*, p. 229
[15]Michael Ath. Kalinderis, *Baron Konstantin E. Bellios, 1772-1838*, p. 29
[16]Michael Ath. Kalinderis, *Baron Konstantin E. Bellios, 1772-1838*, p. 24
[17]Michael Ath. Kalinderis, *Baron Konstantin E. Bellios, 1772-1838*, p. 27

Department needs[18]. In an effort to help meet Greece's educational requirements, he established the Bellian Foundation. He allocated thirty thousand fiorins, whose interest sufficed to educate two Greek students annually. He authorized the Bavarian government to administer the Bellian Foundation. The Bellian beneficiaries completed their studies in Bavaria and returned to Greece to assist with her organizational needs. Stipulation for scholarship was their return to Greece. Candidates from Vlaste, Kastoria, Siatista and other Macedonian towns received preference for scholarships over other Greeks[19]. The scholarships are still given.

Konstantin Bellios traveled to Greece to evaluate his effort's progress. Convinced of an immediate need to protect dispersed antiquities, he initiated establishment of the Archaeological Society in Athens[20]. The absence of a program to resettle Macedonian war victims and refugee families concerned him. He organized a campaign among friends in Vienna and Bucharest to collect funds to help them move in their new community, New Pella, in the city of Atalante.

The young nation recognized his extremely precious contributions to the young state. Its youthful German ruler, King Othon, presented him with the Golden Cross of the Royal Savior Regiment. At a dinner given by the king in his honor, the baron presented the king with an eight-hundred-year-old sword and a golden icon of the Virgin Mary holding Christ in her arms. He presented the Queen a small but rare edition of Homer's classics. Upon leaving the king's dinner, Bellios called on all Greeks to honor and respect their king as ancient Macedonians did to their kings[21]. He returned to his base in Vienna. Prior to his death he granted permission to Siatistian scholars Demetrios and Nickolaos Argyriades to write about his actions regarding his assistance to newly born Greece. Argyriades's brothers exemplified his utter devotion to one's ideals, to humanity, and justice. With his last will, prepared prior to his death in 1838 in Vienna, Bellios donated his two-thousand-volume library to Athens University. His books today are housed in the Athens

---

[18] Michael Ath. Kalinderis, *Baron Konstantin E. Bellios, 1772-1838*, pp. 40,41
[19] Michael Ath. Kalinderis, *Baron Konstantin E. Bellios, 1772-1838*, p. 35
[20] Michael Ath. Kalinderis, *Baron Konstantin E. Bellios, 1772-1838*, p. 48
[21] Michael Ath. Kalinderis, *Baron Konstantin E. Bellios, 1772-1838*, p. 59

National Library. Siatistian Theodore Manouses from Vienna was one of the four executors of his will. Manouses, appointed member of the Holy Synod in the newly formed Church of Greece, supervised disposition of Bellios's properties and ensured utilization of funds for construction of Elpis Hospital in Athens. Bellios's spiritual children, the beneficiaries of his foundation, respected and followed Bellios's concern for others. Bellios never married.

Vlaste's Doumbas family competed with Bellios in progress and generosity. Stergios Doumbas, born in Vlaste in 1794[22], moved to Serres along with brothers Theodore and Michael[23]. The brothers' joint effort, honesty, and perseverance enabled them to excel among other merchants. Their keen judgment led them to Vienna. Like Karajan and Bellios, they pursued their business expansion emphasizing education as well. Their children became scientists and politicians. Stergios's son Nickolaos, born in Vienna in 1830, became a parliamentarian and an important exponent of Europe's liberalism.

The French, Serbian, and Greek revolutions had a tremendous impact on Nickolaos Doumbas. His family's wealth and influence on the financial and political circles in Vienna, combined with Europe's sweeping Philhellenism, helped him in politics. In 1888, he served as secret adviser to the emperor[24]. His exemplary behavior in the Austrian Parliament earned him dignity and respect. Doumbas's immense interest in music and arts encouraged and helped many unknown artists to become famous. His association with German composers Johannes Brahms and Richard Wagner, painters Rudolph Alt and Hans Makart, and architect Theophilus von Hansen resulted in conceiving impressive ideas and making important decisions. Their implementation transformed Imperial Vienna into a Hellenistic city where the arts blossomed. Sculptors Kaspar Clemens Zumbusch, the builder of Beethoven's statue; K. Kundmann, the producer of the marble complex of goddess Athena positioned in front of the Austrian Parliament, archaeologist Otto

[22]Michael Ath. Kalinderis, *Life in the Community of Vlaste During the Turkish Occupation*, p. 134
[23]Polychrones K. Enepekides, *Macedonian Cities and Families,1750-1930*, p. 295
[24]Stephan J. Papadopoulos, *Educational and Social Activities of Macedonian Hellenism During the Last Century of Turkish Occupation*, pp. 53, 54

Bendorf, and others worked with him. Each one separately and all of them collectively contributed their knowledge. Statues depicting Greek mythology scenes and figures decorated Vienna's public buildings and parks. Vienna's elevation to exceptional beauty in the second half of the nineteenth century is primarily due to efforts of Nickolaos Doumbas, descendant of Macedonian Greek settlers[25].

Nickolaos Doumbas initiated and coordinated the activities for construction of Vienna University, Austrian Parliament, City Hall, and Applied Arts Academy buildings. His efforts and financial assistance were responsible for construction of the world-renowned Musikverein building, with among the best acoustics in the world, where the famous Vienna Philharmonic Orchestra festivals are held annually. Doumbas was cofounder of the famous Viennese Choir and helped establish the Arts Society and the Museum of Applied Arts. He financially assisted authors, educational societies, and schools, the Ecumenical Patriarchate, and a multitude of philanthropic institutions especially in Macedonia[26]. He never forgot his ancestor's mother country. He visited Athens and decorated the main entrance overhead of Athens University. He repeatedly assisted young Greek boys and girls seeking assistance to study at German and Austrian universities, agricultural schools, and other institutions of the Arts. Vienna, the city to which he gave his soul, honored his efforts and achievements. Upon his death the artists' street became Dumba Street[27]. The Austrian government appointed as ambassador to Washington Konstantinos Doumbas, a later-generation family descendant.

Stergios Doumbas built several schools in Macedonia. Vlaste's and Serres' school, in 1843 and 1853 respectively, were his projects[28]. His significant donation built Monastere's High School. The family made several grants to the schools of Kastoria and Salonica. Athens University and Arsakeion School in Athens received considerable financial assistance. Schools in other Macedonian communities, e.g., Kozane, received donations as well. The Doumbases assisted wherever need existed. Family members granted Serres its hospital and its kindergarten.

[25]Polychrones K. Enepekides, *Macedonian Cities and Families*, p. 303
[26]Polychrones K. Enepekides, *Macedonian Cities and Families*, pp. 300-304
[27]Polychrones K. Enepekides, *Macedonian Cities and Families*, p. 296
[28]Stephan J. Papadopoulos, *Educational and Social Activities of Macedonian Hellenism During the Last Century of Turkish Occupation*, pp. 49, 118, 136, 169, 179

Barons, Bankers, Benefactors / 167

Baron George Petros von Spirta, descendant of a Kleisoura family, concentrated in education as well. The Spirtas spread over to the cities of Kovilj, Ruma, Sisak, and Vienna[29]. Grandfather George K. Spirtas went to Semlin in 1739[30]. He was a successful trader. His sons Pavlos and Petros succeeded him in business. Ownership by Spirtas's family of thirteen vessels transporting goods to the ports of the Danube, Savo, and Tisa rivers dominated the local shipping industry. Their steamship under ancient name *Archimedes* and cargo ship *Macedonia* reflected the family's Hellenism. Involved in communal affairs, Pavlos forwarded a report to Austrian authorities with several recommendations aimed at trade improvements. His brother Petros served in the Austrian army as an officer and invested heavily in his business. Semlin's archons elevated him to its Elite Citizens class[31]. Petros served as director of Helleno-Museum, the Greek school at Semlin[32]. His children Christina and George graduated from this school. His son George Petros von Spirta, continuing the family's success, became a baron[33]. Following his father's footsteps he served as president of Semlin's Hellenic Educational Brotherhood. The Spirtas' family building, built in 1840, houses today's museum in Semlin[34].

Siatista, the thriving and vibrant community in Upper Macedonia with a population of eight thousand inhabitants, honored its own barons. In addition to Ekaterine Konstantinou Tzeteres, sister of Adam and Demetrios[35] of Vienna, who donated her library to Geraneia's school in Siatista[36], the families of Hadje-Michael and Manouses deserved and earned their titles.

Pavlos Hadje-Michael married Agnes Hadje-Ioannou Konstantinou. Their son John was born in 1757[37]. Pavlos managed the import-export commercial house established in Vienna in 1750 with his brothers/partners[38]. His enormous success enabled him to

[29]John A. Papadrianos, *The Greek Settlers of Semlin*, p. 30
[30]John A. Papadrianos, *The Greek Settlers of Semlin*, p. 42
[31]John A. Papadrianos, *The Greek Settlers of Semlin*, p. 90. *The Greek Settlers at Yugoslav Countries*, p. 96
[32]John A. Papadrianos, *The Greek Settlers of Semlin*, p. 211
[33]John A. Papadrianos, *The Greek Settlers of Semlin*, p. 170
[34]John A. Papadrianos, *The Greek Settlers of Semlin*, p. 76
[35]John Apostolou, *The History of Siatista*, p. 16
[36]John Apostolou, *The History of Siatista*, p. 58
[37]George Laios, *Siatista and Its Commercial Houses Hadje-Michael and Manouses*, p. 107
[38]George Laios, *Siatista and Its Commercial Houses Hadje-Michael and Manouses*, p. 104

offer 156,000 fiorins for a parcel of land located at Torok Becse in Torontal district. Pavlos's first trip to Hungary was in 1740 at the age of twenty-two. His forty-two years' business knowledge of the area encouraged him to expand his operations into land development. In the 11,726-Joch (acres) estate he acquired, he intended to settle Siatistian families. Emperor Joseph II granted Pavlos and his son John estate ownership in 1782[39]. Pavlos took up Austrian citizenship in 1784. Father and son each bought their own homes in Budapest. In 1785, Pavlos terminated the partnership with his brothers and concentrated his efforts in developing the purchased land. Everyone, owners and residents, worked intensively. They introduced better quality grain seeds and improved methods for production of wine, honey, tobacco, wool, skins, lumber, and related products. Importation of Thessalian horses and cross breeding produced impressive results. Better horses strengthened the empire's cavalry. Pavlos and his son assisted Austria and her ally Russia in their war with the Ottomans. They even maintained their allegiance to them opposing the French Revolution of 1789. In 1797, Pavlos Hadje-Michael headed the eighty-eight Vienna Greek merchants' donor list, respondents to government's call for financial assistance[40]. Emperor Franciscus II recognized his services in 1798. He awarded the title of baron to Paulo Hadsimihal Sissani and his son Joannis. Pavlos was already eighty years old. The following year Pavlos died. The family buried him in Vienna. His son John followed him to his grave the same year.

 The two Hadje-Michael widows, Pavlos's Agnes and daughter-in-law Klara, John's wife, survived them. Together with Klara's eight children from John, aged eleven to one, they relied on Siatistian Athanasios George Manouses's support. Attorney Dr. Joseph Strahl from the Barons' court exercised the overall supervision. All family heirs received their share from Pavlos Hadje-Michael's estate distribution. Vienna's Greek School, Illyrian church, Jerusalem's Patriarchate, and Siatista's eighteen churches received specific grants[41]. Pavlos's Will provided annual amounts for destitute persons in his adopted

---

[39]George Laios, *Siatista and Its Commercial Houses Hadje-Michael and Manouses*, p. 113
[40]George Laios, *Siatista and Its Commercial Houses Hadje-Michael and Manouses*, p. 125
[41]George Laios, *Siatista and Its Commercial Houses Hadje Michael and Manouses*, p. 136

land. The families continued to live in their own homes in Budapest. Klara Hadje-Michael von Sissani continued to run the Torok Becse estate until she died in 1830. Her thirty-four-year-old daughter Anastasia died in Vienna[42]. Family descendants preserved their identity for three generations. The assimilation process finally prevailed. Manouses's family had the same fate.

Siatistian Konstantine Manouses traded with Venice since early 1700[43]. Konstantinos Manouses had two sons, George and Theodore. The boys expanded their operations to central European cities around 1740 with astonishing results. The family built its mansion in Siatista in 1762.

George married the daughter of Siatistian John Hadje-Konstantinou, who operated a business in Vienna. They had two children, Athanasios and Agnes. Agnes married Demetrios Hadje-Michael, Pavlos's nephew, in 1787. George, a successful businessman, served on the St. George Church Board of Directors from 1784 until his death in 1790. His Vienna firm continued to operate for another fifteen years. Son Athanasios who survived him took over its management, simultaneously continuing his education. His library included a collection of handwritten works of many Siatistian teachers. In 1777, Athanasios copied Johann Friedrich Wucherer's book *Introduction to Physics*. In 1795, he financed Nickolaos Barkozes's translation from Latin into Modern Greek of F. Ch. Baumeister's *Logic*. Athanasios married Maria Kurtowitz in 1791, daughter of another successful Greek merchant settled in Slovenia[44]. George Karajan, assisted by his Siatistian wife Peristera, acted as their best man. Karajan also became godfather to Athanasios's six children he had with Maria. Athanasios became an Austrian citizen in 1791 and a citizen of Vienna in 1796. His extended commercial activities reached Belgrade, Semlin, Constantinople, and Wallachia. In Vienna he served on the Holy Trinity's—the Austrian citizen Greek church—Board of Directors. He was active in community affairs until 1817. His son's sudden death at the age of twenty-two depressed him. Heartbroken, he moved to Trieste where he again got involved in

---

[42]George Laios, *Siatista and Its Commercial Houses Hadje-Michael and Manouses*, p. 141
[43]John Apostolou, *The History of Siatista*, p. 67
[44]George Laios, *Siatista and Its Commercial Houses Hadje-Michael and Manouses*, p. 156

the Greek community by becoming a professor of German at its all-girls school[45]. He died in Trieste a little after 1830.

Theodore Konstantinou Manouses married Siatistian Alexandra Lassiou. The couple had two sons, Christodoulos and John. Alexandra, a product of Siatista's advanced school system under dominant Metropolitan Zosimas, raised her sons with dignity and respect. Christodoulos settled permanently in Vienna, working in the firm of Nickolaos and Pavlos Hadje-Michael in which his father had an interest. He brought with him his Siatistian wife and their son Theodore. He died around 1800. His wife and son became dependents of his brother John, an obligation imposed by Siatistian customs.

John Theodore Manouses, born in Siatista in 1764, went to Vienna in 1780. He traded mainly in Hungary and married in Buda(Pest) in 1794. In 1798, he replaced Siatistian George Poulios as Vienna Trade Commissioner when the later lost his position due to his involvement in Regas's revolutionary activities. John Theodore Manouses became a (Buda)Pest citizen in 1824. He bought two houses in Vienna and served as a Board of Directors member in the church where his cousin Athanasios served. In 1825, his mother, Alexandra, died at the age of eighty-eight. The same year John offered twenty thousand fiorins to purchase a parcel of land in Ohabitza at Krasso district[46]. In his application for the baron's title he claimed he was a descendant of an aristocratic Siatistian family. A certificate from Siatistian Metropolitan Ioannikios confirmed his claim. He strengthened his case by his forty-five years' residency in Hungary, (Buda)Pest citizenship, and various services to the country. Emperor Franciscus I awarded both land ownership and baron's title to John Manouses and his son George in 1827[47]. John Manouses paid only a total of twenty-three thousand fiorins for both. Shrewd and diplomatic, he protected his commercial and political interests at a time when questioning of allegiance was rampant due to ongoing hostilities in the Greek War for Independence. He managed to include the Greek flag colors, light blue background with a white cross, in his family's baron emblem. He died in 1831 at sixty-seven and was buried in

---

[45]George Laios, *Siatista and Its Commercial Houses Hadje-Michael and Manouses*, p. 161
[46]George Laios, *Siatista and Its Commercial Houses Hadje-Michael and Manouses*, p. 162
[47]George Laios, *Siatista and Its Commercial Houses Hadje Michael and Manouses*, p. 174

Vienna. His son George—whose daughter Maria married a well-known lawyer[48], author, and politician in Athens, Greece—survived him.

John's major contribution to Greece was guardianship and guidance of his nephew Theodore, brother Christodoulos's son. With Uncle John's assistance Theodore concentrated in his studies. George Zaviras[49] worked hard on him. Theodore continued studies in Buda(Pest) and Vienna. Brought up with his Siatistian spirit he promptly wrote a collection of Greek—mostly Siatistian and area—traditional folk songs taught to him by his grandmother Alexandra. He presented these songs to his German friend Werner von Haxthausen[50], who loved Greek folk poetry. Johann Wolfgang von Goethe's translation of the songs in German bolstered Philhellenism in Europe[51]. Following normalization of political developments after the Greek Revolution, Theodore repatriated to free Greece. It was perhaps keeping a promise given to his first teacher Zaviras about Hellenism. Multilingual and broadly educated, he joined the faculty of under-establishment Athens University[52]. He became its first professor of history, sociology, and politics. Like Bellios, he established the Manouseion Foundation, providing assistance to two Siatistian youths. The better of the two continued their graduate studies in Europe. The scholarships were for literature, theology, or archaeology. Candidates today are not limited in these three fields but may choose their own[53]. Manouses willed his five-thousand-volume library to Siatista. Today's Manouseios Public Library continues to serve Siatista's population[54].

The benefactors' actions still benefit all communities concerned.

---

[48]George Laios, *Siatista and Its Commercial Houses Hadje-Michael and Manouses*, p. 175
[49]Demetres K. Chadjes, *John M. Trampatzes*, p. 18
[50]George Laios, *Siatista and Its Commercial Houses Hadje-Michael and Manouses*, p. 161
[51]Demetres Fotiades, *The Revolution of 1821*, Vol. II, p. 180
[52]John Apostolou, *The History of Siatista*, p. 67
[53]George M. Bodas, "The Benefactors of Siatista," *Siatistina*, 2/1989, p. 129
[54]Committee of M. Dainavas, A. Dardas, D. Batzios, G. Bodas, D. Siasios, *Siatista, Acquaintance Invitation*.

Chapter 21
Achievements and Mayors

Resettlement of Greek revolutionary fighters and expatriates into Greece required funds and effort. The influx of talent and capital into liberated areas assisted in establishing the infrastructure of the new country. The organization of civil administration, international profile, entity, and purpose had to be formulated and directed. Everything started from the beginning in the devastated, four-hundred-year-long neglected land. Every capable Diaspora Hellene and all Philhellenes gave a hand. Second- and third-generation descendants honored their forefathers. They kept alive the spirit of Hellenism.

Central and northern regions of modern Greece, including Upper Macedonia, remained under Ottoman rule. The revolution in Upper Macedonia subsided within months. The Ottomans destroyed Naousa[1] and Katranitsa[2]. Several communities, including Siatista, through luck or diplomacy, managed to survive. The existence of an independent mother country gave Macedonians an additional psychological boost. Opportunities for trade and education, however, continued to attract them north. Nickolaos Pagounes and the Papademetriou brothers left Vlaste for Belgrade in 1829. George Bonte, born in Vlaste in 1810, became the richest merchant in all of Serbia. Vlaste's Demetrios Georgiou or Georgevic, Boundic, and Kristits went to Serbia as well. Descendant Konstantin N. Kristits became Serbia's Foreign Minister[3]. Wallachia attracted Demetrios Mousicos and Demetrios Feliades, whose successful businesses elevated them to Vlaste's benefactors club.

Konstantinos Germanes's home in Vlaste still carried a mortgage in 1806. Son John Germanes was in Wallachia when the revolution started. He took part in the first battle of

---
[1]Demetres Fotiades, *The Revolution of 1821*, Vol. IV, p. 338
[2]Michael Ath. Kalinderis, *Life in the Community of Vlaste During the Turkish Occupation*, p. 122
[3]Michael Ath. Kalinderis, *Life in the Community of Vlaste During the Turkish Occupation*, p. 63

Ipsilantis's army at Dragatsani. He and his brother eventually settled in Belgrade. In 1834, John Germanes married the daughter of Serbia's ruler Milos Obrenovic. The same year, Obrenovic appointed as Finance Minister of Serbia Kostas Markovic, born of Siatistian parents in Pozarevats in 1795. John Germanes's childhood friend Theodore Hadje-Bakes married Milos Obrenovic's niece, daughter of Efraim Obrenovic[4]. In 1836, Obrenovic appointed his son-in-law John Germanes to serve as Serbia's consul in Bucharest.

Adames Konstantine Germanes lived in Vienna. Constantine von Bellio, prominent Vlaste expatriate and banker, noticed the respect the Greek community had towards him. In 1837, Bellio authorized Adames K. Germanes to collect funds among his friends in Vienna for his financial campaign to assist Macedonian sufferers of the revolution. Adames's son John contributed generously in 1843 and in subsequent years to Vlaste's school fund.

Nickolaos Germanes resided in Belgrade. In 1837 Belgrade Greek community and Vlaste's archons chose him to serve in a three-member committee formed to execute the will of Vlaste's Michael Tegou Bonte, who died in Belgrade. Nickolaos's descendants moved to Rumania[5]. Menelaos, Nickolaos's son, continued his father's work. His banking and finance business won recognition from the Rumanian government and Menelaos became finance minister. His outspoken support of Greece displeased certain conservative politicians. However, he ignored all pressures and forwarded five thousand fiorins to Vlaste and fifteen thousand fiorins to Monastere from Demetrios Mousicos's estate for construction of all-girl schools. The funds willed by Mousicos in 1870 intended to establish and operate the above schools in the two Upper Macedonian towns.

Vlaste settlers of Semlin welcomed their hometowners Demetrios Poulios and his brother's son Demetrios Poulios. Brother John, Vlaste's priest, had eighteen sons and four

[4]Michael Ath. Kalinderis, *Life in the Community of Vlaste During the Turkish Occupation,* p. 63. Theodore Hadje-Bakes's sister married Siatistian Naoum Demetrios Moraitis, son of international trader Demetres J. Moraitis. John A. Papadrianos, *The Greek Settlers of Semlin,* p. 72, note 214. *The Greek Settlers at Yugoslav Countries,* p. 158
[5]Wallachia and Moldavia united in 1857 and formed Rumania.

daughters[6]. Young Demetrios invited his younger brother Athanasios to join them. The two brothers, brought up by their priest father with Hellenic values, assisted uncle Demetrios with his business. Athanasios, anxious to improve his education, accepted a grant from his Vlaste compatriot Konstantinos Petrovic[7]. Athanasios, like many of his friends, married a Serb, Maria Rogulic. Their marriage produced three boys and a girl. The two sons, the oldest Dimitrije Puljo and the youngest John, operated their own printing shop[8]. They published books, magazines, and newspapers in Serbo-Croat and German languages. They also printed Dr. Milivoje Babic's newspaper *Srpski Odjek*. The newspaper campaigned against the Austrian-Hungarian decision to annex Bosnia-Herzegovina[9].

Semlin's thriving Greek community included Upper Macedonian Karamatas's family from Katranitsa (Pyrgos)[10]. Dimitrije Karamat arrived in Semlin in 1745. His wife dressed in men's clothes to evade detection by Ottomans, who objected to women following their husbands outside their jurisdiction, joined him shortly[11]. Dimitrije Karamat, with brother Athanasios, bought and traded animals, mainly pigs. Their entrepreneurship extended to purchasing newly born animals from South Serbia for growth and resale in northern markets and Vienna. Their wealth and acceptance pushed them up in the social ladder. Austria's emperor Joseph II visited their household in 1788, an impressive building in Semlin[12]. Demetrios's son John concentrated in educating his children. One of them, Athanasios, became a politician. In this case, as it happened with Menelaos Germanes's case above, his family fortune and education helped him attain the position of finance minister in newly formed autonomous Voivodina (Vienna) in 1848. Athanasios's own son John, named after his grandfather, concentrated in literature. He operated his printing shop and a bookstore. This third-generation descendant practiced Hellenism in its true aspects.

[6]Michael Ath. Kalinderis, *Life in the Community of Vlaste During the Turkish Occupation*, p. 86
[7]John A. Papadrianos, *The Greek Settlers of Semlin*, p. 177
[8]John A. Papadrianos, *The Greek Settlers of Semlin*, p. 217
[9]John A. Papadrianos, *The Greek Settlers of Semlin*, p. 219
[10]John A. Papadrianos, *The Greek Settlers of Semlin*, p. 43
[11]John A. Papadrianos, *The Greek Settlers of Semlin*, p. 54
[12]John A. Papadrianos, *The Greek Settlers of Semlin*, p. 212

National origin was secondary to human dignity and respect. His shop printed items in Serb, Croat, and German languages. The magazine *Javor* published many plays inspired from Hellenic classics. Contributors were archmandrite Ilarion and his brother Dimitrije Ruvarac and authors Milan Resetar, Jasa Prodanovic, and Milan Milicevic[13].

Semlin citizenry respected the Greek settlers' hard work and devotion to their city. At least three Upper Macedonians reached Semlin's mayoralty office. Prerequisites for mayor or councilman were stiff. They limited entitlement to elite citizens enjoying integrity with fluency in German, knowledge of Serb language, and possession of managerial skills to supervise operations of the city institutions[14]. George Kalligraphou from Bogatsiko possessed all the above. His own and his sons' standing in all community circles excelled. His son Konstantinos managed their businesses. Son John was elected a mayor in 1803. He stayed in office until 1807. Austrian authorities utilized his services as mediator in their negotiations with restless Serbian groups, sympathizers of revolutionary Karadgeordgevic against the Ottomans. John's son Theodore, however, favored the revolutionaries. The authorities intervened and arrested him in 1812[15].

Vlaste's family Petrovic also reached high respect and business achievement. The financially well-off brothers Konstantinos and Lazarus were generous in their assistance of church and Semlin's Helleno-Museum school. Konstantinos's two sons, Athanasios and Demetrios, thoroughly adopted Hellenism. They also transplanted it to Athanasios's son Konstantinos. He became mayor in 1872. His broad education commanded respect of all Semlin citizens. He studied physics and chemistry in Vienna. He spoke Serbian and German plus Modern and Ancient Greek. His administration accomplished the construction of a hospital and the installation of a citywide gas lighting system. His other proposed plans remained on the planning board. Konstantinos Petrovic was a theoretician and philosopher. He resigned from his office in 1874. The same year

[13]John A. Papadrianos, *The Greek Settlers of Semlin*, pp. 214, 215
[14]John A. Papadrianos, *The Greek Settlers of Semlin*, p. 84
[15]John A. Papadrianos, *The Greek Settlers of Semlin*, p. 92

his cousin Maria, daughter of Demetrios Petrovic, built at her expense a second Orthodox Church at Semlin's cemetery. (Theodore Apostolou donated the first one in 1787.) She dedicated it to Saint Demetrios. Its basement crypt accommodated her family's grave[16]. Her cousin Konstantinos, however—who fifteen years before resigned from the mayor's office—in 1889, a year prior to his death, switched from Eastern Orthodox to Catholicism. His philosophical mind was restless until his very last days.

Katranitsa offered its own son for Semlin's service. Morfes's family settled in Semlin prior to 1800. Pavlos Morfes took an active part in politics. In 1848, he participated in a committee sent to Vienna to reiterate Semlin's loyalty. His son Panagiotes, appropriately educated, worked in a business establishment in nearby Ruma. He relocated to Belgrade working for the Greek firm of Paranos. The company supplied the Serbian army with food provisions. Morfes handled the company's activities with the Serbs. His behavior impressed Serb battalion commander Djoko Vlajkovic. Their acquaintance improved and ended up with Morfes marrying his daughter. He returned to Semlin after marriage in 1881. Panagiotes's education, performance, and Serbian wife helped his political aspirations. The following year Panagiotes Morfes became a councilman. His maturity and initiative in the city council impressed Semlin's constituents. In 1884 they elected him mayor. His eight years in office were full of accomplishments. The city procured a 504-acre public land for its needs, established a city park, built a pier at the River Danube, expanded pavement of existing streets, and improved the water supply system. The construction of public buildings marked his personal success. His last projects were construction of a new city hall in 1887 and a hospital in 1891. Morfes's preference of autocratic government for results disappointed many Semlin Democrats. Serb prominent citizens attacked him through the newspaper *Novo Vreme*. Morfes lost the 1893 election, although his Hungarian friend Ignaz Soppron with his newspaper actively supported him[17]. Morfes returned to his Hellenic trait, business.

[16]John A. Papadrianos, *The Greek Settlers of Semlin*, p. 110
[17] John A. Papadrianos, *The Greek Settlers of Semlin*, pp. 95, 97

Austro-Hungarian Empress Elizabeth (1837–1898) believed in Hellenism for promotion of trade and industry[18]. She acquired a high-level efficiency in Modern Greek through her nine Greek teachers. Two of them hailed from Upper Macedonia. One, Konstantinos Chrestomanos (1854–1904), hailed from Meleniko. Elizabeth, in her 1898 book *The Book of Empress Elizabeth*, discussed their efforts. The other, Roussos Rousopoulos, hailed from Bogatsiko. Both of their fathers were professors who studied in Germany. Both had German mothers. Athanasios Rousopoulos (1823–1898), Roussos's father, was a Bellian Foundation recipient[19]. He became an archaeology professor at Athens University. His German wife, Louise Murray, had with him eleven children. One of them, Othon, became a professor at Athens Military Academy. His efforts led to establishment of Superior Industrial Institute at Piraeus. Othon's brother Roussos studied law at Athens University. Empress Elizabeth selected twenty-six-year-old Roussos Rousopoulos through Baron Perfall's Greek wife. Elizabeth renewed Rousopoulos's one-year contract twice.

Rousopoulos accompanied his twenty-five-years'-senior pupil on her trips, teaching her Greek. Together they traveled to sunbathed Mediterranean cities. Elizabeth spoke Hungarian, German, English, French, and Greek. She enjoyed conversing in Greek in Cairo, Alexandria, Tynis, Algiers, and cities with a substantial Greek element. Elizabeth named her palace on Corfu Island "Achilleion" at the suggestion of Rousopoulos[20]. Through her efforts in 1891 Roussos Rousopoulos became a professor of Modern Greek at Eastern Commercial Academy of Budapest and the University of Budapest. Roussos never married. Upon his retirement, he moved to Athens and died at the age of ninety-three[21]. He strengthened the spirit of Hellenism by his association with Empress Elizabeth and his teaching in the Budapest institutions.

---

[18]Polychronis K. Enepekides, *Macedonian Cities and Families, 1750-1930*, p. 290
[19]Michael Ath. Kalinderis, *Baron Konstantinos E. Bellios, 1772-1838*, p. 37, note 2.
[20]Polychronis K. Enepekides, *Macedonian Cities and Families, 1750-1930*,
    p. 289
[21]Polychronis K. Enepekides, *Macedonian Cities and Families, 1750-1930*,
    pp. 273, 277

Chapter 22
Education—An Objective

Helleno-Museum, Semlin's Greek school, continued to offer quality education to young boys and girls. The Greek revolutionary activities forced the Imperial Court and Vienna's War Council to re-evaluate their attitude. They ruled that they would appoint teachers. This change of position by the authorities prompted director Zachariades's resignation. The Serb city of Sabac's school gained from this move by utilizing his talent[1]. In 1823 the Helleno-Museum population numbered 123 students while Vienna's school registered only 70. Trieste's Greek school at the time enrolled 185 students[2]. Settler-expatriate-merchant from Kozane, George D. Zeses, financed in 1826 the book *Review of Natural History*, translated from Latin into Modern Greek by George D. Kleides, teacher at Helleno-Museum and also from Kozane. Prominent Semlin merchants continued investing in the school. Their return was better preparation for their children. Naoum Peschares's two sons graduated from there. Nickolaos attended it in 1820 and Petros in 1836.

Serb school supporter Stojan Pavlovic from Nis sent his son Demetrios to Helleno-Museum. He simultaneously financed several of its publications. Efronios Raphael Popovic, bishop of Budapest's son, taught there in 1830. His thirty-year accumulated knowledge from teaching at Pest, Vienna, and Temesvar proved extremely valuable to the students. In 1837, Efronios Popovic moved to Iasi in Moldavia[3]. Nikodemos from Kozane replaced him. Teacher Argyrios Demetriou and Siatistian Konstantinos Papageorgiou followed Nikodemos's service. In 1853 the Educational Brotherhood board, in an effort to assist with the education of all Greek schools everywhere, financed George Karavelopoulos's *Encyclopedia*. The Semlin-printed publication reached many Diaspora Greek schools.

[1] John A. Papadrianos, *The Greek Settlers of Semlin*, p. 158
[2] John A. Papadrianos, *The Greek Settlers of Semlin*, p. 160
[3] John A. Papadrianos, *The Greek Settlers of Semlin*, p. 166

Fifteen years later, in 1868, far-sighted individuals established the Hellenic Educational Union. An Emperor's directive granted its permission. Its main objective was elevation of the school into a Superior Commercial Academy in Greek language[4]. They were confident that Hellenic-trained, Greek-speaking individuals would enhance further international stability through trading. The unexpected constant shrinking of the Greek population in their community, however, forced the school to review its curriculum. Only twenty hard-core Hellenes remained in Semlin by 1875[5]. Konstantinos Petrovic, cousin Maria Petrovic-Charisiou, Panagiotes Morfes, John Karamatas, George P. von Spirta, and John Poulios, all Upper Macedonians and Elite Citizens of Semlin, were amongst them. By the end of nineteenth century, the Hellenic Educational Union's fund exceeded the respectable sum of one hundred thousand fiorins. In 1912, its Board of Directors, with George von Spirta's initiative, turned them over to Semlin's Serbian community[6]. The Serbs had to develop their own educational objectives.

Vienna businessman George Sinas from Vlaste shared the feelings of his compatriots Bellios and Doumbas. He donated respectable sums to liberated Greece. He built and equipped the Athens Planetarium. The Greek government in 1834 appointed him consul in Vienna. His son Simon (1810–1876) followed his father's footsteps. Guided by his Hellenic spirit and background, he continued assisting the Planetarium and the Educational Society in Athens. His thorough satisfaction and recognition, however, came through his major contribution of building the Athens Academy. The city of Athens honored his actions and named after him the street adjacent to the Academy. The Greek government appointed him ambassador to Vienna[7].

In Constantinople lived Konstantine Thomaides and George Tsiotses, later named Vranakis, from Vlaste. Vranakis, a Bellian Foundation recipient, became a multilinguist by studying German, Serb, French, and Turkish. Ottoman authorities utilized his services in their postal service[8]. Vranakis discharged his moral obligation to

[4]John A. Papadrianos, *The Greek Settlers of Semlin*, p. 174
[5]John A. Papadrianos, *The Greek Settlers of Semlin*, p. 75
[6]John A. Papadrianos, *The Greek Settlers of Semlin*, p. 178
[7]*Encyclopedia Avlos*, p. 3278
[8]Michael Ath. Kalinderis, *Life in the Community of Vlaste During the Turkish Occupation*, p. 145

Bellios by leaving his estate to build a boy's school in Vlaste. Vranakis's sponsor to Ottoman service, Konstantine Thomaides, operated his successful tobacco business in Constantinople. Thomaides enjoyed Sultan Hamit's trust and favors in exchange for his supplies of fine, choice tobacco. Thomaides built an allgirl school in Vlaste in 1860. Ten years later, with the cooperation of Upper Macedonians' Metropolitan Ioannikios of Nicea, priest Noukas, and Demetrios Konstantinides[9], Thomaides initiated the establishment of the Macedonian Educational Brotherhood in Constantinople. He became its first president, serving from 1871 to 1878. Through persuasion of Sultan Hamit he secured a permit to establish a higher learning school in Tsotyli, a town near Siatista. In an effort to enthuse others to participate in the financial campaign and reach the required amount, he donated his own Constantinople home. Thomaides joyfully attended the dedication ceremonies in Tsotyli. The school was opened in 1873.

Siatistian Zosimas's Hellenic values continued to appear in Diaspora Siatistians. George Nickolaou Zihnizares and his sister Vasilike settled in Iasi, Moldavia. Friendly and responsible, Zihnizares operated a pharmacy. His success and comforts ended with his death in 1810 and with no will. His sister Vasilike, together with their nephew Thomas Nerantzes, inherited his estate. They immediately allocated one-third of it prior to splitting it to support the operation of Siatista's school. Vasilike wrote to Ecumenical Patriarch Cyril VI in 1816 requesting assistance. She specified her requirement for establishment of a committee by Constantinople's Greek Merchants Association to receive and manage the fund under his supervision. Its interest, paid semiannually, forwarded to Siatista's school committee, would meet school costs and pay the teachers' salaries[10]. Siatistian children deserved the benefit their predecessors enjoyed a century before. Everyone's praise and enthusiasm as a result of this action impressed young John Trampantzes.

Father Michael Trampantzes lived in Siatista since about 1760. He and his wife Polyzotra (translated "source of life") raised six children. They were Thomas, Demetrios, Raphael, Malamate, Vasilike, and John[11]. Endowed with Siatista's Hellenic

[9]Demetres N. Tsigaridas, *Macedonian Educational Brotherhood*, Vol. 7, p. 11
[10]George Laios, *Siatista and Its Commercial Houses Hadje-Michael and Manouses*, p. 99
[11]Anastasios N. Dardas, *John M. Trampantzes, 1813-1890*, p. 17

education, Thomas and Demetrios left Siatista around 1800 at an early age. Their destination was Wallachia. A thriving Siatistian community there promised employment and success. Raphael, the third son, joined them within a few years. The girls stayed behind, protected by Siatista's family and culture. Their dowries were certain to arrive through their parents when appropriate. John, the youngest son, joined his brothers in 1825 at the age of twelve, escaping the Greek revolutionary turmoil.

Thomas, strict adherent to Siatista's customs, returned home to prepare taking over the head-of-the-family role. Siatista devotionally maintained a patriarchal society. Thomas married and raised his family in Siatista. He had three daughters and three sons. Two of his sons, Christos and George, went to their uncles' in Wallachia to continue their father's efforts. The income flow from Wallachia was needed. Daughters Helen, Anastasia, and Vasilike stayed home with their brother Konstantinos. Grandfather Thomas enjoyed his eleven grandchildren from Konstantinos's two marriages.

Thomas's brother Demetrios settled permanently in Wallachia. His family included two daughters and a son from his marriage. His son Michael settled in the city of Mertjei. His first daughter, Margiola Christake Posesku, raised five grandchildren for Demetrios[12]. His second daughter, Anna, married Polychrones Konstantinesku. From the suffixes -sku it is obvious their husbands were Rumanized Greeks (Wallachs and Moldavians became Rumanians in 1857) or Rumanians.

Thomas's other brother Raphael also settled in Rumania. His business ventures led him to ownership of the Fuistor estate property. He had two grandchildren from his only daughter Kasitsa. In Siatista, Thomas's oldest sister, Malamate, married Papaelias from the nearby village of Mikrocastro. Malamate's daughter, Anastasia, had nine children with numerous descendants. Thomas's younger sister, Vasilike, married Nickolaos Gargachuya. Their son Demetrios had ten children, five each, boys and girls[13]. The family tree really grew in Siatista from the girls' side.

[12]Anastasios N. Dardas, *John M. Trampantzes, 1813-1890*, p. 22
[13]Anastasios N. Dardas, *John M. Trampantzes, 1813-1890*, pp. 22-25

Thomas's youngest brother John, born in 1813, followed his brothers' trading activities after receiving the necessary education to become familiar with Wallachia conditions. Prudent guidance and assistance led him to his decisions. However, the enthusiasm he felt during his childhood with Vasilike Nickolaou's grant for a school influenced his plans. He pursued his fundamental objectives, commerce and education, from a very young age. Knowledge of local behavior and keen judgment gave him an advantage. The outbreak of the Russo-Ottoman war of 1877 found him in the city of Slatina, close to where the Greek Revolution started fifty-six years before. His warehouses were full of wheat and horses' foodstuff. The demand for these supplies skyrocketed along with their prices. The Russians singled out his substantial economic power and social respectability. John Trampantzes provided the Russian cavalry with the required grains. His profits elevated by far his already enormous wealth. At the end of the war, his only concern was its proper utilization. He was already in his mid-sixties.

John M. Trampantzes returned to Greece in 1878[14]. He remembered Polyzotra's (his mother's) send off words: "God may be with you. We will be praying for you. Do not forget Siatista." He was anxious to help his birthplace, which was still under Ottoman rule. He settled in Corfu Island for health and safety reasons. He split his time with Athens, where he maintained an apartment. Visiting Karlsbad, Austria, he revealed his feelings to Siatistian Nickolaos Samaras. Trampantzes wrote to Siatista's archons outlining his objectives. He asked about their needs. The response he received specified revitalization of the existing Hellenic school. Trampantzes found this request very insignificant. Aware of the need identified by the Macedonian Educational Brotherhood of Constantinople for higher education in the area, he decided establishment of a similar institution. The "Trampantzeion Gymnasium" he envisioned included sufficient endowment by him for continuous operation. It was an appropriate project. The contracted architect Pipiliagas from Vlaste, knowledgeable with local conditions, constructed a modern-for-its-time, spacious,

[14]Anastasios N. Dardas, *John M. Trampantzes, 1813-1890*, pp. 29, 30

and efficient building. It was ready in 1888. It functioned the following year.

Trampantzes donated the school to Siatista's Eastern Orthodox Metropolis. It functioned under the Ecumenical Patriarchate. The Patriarch proudly blessed the gift and sanctioned its operation. It was a necessary move to prevent Ottoman intervention and possible harm. The Patriarchate honored the donor's specific requests. The school operated academically on the basis and system used by the Superior School of the Patriarchate at Constantinople. Vlaste's school followed the same method. A teacher from Siatista's Gymnasium supervised Vlaste school's annual Graduation Examinations[15]. The founder of Trampantzeion Gymnasium endowed it with an enormous fund. Its earned interest assured payment of its operational costs and all faculty salaries. A five-member prominent citizen committee headed by the Metropolitan administered the fund. A donor's additional smart move further enhanced the institution's importance. Trampantzes accepted Stephan D. Roses's advice and financed a Teachers' Training Manual. Roses, professor of Corfu's Gymnasium and Arsakeion All-Girl School in Athens, composed the publication, which was published in Athens in 1889[16]. The manual proved immensely useful as it helped prepare graduates to be teachers. Well-trained, they taught schools at other communities in the region and elsewhere. They enhanced education in an area which liberated Greece had no access to and could not help for another quarter of a century, although several Siatistians continued their studies in Athens or other cities invited by their relatives for this purpose.

John Michael Trampantzes's deed met wide praise and recognition. He received the Golden Cross of our Savior Jesus Christ, awarded him for his outstanding service. Siatista erected his marble bust in front of the Gymnasium and named the square after him[17]. The most important honor bestowed to the donor, however, remains the appreciation of Siatistians and area

---

[15]Michael Ath. Kalinderis, *Life in the Community of Vlaste During the Turkish Occupation*, p. 107
[16]Anastasios N. Dardas, *John M. Trampantzes, 1813-1890*, p. 41
[17]Anastasios N. Dardas, *John M. Trampantzes, 1813-1890*, p. 57

students, including the author, who attended the school. The spirit of Hellenism cultivated in Siatista continues to provide them strength for enhancing themselves and their fellow men. Several Trampantzeion Gymnasium graduates continued their studies in the Western Hemisphere. Among them are Siatistian brothers Naoum and Thomas J. Perikleous, who with their brother-in-law Naoum N. Basias migrated to the United States in September 1907. Naoum Perikleous found employment at a Greek's confectionery store in Philadelphia. His letters home, available at Manouseios Public Library in Siatista, are revealing. Two-thirds of his first twelve-dollar monthly salary (plus room and board) he sent home regularly to repay the debt his parents incurred to cover his tickets to America. His social background and solid education, however, quickly paid dividends. He fully mastered his English. In April 1910, he accepted the position of manager and secretary of the Pan-Hellenic Union (PHU), Philadelphia branch, offered to him by Mr. Stefanou. His agreed remuneration, covering wages and expenses, was 10 percent of receipts. In September 1912, the organization's Pittsburgh branch, impressed with his performance in Philadelphia, offered him the same position in Pittsburgh. In the meantime several opportunities opened up. Philhellene Americans proposed his participation in producing and presenting ancient Hellenic plays to the American public. Theatrical performances would enhance both his social status and finances.

Events in Macedonia interrupted Perikleous's plans. Siatista, liberated by the Greek army on November 4, 1912[18], became part of mother Hellas. In his letter to his father of November 13, Naoum stated:

> *"Here we have abundance of the press with their opinions and critiques of all distinguished world diplomats. They all recognize Venizelos's (the Greek Prime Minister) diplomatic score. I decided to visit you but, because Pan-Hellenic Union asked me to assist them, I postponed my trip. PHU received a request from the Greek foreign ministry to assist with Greece's*

[18]Panagiotes G. Siapantas, "The Battle of Siatista of November 4th, 1912," pamphlet Nov. 1995

mobilization. We sent to them so far 20,000 men (Greek immigrants). We collected 1,000,000 francs for the war's needs and 500,000 francs for Greece's Red Cross. We now solicit funds from America's Greeks for a 5,000,000-franc loan for the Greek government. Everyone contributes generously and enthusiastically. . . . We received letters from 13 American aristocratic young ladies offering their volunteer services as nurses. Many of them left already according to newspaper reports while others are due to follow. Two American Army officers, retired, volunteered enlistment in the Greek army as ordinary soldiers. The above pertains only to this branch. There are 128 branches existing throughout the country and they all received similar offers. I do not exaggerate if I say Greece could have 5,000 volunteer nurses and that many more soldiers from America if would only accept them[19]*."*

Siatistians' Hellenism was alive wherever they lived.

---

[19] Anastasios Ch. Megas, "Migration to America," *Siatistina*, 5-6/1991, pp. 26-28

Chapter 23
Cultural Behavior

Persistent efforts by Siatistians for education and advancement paid off. Upper Macedonians enhanced Hellenism's virtue of individual excellence. Relatives and friends readily assisted in cases of personal hardships and accidental individual misfortune. Archons or church resources came in as last resort. A feeling of affluence prevailed.

Siatistians confidently concentrated on their own tasks. Everyone knew each other in the community. Electricity, telephones, and automobiles were unknown. Horses and mules transported their goods, tools, and equipment. They willingly followed on foot except on special occasions. It took Siatistians ten hours to walk to Kastoria, five hours to Kozane, and four hours to Tsotyli. Men, women, and children walked to the vineyards starting before daybreak.

Siatistians meticulously cultivated most of their limestone-dappled slopes. Nearly seventeen hundred hectares of vineyards spread across the clay-gravel inclines[1]. At harvest time, neighbors joined in for safety and efficiency. Their trips to the vineyards with horses loaded with homemade bread, cheese, cheese-pies, meatballs, and pickled vegetables provided optimism and strength. The wine, ever present among Siatista's men, maintained its taste in special wooden jugs of two to three liters capacity. Water carrying was essential due to scarcity of springs or fountains in the area. A community-hired employee stood watch and protected the vineyards from unwelcome visitors. He knew almost all Siatistians' properties and their borders. He monitored all passers-by and events. Nearing harvest time vineyard owners in person stood watch to discourage intentional errors during night hours. Organized teams in early-rising grape picking attained their goal efficiently. They capitalized all efforts, livestock, and installations through their cooperation. They led their horse-loads of grapes home all

[1] Miles Lambert Gocs, *Wines of Greece*, pp. 131, 132

day and night where barefooted relatives and friends welcomed their challenge. They climbed on the lengthwise split-in-half huge barrels and stamped on the grapes thrown in. The wine produced filled Siatistian wine cellars and maintained their prosperity. Dry red, dry white, and sweet white wine came in different varieties. *Eliasto* wine was Siatista's specialty. They crushed the well-ripened, specially selected grapes after their weeklong exposure to the sun or six-week open-air exposure. *Eliasto* wine sold ten times the price of the town's highly esteemed dry red[2]. Wine production was a festive activity. Eating, drinking, singing, and partying were part of the process. The quantities of wine produced provided them with happiness and financial security.

The supply of foodstuff and other necessities was of paramount importance. The wheat they produced in their small fields or flour they procured through sale of their wine and money sent by expatriates filled the available lengthwise split-in-half barrels or sacks. Walnuts, almonds, chestnuts, figs, and a variety of food items also found their way into storage, mostly in wooden or ceramic containers. Siatistians purchased all their food supplies since they produced only wine, some grains, and some milk products. Nearby Eratyra and Pelekano sold them their vegetables. Kastoria fishermen supplied them with fish, and Sisani's famous bean growers provided their main staple meal. Vlaste and Samarina provided Siatistians with cheese while Galatine exclusively supplemented their milk, a basic requirement for Siatistian homes on a daily basis. Area residents stockpiled leeks standing up on the garden's wall with their roots in the ground for continued freshness. Dried onions and garlic hung from the cellar ceiling wooden beams, while quantities of cabbage found their way in specially made, long-necked upright barrels filled with salted water. The housewives pickled eggplants, tomatoes, cucumbers, and peppers. The up-to-forty-pound red pumpkins had special place in their winter supply. Siatistians' exclusive recipe produced their specialty, sweet pumpkin pie (similar to apple pie). Church committees distributed such pies, donated to the church by wealthy families, to every Siatistian home on Epiphany Day, collecting in return

[2]Miles Lambert Gocs, *Wines of Greece*, p. 133

their new-year's monetary contribution. Preparation of pasta varieties early fall concerned all housewives. New recipes brought in by expatriates quickly passed around to relatives and friends.

The kitchen fireplace burned daily. Siatistians used firewood purchased from surrounding village woodcutters. The villagers' early morning visits to not-so-near woods enabled them to bring their horse loads on time for the day's open-air market. Siatistians ordered enough loads to last all winter. The house's heat depended on firewood. The fireplace corner displayed a pot full of water permanently placed on a tripod. It provided hot water for a cup of coffee the housewife offered to her visitors or an aromatic, delicious, and healthful cup of tea. Natural, locally grown tea in close-by mountains of Bourinos and Siniatsiko offered cold treatments, revitalization, and longevity. Hot water was precious for personal hygiene, dish washing, and miscellaneous clothes washing. The main family wash took place by hand in specially constructed metal tubs. This was a major chore. Housewives carried enough water from springs and fountains as far as a mile away. Bread preparation, though top in priority, followed the family wash day in housewives' concerns. Baking was done at privately operated bakeries found in every neighborhood. Bakeries were profitable, and fathers passed them on to their sons.

Housewives had to care for other, not so familiar tasks. Coffee beans, imported by merchants or supplied by expatriates, had to be baked and pulverized at intervals for their aroma and freshness. In good weather they emptied the beans into a round hole, one foot in depth and in diameter, carved into a solid hard rock with all its surfaces smoothed out. They beat them for hours with a long and heavy round metal rod, two feet long and two to three inches in diameter thickness. After hours of beating, they produced the required fine powder. The coffee aroma and the noise from constant beating invited all neighboring housewives. At the end of the day, with all of their chores out of the way and before their men came home, women spontaneously appeared at the yard's main gate. The host served them with her freshly pulverized aromatic coffee. They chatted and briefed themselves on community news. Small children accompanying their mothers played hide-and-seek until dark when exhaustion and fear from darkness drove them to their mothers' company. They listened to all sorts of true and fictitious stories and myths. Adults' exchange of ideas often inspired inquisitive mothers. The coffee-pulverizing process became much simpler with the introduction of metal grinding mills brought home by expatriate returnees. The mills made the rounds from home to home, helping friends and neighbors. The habit of evening gatherings, however, remained.

The Eastern Greek Orthodox Church celebrates a specific day annually for each of its Saints. These name-day observances necessitated lengthy preparations. The hosts prepared a variety of sweet treats for the celebrations. The visitors selected their choice from the ones offered. Siatistians transformed into superb servings little, long-shaped eggplants and tomatoes, choice grapes, appropriate roses, brought-in fresh figs, and locally grown quinces. Their unique specialty was white pumpkin treat. The red pumpkin was only for pies. In both cases, they cleared them from its outside shell first. For the sweet treat they shaped it in cubed pieces about two inches in dimensions, and after boiling them they marvelously prepared them to a delicious taste. The pumpkin sweet served with famous *Eliasto* wine identified Siatistian association in distant lands. All expatriates visiting home carried back to their adopted lands both items. Pumpkin sweet was the main serving on all festive gatherings.

Name-day celebrations provided an opportunity for enjoyment as well as social exposure. During that day both panels of both yard gate and home main door opened. At the main house entrance, beautiful young marriageable women dressed in their best stood ready to host all visitors. The honored individuals attended church services and received the Metropolitan's blessings, simultaneously placing their gift on the elder's tray. When the service was over, relatives and friends accompanied them home. Neighbors, associates, and acquaintances kept on coming. Siatistians visited honored individuals in waves of groups. Friends meeting outside the church walked in every wide-opened door they came across. They knew them all. Celebrating, crowded homes were unable to treat all well wishers through all the servings. The hostesses often treated the standing visitors, accepting their wish Chronia Polla (translated "Many Years") for honored individuals at the entrance of the house. Respects had to be paid to all celebrating individuals. Following the considerable tiresome visitation parade, the family, close friends, and neighbors returned to their base. The party was in process. The local, traditional musicians arrived, the hostesses kept on serving sweet treats, cakes, almonds, walnuts, and snacks with wine until they all joined the dance. Siatistians looked for opportunities to party and dance.

All hostesses and maturing young girls paraded back and forth, passing trays full of snacks, goodies, and wine. Marriage promoters and probable in-laws found an opportunity to evaluate their assets. Positive comments often brought reciprocal responses. Single, marriage-minded men identified the girls' beauty and appearance, their willingness and efficiency, their politeness and attractiveness. Favorable reaction by a girl to a boy's expressed interest enthused parents and relatives. The musicians contributed by playing dancing tunes. All parties full of euphoria ate, drank, and joined the circle dancing until dawn of next day.

Parents or marriage promoters usually arranged marriages. No promoter ever received any fees. The intermediaries enjoyed life-long respect and honors from the newlyweds, especially from a contented bride. Dowries were part of all arrangements. Parents of several girls could go broke granting dowries and paying marriage costs. The parents' approval or rejection was final. Michael Ath. Kalinderis[3] wrote in his book: "The girls were not asked (for marriage), they were promoted. A girl engaged to be married and disengaged had difficulty finding a husband, especially if the groom went in and out of the house. Parents of boys were privileged. The ones who had girls had to exhibit exemplary behavior. Father and brothers had to think of the girls. Older girls had to marry first and all girls had to marry before the boys." An unquestionable asset of an expatriate brother was sending money to marry off his sisters. He could not get married unless his sisters did. Girls were kept inside from a very young age. One or two years' schooling sufficed. They

[3] Michael Ath. Kalinderis, *Life in the Community of Vlaste During the Turkish Occupation*, pp. 239, 240

placed emphasis on housekeeping and management. Girls could visit relatives' or neighbors' weddings or join other girls their age in watching community festivals from a distance. Visits to religious fairs were permitted at the side of chaperons. Similarly chaperoned they attended Easter services. Matchmaking intensified at springtime when flowers blossomed. Often they made marital arrangements at a much younger age without the children's knowledge. They were spoken for even at their birth. Parental commitment was final. Respect and honor commanded Siatistian society. Girls became brides at the age of twelve or thirteen in some cases. Girls had to marry by their twentieth birthday or accept a widowed man for a husband or even stay single.

Marriage ceremonies lasted for two weeks. Partying at the tunes of local clarinet, trombone, and cornet players involved a big segment of the community. They sustained it alternately at the groom's, the bride's, the best man's, or the close relatives' homes. The couple and their relatives exchanged all kinds of gifts, personal or household items. The two-week period was enjoyable and exhausting. The Sunday's church ceremony occurring after morning services developed into an all-are-welcomed dance party at the main square lasting all day. The entire procedure certainly was impressive and costly. Many times it left its marks on all participants. Amounts spent were enormously disproportionate to their earnings in some cases. I remember my father saying he spent my mother's dowry on the wedding and had to start from scratch. Direct and indirect consequences on the couple's lives occasionally followed on the relationship of blood and in-law relatives as well.

Family was, and remains, the basis of Siatistian society. Couples worked at it from their first night together. Nightlife consisted of work around the house knitting and sewing. Even these tasks were difficult with only the light of a hand-carried oil lamp. Their use was costly and limited. Most everyone went to bed early. Women were continually pregnant and gave birth at home, with the help of midwives or mothers-in-law. The new mother stayed inside the house for forty days. They wrapped the baby around with a wide cloth belt completely. The baby moved no hands or legs, except when they undressed it to clean it, which was regularly. This continued for about one year. Breastfeeding continued from one baby to another. Medical supervision by doctors was rare. Grandmother's practical knowledge weighted heavily, providing confidence and hope. Children played with homemade dolls often made through their talent. Girls aged five or six helped their mothers in raising their younger brothers and sisters. It was most difficult on winter days. Their only entertainment consisted of their own disposition, good spirit, and singing. Family gatherings around the fireplace in the evenings hammered closeness and understanding through baking corn and chestnuts. The women knitted woolen blouses, socks, slippers, and the like. Fur craftsmen worked on their furs, supplementing the day's work. Mothers with expatriate husbands stayed by the fireplace late, writing letters to their husbands. They urged them to keep on thinking about their children's future. I vividly remember my mother's letters to my father. The girls' dowries and the boys' schooling concerned them both. The boys could take up apprenticeship as experienced craftsmen if unable to continue studies outside Siatista. Early decision was necessary in such a case. Young apprentices had absolute respect for their craftsmen. Often they resided in their homes. Many times the craftsmen adopted them or even married them to their daughters.

Regardless of problems, however, Upper Macedonians raised considerably large families. They seldom stopped at less than five or six children. My mother was the eighteenth child in her family. Isolated in the mountainous region Macedonian culture survived all outside downgrading influences. Siatistians retained their pure personality, noble sentiments, and brilliant sagacity[4]. It was the result of centuries-old Hellenic culture, customs, and tradition[5]. Anastasios M. Tamis wrote in 1994 in his book, *The Immigration and Settlement of Macedonian Greeks in Australia*, (Bundoora, Victoria, 1994): "Macedonian Greek culture formulates certain unique living patterns.... To leave a neighbor at the front door without inviting him in is considered to be a rudeness which displays malice." The "families are in close

---

[4]Konstantinos E. Siabanopoulos, *The Museum of Kozane*, p. 4
[5]Anastasios N. Dardas, *Establishment and Operation of Trampantzeion Gymnasium of Siatista Under the Church's Supervision*, p. 327

contact in entertainment and celebrations. The happiness of a Macedonian Greek family is shared by other families who gather together sitting around the table drinking, singing and dancing. Friendliness is a custom, part of the culture, not a mode of behavior that can be obtained by way of education. . . ." Whether elderly dependents share the facilities of their son's house or visit their children's families, they are involved in the decision-making processes of the household and are active in the upbringing of the children regarding religion and language. It is thought to be insulting and a social stigma to put the old people away in institutions and nursing home[6]. Siatistian's donation twenty years ago of a Home for the Aged remains unused. Old folks continue to be taken care of at home by their children.

---

[6]Anastasios M. Tamis, *The Immigration and Settlement of Macedonian Greeks in Australia*, p. 177

Chapter 24
Annual Festivals

Siatistian culture perpetuated many of its centuries-old customs. Traditional recreational activities remained well entrenched. Beyond the annual name-day celebrations and weddings sustained at family level, Siatistians observe many community-oriented festivals. The year-end season offers excellent opportunities for partying.

The three-day Christmas holiday is preceded by weeks-long seasonal activity. Groups of teen-aged boys of every neighborhood compete in picking up dried-up branches and grasses from surrounding mountainsides. On the night of December 23, they build open-air fires in their neighborhood. All ages take part in driving a seven- to eight-foot-long wooden pole into a pre-dug hole in the ground and stockpiling the collected grass around it until it reaches six or seven feet high and four to five feet wide. They carefully place the grass solidly all around it. When darkness falls, young and old gather around, ringing all sizes and types of bells used by the shepherds for their animals over the years. The commotion created attracts all within hearing range. The boys, under parents' supervision and observing all precautions, lit the fire. The happy atmosphere raises their spirits. People sing centuries-old songs reminiscing about Siatista's past and dance around the fire. Archons and town supervisors visit all neighborhood fires wishing Siatistians well. The clergy stayed away from the fires for centuries and still do today, although some suggest the fires represent the ones shepherds lit at the time of Jesus's birth. The likelihood is that the fires have a pre-Christian origin and settlers brought them with them. The local musicians visit the most prominent fires in addition to the two main ones at the town's central squares. Archons and influential Siatistians join the people's circular dance around the fire. Now, video cameras, operated by locals, expatriates, and TV teams, record this unique event.

Early-morning hours the next day all children knock at the doors of homes of friends and neighbors, singing Christmas carols. The boys, up to the middle of the twentieth century, had a special song for every family circumstance. Their specific verses fitted appropriately every household[1]. They expressed wishes for longevity to advanced age couples, good luck to marriageable young women, happy reunions to homes with expatriates, health and logic to young couples with small children, respect and social advancement to homes with educated people, and success for every imaginable circumstance.

The following verses applied (author's translation):

To elderly couples:

*"Hope you live for one hundred years
and more, to get white-haired
like Mount Olympus and the white dove."*

To a shepherd house:

*"Here they have one thousand sheep and two thousand goats,
(the shepherd) with his flute entertains them
and with his courage he rounds them up,
Don't take them down to the valleys,
down to green meadows."*

To mule caravan operators:

*"Our master was going over a marble bridge
With his iron horse and its golden saddle
Our master went to Ioannina, went to Salonica
To bring you curly hair and silvery hair-tails."*

To the homes of expatriates:

*"And the good news arrived, (that) the master is on his way home
From the town of Wallachia and from Bucharest
He was nearing Danube River, to come across it."*

And, for the home of the archons they reserved the following verses:

*"We came to pay respect to the master of this house,
Who is famous among us, famous everywhere,
In Constantinople and in Venice (use him) as an example,
And in Siatista he is, a strong-based tower."*

[1] Vasilike G. Siasiou, "Caroling in Siatista," *Efemeris,* Siatista's newspaper, 11/1996

While the verses differed, the tune remained the same, following their mountainous dance "Tsamiko." Contrary to modern caroling all over Greece at Christmas time, Siatistians never presented them with money. They probably considered it degrading since all families had money or to eliminate bad feelings on the part of the ones that did not have it. The elders received immense satisfaction out of giving, knowing that their neighbors constantly remember them. Christmas holiday quickly culminated into the year-end celebration.

On New Year's Day, good-spirited Siatistians dressed in masquerading outfits. Their converted appearances presented bears, bull fighters, wood cutters, professors, politicians, misfits, and anything they thought would make Siatistians laugh and bring humor. Enthused groups danced in the town's streets, visiting homes of friends and relatives. Young men continued into the following day with the help of local musicians' drums and clarinets. They rested, only to carry on January 6, Epiphany Day, for a more formalized and dynamic repeat performance. The spirit was considerably greater when expatriates, realizing their visit home was about to end, wholeheartedly participated. The custom continues today in Siatista and Kastoria on Epiphany Day only, contrary to other parts of Greece, which hold festivals forty days prior to Orthodox Easter.

A purely Siatistian exclusive, not known to take place anywhere in the world, is the August 15 festival. Macedonian respect for horses is traditional: Alexander based his conquest on the swiftness of his cavalry. In Siatista[2] the horse played a predominant role for centuries. In our days, Siatistians relive the ancient Athenians' custom where horse-riders honored the goddess Athena at the Panathenaic ritual procession[3]. Siatista's once-a-year frenzy far surpasses the purely religious Assumption of the Virgin ceremonies. The festival developed over the years of prosperity and happiness. It provided an opportunity for Siatistians based in foreign lands to return home and see the family, join friends in get-togethers, test delicious home-made snacks, drink home-grown quality wine not

[2]James C. Siotas, "Horses, Food, and Wine," *The Athenian,* 8/1996, pp. 18, 19
[3]Boardman, John, *Greek Art, 4th Edition,* p. 148

available where they lived, and, for the single ones, meet maturing young girls they could choose from to marry.

Considerable wealth, determination, and effort went into this affair and continues to go, even nowadays. Families and friends enthusiastically participate in a spirit of joy and welcome. The whole town is on alert. Several families own horses today specifically for this purpose. Many horses are rented from area owners in advance. Few days prior to the event they are brought home so they can be cleaned, fed, and rested for the important day. The festival begins the day before when the horses are taken to the nearby River Aliakmon for a thorough, almost reverential, scrub and rinse. This ritual allows the participants to discuss their problems and to coordinate their own group. Their performance should outlast or surpass in beauty, spirit, and enjoyment the other groups.

The horses are lavishly decorated. A red flokati rug covers the horse's saddle. Sunflowers are placed on the animal's head and multicolored bead strings are hung around the horse's neck[4]. Multicolored ribbons are tied on its mane and tail, and some decorate even the horse's legs. The riders identify their groups wearing their own uniforms and colors. One group wears white shirts with red, dotted scarves while another uses black shirts with white scarves. A third group uses red shirts while others wear almost identical trousers.

Emphasis is placed on three areas: decoration of horses, uniformity of dress, and traditional musicians. This last requirement is almost always the most difficult to fulfill. Siatista's rhythmic, hard-charging musical patterns have a way of entering deeply into the soul. Where does the music come from? Musicologists believe its roots are in medieval Byzantine celebrations; others insist the spirit lasts from Kolokotronis, the legendary leader from the Greek War of Independence days. In any case, it has little to associate it with the standard Syrtaki tunes only too-well-attached to foreign images of Greece today. Available bands knowledgeable of this unique music cannot satisfy the big demand. They are contracted for a year in advance. Search, therefore, becomes necessary among the

[4] Zane Katsikis, "Siatista, A Wealthy, Secretive Northern Town," *Athens News*, 2/6/1998, p. 11

neighboring, and often not-so-neighboring, communities. The best clarinet, cornet, and trombone players are sought. The horse riders pay particular attention to the band's repertoire as well as to its members' stamina. August 15 was and is an extremely long and strenuous, though enjoyable, day. Younger-aged celebrators continue partying for two or three days, if a weekend follows.

When the big day arrives, all family members are busy. There are families with two or three members participating in the riders' groups. Preparation of horses becomes everybody's responsibility. Others ready the snacks and wine taken by the celebrators to the Virgin Mary's monastery. The mother, the head of the household, with a tray full of glasses of fine local wine, treats arriving members of the group. As the time nears and the musicians arrive, it is time for another glass of wine. A well-meant "best wishes for ever" or Chronia Polla is heard and the drummer begins. All musicians join. The tunes played are inspiring. The men mount their horses in a festive mood. They take off for the long day. The distinct sounds of many horses clattering on the streets accompanied by clarinet notes stir the populace ready to spill out onto the streets. The air is filled with music from other bands as well. Each plays a different tune. Unlike marching music, the tunes played are dance-oriented, uniquely used in the area. Most songs express courage and liberty, like the following[5]:(author's translation)

> "Brightness cover the mountains,
> Brightness cover the meadows,
> Brightness reflect their movements,
> Of Kolokotrones (father and son, leaders during the Greek Independence War),
> With plenty of silver around them, and silvery weapons,
> They never care to dismount (from their horses), to step on the earth,
> On horses they go to church,
> On horses they pray in front of the altar,
> On horses they take their blessing, from the priest's hand"

Some speak of love and affection. Others denote success and nostalgia. All songs reaffirm will and determination to live,

[5]Naoum Ch. Tsitsares, *Songs of Siatista*, edited by Nicos (Potamites), Psimmenos, p.52

enjoy, and proudly die pursuing the above. Life values were, and are, at their highest esteem in this society.

By early morning most groups pass the two main squares. They begin from the lower part, Geraneia, and pass through Chora on their way to the monastery through the mountain path. As riders pass, close friends and relatives offer their hands for a warm handshake. The age-old-standard wish, Chronia Polla, can be heard above clopping hooves, neighing horses, and throat-rattling trombones. These two words represent a multitude of individual wishes. In Turkish occupation years, it was a standing wish for freedom long denied by their conquerors. It was especially meaningful to freedom fighters in difficult times when action was necessary. They often used similar festive gatherings for secret discussions and clandestine operations with distant communities.

One by one, the groups leave the St. Athanasios area at the Northwest edge of Siatista. The riders arrive at the monastery, singing on their way. They dismount their horses and let them loose on the grounds. They join the crowd and enter the church to light a candle. They pay their respects to the Virgin Mary and pray for guidance and strength. Following a brief respite, with snacks and wine on the monastery's open grounds, the riders remount their horses. Music, singing, and festive moods accompany them on their way back. Town spectators gather in front of St. Athanasios church, the assembly point for a parade by all mounted groups through the crowded streets to the square of Geraneia. The people welcome them noisily applauding and hand clapping. Close friends, old and young, join them on the way downhill to the first main square. Each band plays its own tune to distinguish them from others preceding or following. Horse riders often enter the town five abreast. Musicians do their best to stir them to dance standing on their saddles. Horses rear on their hind legs and the tempo accelerates.

Everyone walks and dances to the tune of the musicians. The riders dismount occasionally, leaving their horses to small children, and join the foot dancers. The procession reaches the square where the community's elders committee officially welcomes them. Everyone does his or her best to impress everyone and get the best in satisfaction. Monetary awards were not given. All groups, horses, riders, musicians, families, and friends squeeze in the little square. The pandemonium created lasts an hour or so. As the spectators begin leaving for lunch, bringing with them their out-of-town guests and friends, the groups go back on the road to the lower square. The festive mood continues on the one-mile road. Many celebrators follow the horsemen. There is a repeat performance of what happened in the upper square. Plain citizens mix with celebrities and live it up. The spacious square of Geraneia allows tethering horses in a corner. Some are taken to close-by homes. Tables are set up to wine and dine the groups taking turns while others continue dancing. There is no interruption of the dancing as groups take their break.

The partying continues late in the day. Petroleum lamps were lit in the old days and the spirit remained high. Modern-day electricity with powerful speakers spreads the music to ravines and surrounding mountains. Cars bring spectators from miles around. Video cameras record this magnificent event. Its impact on the psychosynthesis of Diaspora Siatistians is inestimable. They arrive from America, Europe, and Australia to relive their childhood excitement. They are thrilled witnessing a further improvement: seeing young women in their teens participate with grandfather and grandchildren, riding horses together, contrary to old-time festivals where women were only spectators. A palpable energy imbues all with the sense that the scene unfolding is not only a gleeful midsummer distraction. It is also a direct link with Siatista's long and proud past.

It is an event worth attending. Siatista continues pursuing happiness through individual excellence and international cooperation. The Spirit of Hellenism goes on.

First copy of the *Efemeris* newspaper of Vienna published by Siatistian Poulios Biothers.

Siatista: A wealthy, secretive northern town

By ZANE KATSIKIS
SPECIAL TO THE ATHENS NEWS

CLATTERING hooves on stone streets bear out an insistent tattoo interwoven with wafting notes from strident clarinets as mounted riders stand and dance on their patient horses. It is the mid-August *panigyri* in Siatista. Far northwestern Macedonia is well off the beaten tourist path. If travellers venture into the remote area it is usually to the pristine Prespa Lakes or the old Byzantine city of Kastoria.

Siatista, a lively, bustling town of some 8,000 inhabitants 28km west of Kozani is rarely thought of by foreign visitors as a vacation idyll. Locals know it well and flock to it during the remarkable August 15 festivities.

Tucked into the folds of the Mount Sniatsikon range, 950 metres above the narrow plain of the Aliakmon River, Siatista dates its founding back to the late 14th century, when low country Greeks retreated into the hills to escape the ever encroaching Ottoman hegemony. Even today the amphitheatre-shaped town overlooking the barren slopes of Mount Velia is hidden, away from the main Kozani-Kastoria road. Look for the turnoff after the combined service station-restaurant at Bari.

Little is known of Siatista's origin, though some observers point to unexcavated local mounds as proof of ancient settlements in the area. The name could come from the local Greco-Vlach slang *siar* meaning thirst (for a perceived lack of year-round potable water), or it could be the Turkish *sar* for fortress. Many believe it comes from the German *shatzstadt*, which translates as "treasuretown".

In any case, Siatista became well-known in medieval Europe. As early as the 16th century, furriers from Siatista were established in Vienna, trading their skins for whatever commodities they could transport on horseback through the Balkans and then exchange in Siatista. By the late 18th century industrious townspeople had created some 200 commercial ventures in Siatista with branches in many European capitals and were well-known to the Austro-Hungarian nobility.

Thriving commerce led to a lifestyle of ease and influence. One of the first Greek newspapers, *Efimeris*, was published in Vienna in 1790 by Siatistans and, in the time-honoured Greek tradition, wealthy Siatistan expatriates began to return, constructing a series of remarkable, ornately decorated, multistoried stone and wood houses that shock those used to the tiny cubist white and blue Aegean isle dwellings.

Despite its discreet site in the hills far from prying Ottoman eyes, imperial tax collectors, and especially renegade marauders, managed to find the town several times during the 1700s. The grand houses, designed to interconnect, often became sort of multi-turreted fortresses.

These traditions of self-banishment, trade, self-defence and isolation have led to a unique sense of place that is celebrated along with the Orthodox Christian Assumption of the Virgin Festival. Every year on August 14 and 15, Siatistans from throughout the diaspora return for a series of festivities that link homecoming, religious observance and old-fashioned good time partying.

After memorial religious services at dusk on the 14th, the merriment generally begins in the low town, Gerania, square around fires, squatting musicians and blearing trumpets. Early the next morning, the bands of mounted riders led by their musicians respectfully file out of town, up the single road from Yerania past the 1677 Agia Paraskevi church through the Chora neighbourhood to pay their respects to the Virgin at the Monastery of the Panigyra at Mikrokastro. Then the 150 or so riders begin the increasingly boisterous 12km journey back to Chora. The gaily decorated horses and the oddly rhythmic music, whose Byzantine origins are lost, create an ambiance difficult to describe but certainly not from our era.

The triumphant processional return to Siatista past large crowds of onlookers and wellwishers in no way resembles the rather solemn departure from Yerania.

Few alive today have ever experienced so many uniformed and mounted riders aligned behind musicians returning home from a successful campaign. Go to Siatista and see for yourselves, then stay several days, to discover a little-known though deserving part of Greece.

Traditional religious festivities at the thriving Macedonian town of Siatista

▶ **How to get there:** From Athens all KTEL buses, OSE trains and OA flights transit via Kozani. From Kozani, a taxi will cost about 3,000 drs for the 20-minute trip. Local buses operate many times per day from the central bus station.

▶ **Where to stay:** The recently renovated 24-room Archontikon hotel (tel 0465-21298, fax 22835) is the only place to stay in the small town where every expat Greek seems to have kept his ancestral home in condition for an eventual return.

▶ **Further reading** *Siatista*, published in Greek, English and German, in Melissa Publishing House's Greek Traditional Architecture series is a fine source of information on the unique building style. *Siatista, Macedonia and Our Ancestors* (1995) by James Sotsantsas is a lively, informative recollection of one Siatistan expatriate's love affair with his home town. The Siatista Friendship Association (tel/fax 0465-21386) can also provide information in Greek and English on the town and can possibly help finding local lodgings.

Article from the *Athens News* February 6, 1998.

Bibliography

Apostolou, John. *History of Siatista*. Athens, 1929.

Arch, G.L. "Greek Intellectuals and Merchant Benefactors of National Education in Russia in the 18th and 19th Century." International Chamber of Commerce, Greek National Committee. *1000 Years of Hellenism-Russia*. First edition. Athens: Gnose, 1994.

Arnakis, George Georgiades. *Americans in The Greek Revolution. George Jarvis*. Salonica: Institute of Balkan Studies, 1965.

Arrian, translation of A. De Selincourt. *The Campaigns of Alexander*. New York City: Dorset Press, 1971.

Avlos Encyclopedia. Athens, 1961.

Babouskos, Konstantinos. "Ecclesiastical Relationship of Serbs and Ecumenical Patriarchate in the 19th Century." *Helleno-Serb Symposium*. Salonica: Institute of Balkan Studies, 1979.

Bakalopoulos, Apostolos E. *History of Thessalonike*. Thessalonike: Institute of Balkan Studies, 1993.

Bakalopoulos, Konstantinos. *Macedonia and Turkey, 1830-1878*. Thessalonike, 1987.

Beikou, Despina-Rizos, D.N. *Siatista Architecture*. Athens: Mellisa, 1989.

Boardman, John. *Greek Art*. 4th ed. New York City: Thames and Hudson, 1999.

Bodas, George M. "Benefactors of Siatista." *Siatistina Magazine*. Salonica, 2/1989.

Bodas, George M. "Siatistian George Papazoles or Papazoglou." *Elimeiaka Magazine*. Salonica, 27/1991.

Bodas, George M. "Siatistian 'Filike Etaireia' member Nickolaos Laspas." *Elimeiaka Magazine*. Salonica, 35/1995.

Chadjes, Demetrios K. *John M. Trampatzes*. Athens, 1969.

Churchill, W. S. *The Second World War.* vol. V. pp.470-471. London: 1952— "Hellenism, The Pedestal of Christianity." Methodius G. Fugias. Athens: Apostolic Press, 1993.

Committee of: Dainavas, M., Dardas, A., Batzios, D., Bodas, G., Siasios, D. *Siatista Acquaintance Invitation.* Siatista, 1993.

Committee of: Liamades, N., Makris, D., Bellos, A., Papaioannou, L., Siabanopoulos, K. *Acquaintance with the Prefecture of Kozane.* 1970.

Dardas, Anastasios, N. "Zosimas's Episcopal Service in Siatista (1686-1746)." *Siatistina Magazine.* Salonica, 2/1989.

Dardas, Anastasios, N. *John M. Trampantzes, 1813-1890.* Salonica, 1988.

Dardas, Anastasios, N. "Nikeforos of Achris Episcopal Service in Siatista (1746-1769)." *Siatistina Magazine.* Salonica, 3/1990.

Dardas, Anastasios, N. *Siatista's Participation in the Holy Struggle of 1821-1830.* Salonica, 1981.

Dardas, Anastasios, N. "Siatista's Schools." *Elimeiaka Magazine.* Salonica, 16-19/1987.

Dardas, Anastasios, N. *The Establishment and Operation of Trampantzeion Gymnasium of Siatista with the Supervision of the Church.* Salonica: Vlatadon Church, Institute of Patriarchal Fatherly Studies, 1997.

Dardas, Anastasios, N. "The Episcopate of Sisani, (? 1686)." *Siatistina Magazine.* Salonica, 1/1989.

Dardas, Anastasios, N. *The Metropolitan Church of Saint Demetrios.* Siatista, 1995.

Dardas, Anastasios, N. "The Metropolitan of Prespa and Achris Anthimos (M. E. Toumpalides)." *Siatistina Magazine.* Salonica, 11/1994.

Dardas, Anastasios, N. "The Monastery of Virgin Mary at Mikrocastro." *Siatistina Magazine.* Salonica, 5-6/1991.

Daskalakes, G. D. *The Ages-Long Development of Hellenism in Macedonia.* Athens, 1992.

Droysen, J. G. translation of R. & H. S. Apostolides. *The History of Alexander the Great Heirs*. Athens: Credit Bank, 1993.

Enepekides, Polychrones, K. *Macedonian Cities and Families, 1750-1930*. Athens: Estia, 1984.

Filios, George, N. "How Siatista Received Its Name." *Efemeris* newspaper. Siatista, 11-12/1995.

Fotiades, Demetres. *The Revolution of 1821*. Athens: N. Votsis, 1997.

Fugias, Methodius, G. *Hellenism, The Pedestal of Christianity*. Athens: Apostolic Press, 1996.

Gafurof, B., Tsiboukides, D. translation of George Stergiou. *Alexander the Macedon and the Orient*. Moscow, 1980. Athens: Edition Papademas, 1992.

Ganoules, G. Th. *The Administrative Organization of Siatista During the Turkish Occupation*. Siatista Memoirs album, Salonica, 1972.

Gantonas, Nickolaos. *Galatine*. Salonica, 1987.

Gavrilovic, Slavko. "The Greek and KoutsoVlachs Natives of Macedonia and Merchants of Semlin in the Face of the First Serbian Revolution." *Helleno-Serb Symposium*. Salonica: Institute of Balkan Studies, 1979.

Gocs, Miles-Lambert. *Wines of Greece*. London-Boston: Faber and Faber, 1990.

Golden Home Encyclopedia. New York, New York: Golden Press Inc., 1961.

Hammond, G. N. *Problems and Achievements of the Great Macedonian Kings Phillip and Alexander*. Salonica: Macedonian Studies Society, 1982.

Hammond, G. N. *The Allied Military Mission and The Resistance in Western Macedonia (in World War II)*. Salonica: Institute of Balkan Studies, 1993.

Kalinderis, Michael, Ath. *Baron Konstantin E. Bellios, (1772-1838)*. Salonica: Macedonian Studies Society, 1973.

Kalinderis, Michael, Ath. *Life in the Community of Vlaste During the Turkish Occupation*. Salonica: Macedonian Studies Society, 1982.

Kalinderis, Michael, Ath. *Metropolis of Sisani and Siatista Register (1686-)*. Salonica: Macedonian Studies Society, 1974.

Kanatsoules, Charilaos. *Theohares G. Tourountzias, (1776-1798)*. Athens, 1985.

Karathanases, Athanasios. "Stefan Zivkovic and the Greek Family Douzes (6/1815)." *Helleno-Serb Symposium*, Salonica: Institute of Balkan Studies, 1979.

Kardases, Asemakes, A. *The City of Demetsana*. Athens, 1984.

Kasomoules, Nickolaos. *Memoirs of the Greek Revolution, 1821-1833*. Fotiades, Demetres. *The Revolution of 1821*. Athens: N. Votsis, 1977.

Katsikes, Zane, G. "Siatista, A Wealthy, Secretive Northern Town." *Athens News*, 6/2/1998.

Kitromelidou, P. *The Political Contents of the Greek-Russian Spiritual Relationship During the Turkish Occupation*. International Chamber of Commerce, National Greek Committee. *1000 years Hellenism-Russia*. Athens: Gnose, 1994.

Korkas, John. "Details from the Liberation of Kozane," *Elimeiaka Magazine*. Salonica, 35/1995.

Koukkou, Helen. *John Kapodistrias*. International Chamber of Commerce, National Greek Committee. *1000 years of Hellenism-Russia*. Athens: Gnose, 1994.

Koutras, Nickolaos, K. *The Truth About the Central Region in the Balkans*. Athens, 1993.

Krestic, Vasilije. "On Some Echoes of Greek Insurrections in Serbian Literature." *Helleno-Serb Symposium*. Salonica: Institute of Balkan Studies, 1979.

Laios, George. *Siatista and Its Commercial Houses Hadje-Michael and Manouses*. Salonica: Macedonian Studies Society, 1982.

Lake, J. W. *The Works of Lord Byron*. Vol. II. p. 430. Paris, France: Jules Didot Sr. Press, 1825.

Laskares, Elias. "Byzantine Emperors." *Eleftheros Typos* newspaper edition. Athens, 1995.

Leake, William M. *Travels In Northern Greece in 1805*. Siatista Memoirs album. Salonica, 1972.

Lioses, Polykarpos. (Metropolitan of Siatista). *The Metropolis of Sisani and Siatista*. Siatista Memoirs album. Salonica, 1972.

Lioufes, Panagiotes N. *History of Kozane*. Athens, 1924.

Loucatos, Spyros D. "Serb, Montenegran and Bosnian Fighters of the Greek Revolution." *Helleno-Serb Symposium*. Salonica: Institute of Balkan Studies, 1979.

Macrakis, Lily A. "Introduction, International Chamber of Commerce." National Greek Committee. *1000 years Hellenism-Russia*, Athens: Gnose publishers, 1994.

Maligoudes, Faidon. *Salonica and the World of Slavs*. Salonica: Vanias, 1992.

Martis, Nickolaos. "Macedonia, Hellenism's Advanced Shield." *Makedonika Themata* bulletin. issue 3-4/1995, Edessa.

Megas, Anastasios, Ch. *The Archives of Zoupan-Moraites-Pericleous Family*. Siatista Memoirs album. Salonica, 1972.

Megas, Anastasios, Ch. "Schools and Church in Siatista the First Half of 19th Century." *Siatistina Magazine*. 1/1989.

Megas, Anastasios, Ch. "Migration to America," *Siatistina Magazine*. Salonica, 5-6/1991.

Meliopoulos, Paraskevas, J. "The Slavo-Macedonians of Skopja, Descendants of Homeric Greeks." series of articles in *Dytike Makedonia* newspaper. Kozane, 1992.

Metsakis, Konstantinos. *Macedonia Throughout the Centuries*. Salonica: Institute of Balkan Studies, 1979.

Nicol, Donald M. translation of Pericles Fefkas. *The Despotate of Epirus*. Ioannina. Epirus, 1974.

Panagiotou, John P. *The Holy Community of Mt. Athos.* (pamphlet). 1981.

Papadopoulos, Stephanos, I. *Educational and Social Activities of Hellenism in Macedonia During The Last Century of the Turkish Occupation.* Salonica: Macedonian Studies Society, 1970.

Papadrianos, John, A. *The Greek Settlers of Semlin.* Salonica Institute of Balkan Studies, 1988.

Papadrianos, John, A. "The History of the Slaveno-Serbs by Triantafyllos Doukas of Kastoria and Its Significance with Regard to the First Serbian Revolution." *Helleno-Serb Symposium.* Salonica: Institute of Balkan Studies, 1979.

Papadrianos, John, A. *The Greek Settlers at Yugoslav Countries.* Salonica: Vanias, 1993.

Papathemelis, Stellios. "Macedonia, The Historical View." *Elimeiaka Magazine.* Salonica, 16-19/1987.

Papoulides, Konstantinos, K. "The Greeks of Russia in the 19th Century and the Beginning of 20th Century." International Chamber of Comerce, National Greek Committee. *1000 Years Hellenism-Russia.* Athens: Gnose, 1994.

Patrineli, Ch. G. "The First Teachers In Kozane's Schools." *Elimeiaka Magazine.* Salonica, 36/1996.

Perros, George P. "The First Greek in Congress." *The Ahepan* magazine, Washington, D.C., Fall 1998.

Plevris, Konstantinos, A. *Socrates Facing His Death.* Athens, 1991.

Rogof, A. "The Russo-Hellenic Cultural Relationship From the Second Half of the 15th to the 17th Century." International Chamber of Commerce, National Greek Committee. *1000 Years Hellenism-Russia.* Athens: Gnose, 1994.

Sfekas, George. *Bourinos, The Beautiful Mountain of Western Macedonia.* Siatista, 1996.

Siabanopoulos, Konstantinos, E. *The Museum of Kozane.* Kozane, 1992.

Siapantas, Panagiotes, G. "The Battle of Siatista on November 4th, 1912." November 1995 newsletter, Athens.

Siasios, Demetrios, G. "The Siatistian Traders, Their Trips and Their Songs." *Siatistina Magazine*. Salonica: 13/1995.

Siasios, Demetrios, G. "Zosimas' School." *Siatistina Magazine*. 7/1992.

Siasiou, Vasilike, G. "Hadje-Michael/Kanatsoules Mansion Calendar." Siatista, 1997.

Siasiou, Vasilike, G. "Caroling in Siatista." *Efemeris* newspaper. Siatista, 11/1996.

Siotas, James, C. "Horses, Food and Wine in Siatista." *The Athenian* magazine. Athens, 8/1996.

Strakales, Miltiades. *The Development of the Mayors Office in Siatista*. Siatista Memoirs album. Salonica, 1972.

Tamis, Anastasios, M. *The Immigration and Settlement of Macedonian Greeks in Australia*. Bundoora, Victoria, Australia: La Trobe University, 1994.

Tifras, Parmenion, N. *Brief History of Bogatsiko*. Athens, 1992.

Tsigaridas, Demetrios, N. "Macedonian Educational Brotherhood." *Chronika* Vol. 7. Salonica, 1991.

Tsirpanlis, Zacharias, N. *The Macedonian Students of the Greek College of Rome and Their Activities in Greece and in Italy*. Salonica: Macedonian Studies Society, 1971.

Tsitsaris, Naoum, Ch., edited by Nicos (Potamites) Psimmenos. *Songs of Siatista*. Dotion, 1994.

Tsolakes, Panos, Gr. *The Boats of Kastoria*. Salonica, 1992.

Valaorites, John., *National Bank of Greece*. Athens, 1988.

Vittes, Fotis. *Stachyologemata* (collection of short stories). Ptolemais, 1981.

Voures, George. "George Papazoglou, A Greek from Epirus at the Service of Serb Ruler Milos Obrenovic." *Helleno-Serb Symposium*. Salonica: Institute of Balkan Studies, 1979.

Zaviras, George. "Siatistian Intellectuals." (from the book *New Hellas* by George Kremos), Siatista Memoirs album. Salonica, 1972.